Christopher McIntosh was born in England in 1943 and grew up in Edinburgh. He studied Philosophy, Politics and Economics at Oxford University and German at London University. Later, he returned to Oxford to take a doctorate in History. As a writer, he has specialized in the history of ideas, central European history and the Western esoteric tradition. In addition to *The Swan King*, he has written two books on the Rosicrucians, a biography of the French occultist Eliphas Lévi and *Gardens of the Gods* (I.B.Tauris).

King Ludwig II of Bavaria in his General's uniform, in a portrait by F. Piloty of 1865.

The SWAN KING

LUDWIG II OF BAVARIA

CHRISTOPHER McINTOSH

I.B. TAURIS

LONDON · NEW YORK

New revised edition published in 2012 by I.B. Tauris & Co Ltd
6 Salem Road, London W2 4BU
175 Fifth Avenue, New York NY 10010
www.ibtauris.com

Distributed in the United States and Canada Exclusively by Palgrave Macmillan
175 Fifth Avenue, New York NY 10010

First published by Tauris Parke Paperbacks in 2003

ISBN: 978 1 84885 847 3

A full CIP record for this book is available from the British Library
A full CIP record is available from the Library of Congress

Library of Congress Catalog Card Number: available

Printed and bound in Sweden by ScandBook AB

Contents

List of Illustrations

'There is a Swan whose name is Ecstasy . . . '
Aleister Crowley, *The Book of Lies*

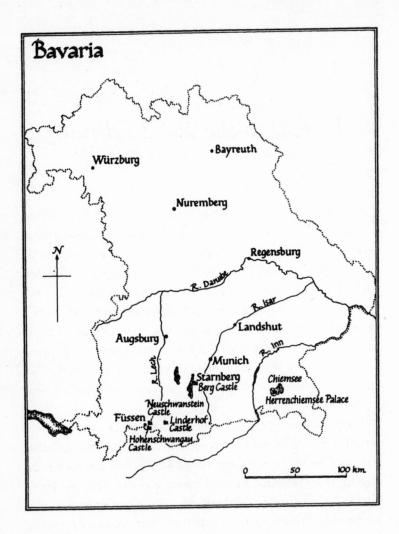

Preface to the 2012 Edition

In the period of nearly three decades since the first edition of this book was published, the figure of King Ludwig II has exerted an ever more powerful fascination and attracted an increasing number of admirers. He features in books, articles, television programmes, films, plays and even a musical. And, in the age of the internet, a search under his name will reveal thousands of entries. At the same time, research on him has advanced considerably since this book first appeared. This new edition gives me the opportunity to present a fuller and more up-to-date view of Ludwig and the various areas of controversy connected with him.

There are four areas of his life that are particularly controversial. First, there has been a persistent rumour that his father was not Crown Prince (later King) Maximilian but rather the dashing royal adjutant Baron Ludwig von der Tann or possibly the Italian Joseph Tambosi, who was a butler in the royal household. According to one theory, Maximilian was not in possession of full potency and von der Tann was asked to ensure the succession. These theories are highly speculative, but I have mentioned them briefly in the chapter on Ludwig's birth and childhood.

The second area of controversy is Ludwig's supposed homosexuality, which is widely taken for granted, although many of his devotees deny it vehemently. Again, this subject has been much written about lately, and much new alleged evidence has come to light. While I have already written about this question in the earlier edition, I now do so more fully in Chapter 15.

A third topic of controversy is the question of whether Ludwig was mad or not, and, if so, what the cause of his madness might have been. The story has often been told of his dethronement on the grounds of a psychological 'assessment' that pronounced him insane, but there are many who reject the madness theory and dismiss the assessment as part of a plot against him. The possibility that his condition was due to syphilis has been aired a number of times, but one recent author on Ludwig who rejects this theory is Heinz Hänfer, Emeritus Professor of Psychiatry at the University of Heidelberg, who has examined this question very thoroughly in his book *Ein König wird beseitigt. Ludwig II von Bayern* (A King is Removed. Ludwig II of Bavaria). In Chapter 18 I shall return to the subject of Ludwig's mental and physical health, examining the question in greater detail than in the earlier edition.

The fourth – and perhaps most hotly debated – issue concerns the cause and circumstances of his death in Lake Starnberg on 13 June 1886. Essentially the speculations on this subject boil down to three basic theories: (a) the murder theory; (b) the theory that Ludwig died accidentally while trying to escape; (c) the suicide theory. The murder theory is a favourite among Ludwig's devotees, but I find it unconvincing for the reasons I give in Chapter 19. The second theory has a romantic quality, but there is little solid evidence to support it. On balance, I continue to believe that Ludwig entered the lake with the intention of committing suicide. This seems to me his most probable motive, given the intensely humiliating and hopeless situation in which he had been placed. Clearly a struggle then took place between the King and his doctor. I have suggested what might have ensued in the struggle, ending in the deaths of both men, but I do not claim that this is anything more than speculation. I have not changed my position on this since the earlier edition, but I have reported on various recent pronouncements on the subject.

A further area where I felt some updating was necessary was in connection with the legend of Ludwig, which even in his lifetime had begun to outgrow the man himself and since his death has grown continuously. Herein lies one of the main reasons why I was attracted to the subject of Ludwig in the first place. I have long been fascinated by the borderland between history and myth – by the way in which history turns into myth and myth in turn influences history. This is a process which is not yet sufficiently understood, although it continually propels historical events and shapes the way we perceive them. One way in which it manifests itself is with national heroes or heroines, who often assume a mythical dimension out of proportion to the reality. We saw this, for example, towards the end of the last century with the near deification of Princess Diana – to the point where a Pakistani waiter in a Hamburg restaurant told me that, out of grief over her death, he had taken two days sick leave. Royalty are, of course, especially likely to be objects of this sort of mythologizing because of the exalted aura that their role gives them. If you add, as in the case of Ludwig, a highly eccentric personality to the point of suspected madness, a passion for creating astonishing buildings, a key role in the life of a great composer (Wagner), alleged homosexual leanings, rumours concerning his parentage, and a mysterious, tragic and premature death, then you have a recipe for a legend of enduring fascination. Accordingly, I have extended the Epilogue to take account of the continuing cult of Ludwig. At various other points in the book I have made changes and corrected what I felt to be omissions in the earlier version.

Ultimately, Ludwig remains what he wanted to be: 'an eternal enigma'. No book can ever fully 'capture' him, but this one, in its revised form, attempts more fully to describe the enigma and the legend and to throw some more light on the reality.

Preface

I first came to learn of the extraordinary, half-mythical reputation of King Ludwig II of Bavaria through an early passion for the operas of Richard Wagner. Even the most superficial study of Wagner's life reveals the crucial role that Ludwig played, by coming to Wagner's rescue at a critical point in his career and supporting him financially and often morally through the years when the *Ring* and other works were being completed and brought to the stage. But I soon discovered that Ludwig was a highly interesting character in his own right. Having started as a Wagnerite I found myself rapidly becoming a Ludwigite as well, and more and more pieces of information about him began to come my way. His life seemed to me to resemble a rich and eccentric cabinet of curiosities, which invited further exploration. The French *fin-de-siècle* poet and aesthete, Robert de Montesquiou, had idolized Ludwig, kept a framed envelope addressed in the King's hand, and built follies in the grounds of his château in emulation of his hero, for Ludwig had been a great builder of extravagant edifices. Huysmans was thought to have based his hero Des Esseintes in *À Rebours* partly on Montesquiou and partly on Ludwig himself. I also discovered that Ludwig's life appeared to hold certain dark secrets.

So here was a man who had been Wagner's greatest devotee, who had built amazing castles, who had been a hero of the decadent French aesthetes of the nineties, and about whom there was more than a whiff of mystery and scandal. My initial curiosity grew into an absorption. I read Wilfrid Blunt's short illustrated book on Ludwig, *The Dream King*, and a number of other works on him, but was surprised to discover that there was no full and satisfactory biography in English. Encouraged by Wilfrid Blunt, I began to collect material with the aim of writing one. I soon found that the large volume of literature about Ludwig included fiction and poetry as well as biography. It was mostly by German authors, but some French and English ones had also contributed. These works ranged from the serious and scholarly to the downright fanciful, and showed the thick accretion of mythology that had built up around the King.

I discovered that Ludwig's admirers, past and present, constituted a diverse and fascinating group in their own right. Apart from the ones I have mentioned, there was the English occultist Aleister Crowley, who included the names of both Ludwig and Wagner in his Collect for the Saints, part of the Gnostic Mass he wrote for his disciples. The relevant passage reads as follows (Ludwig's name is Latinized):

> Lord of Life and Joy . . . though adored of us upon heaths and in woods, on mountains and in caves, openly in the market place and secretly in the chambers of our houses . . . we worthily commemorate them worthy that did of old adore thee and manifest thy glory unto men, Lao-tze and Siddartha and Krishna and Tahuti . . . and these also Thomas Vaughan, Elias Ashmole, Molinos, Adam Weishaupt, Wolfgang von Goethe, Ludovicus Rex Bavariae, Richard Wagner . . .[1]

It is easy to understand Wagner's inclusion in this list, for his operas are powerful symbolic allegories capable of arousing in their audiences something akin to mystical ecstasy. And Ludwig of course deserves a place in the list as Wagner's patron and collaborator. But I think Crowley had something deeper in mind as well. As someone steeped in the western occult tradition he sensed a kinship with both Ludwig and Wagner, for both of them spoke the ancient language of symbol and myth. In particular, the Holy Grail was a motif which was meaningful to both of them and which plays a key symbolic role in the Gnostic Mass.

I was also struck by how closely Ludwig corresponded to the psychological type that Colin Wilson analyses so brilliantly in his book *The Outsider*. Ludwig was an outsider in the same way as the outsiders Wilson discusses: among others, Van Gogh, Nijinsky and Dostoyevsky. Like them he had known that vivid stab of intense experience after which the everyday world seems flat and banal. Like them he sought to reproduce it again and again.

As for the outer facts of that life, many of these have proved elusive to students of Ludwig in the past. Much of the documentary material relating to his personal life is kept in the custody of the Bavarian State Archives, in a department known as the Secret Archive of the Royal House. Permission to see this archive has to be obtained from the Wittelsbach family, who are understandably sparing in giving it for fear of its being used by sensation-mongers. I was kindly allowed to consult the archive and have tried to be as fair to the King as I can while not concealing anything that I consider relevant.

There is one important set of items that I have not been able to consult in the original, namely the series of secret diaries that Ludwig kept between December 1869 and June 1886. My earlier account of the fate of these diaries is somewhat inaccurate, so I now correct the record. The last two volumes of the diaries were held for a time by the then Prime Minister Johann von Lutz, and parts of these were published in 1925 by Lutz's son-in-law, Erwin Riedinger, under the pseudonym of Edir Grein. All the volumes of the diary were eventually deposited in the Secret Archive of the Royal House, where they remain today except for some crucial later volumes that were destroyed during aerial bombardment at the end of the Second World War. In referring to the diaries I have had to rely on the printed extracts.

All that I heard and read about Ludwig raised certain questions in my mind. Why were there apparently so many embarrassing secrets about him? And what was all the concealment about? The explanation, I decided, lay in the four areas of his life over which there had been speculation: his parentage (was his father really Crown Prince Maximilian?), his supposed homosexuality, his alleged madness and its cause, and the mysterious circumstances of his death. Part of my aim in this book has been to look at these issues in as clear a light as possible.

In carrying out the research for this book I have relied heavily on material already published. But I have also made use of original documentary material which has not been fully exploited before. I found much in the Secret Archive that threw new and interesting light on Ludwig's life, and I also examined the dispatches of Sir Henry Francis Howard, British envoy in Munich from 1866 to 1871, which are now in the British Public Record Office at Kew.

In the total picture I have presented of Ludwig I have tried to include a balanced assessment of his character and achievements, something that is lacking in many of the pronouncements about him. The complete man will, I hope, emerge from the pages that follow.

Acknowledgements

M y biggest debt of gratitude is to Gisela Kirberg, who
helped me with research, translated many opaque passages from German, gave constructive criticism and, by sharing
wholeheartedly in the adventure of writing this book, helped to
lighten the burden. Next I must thank Wilfrid Blunt for encour-
aging me to write a biography that would complement his own
admirable work *The Dream King*, and for lending me material
and giving me useful advice. A very special thank-you is also due
to Professor Hans Rall of the Bavarian Academy of Sciences, a
leading expert on Ludwig II and his reign, who read and commented on my manuscript. Although his careful concern for
historical accuracy sometimes bridled at my more daring speculations, Professor Rall was a most gracious mentor, and the
hospitality I received from him and his wife greatly enhanced
my visits to Munich. Another helpful mentor was Dr Michael
Petzet. Yet another was Professor Ronald Taylor of the University of Sussex, who checked the sections of my book dealing
with Wagner. I must also give my thanks to His Royal Highness
Herzog Albrecht von Bayern for allowing me to examine the
papers in the Secret Archive of the Royal House, to the staff of
the archive and to that of the Bayerische Staatsbibliothek.

Finally I must thank the publishers and copyright hold-
ers of the books from which I have quoted, especially the

following: Cassell & Co. (London), Hamish Hamilton (London), von Hase und Koehler, Verlag (Mainz), John Murray (London), George Rainbird (London), Random House Inc. (New York), Karl Rauch (Düsseldorf), Eugen Rentsch (Zürich), Schnell und Steiner (Munich).

1

The Northern Apollo Reborn

The whirlwind of revolutions which swept through Europe in the year 1848 might have passed by the little kingdom of Bavaria had it not been for the indiscretion of an old king and the ambition of an Irish dancing girl of iron will and strong sexual magnetism. The king was Ludwig I of Bavaria, and the dancer was a certain Maria Dolores Gilbert, better known under her adopted name of Lola Montez, of whom Alexandre Dumas said, 'She has the evil eye and is sure to bring bad luck to anyone who closely links his destiny with hers.'[1] The crisis which resulted from Ludwig I's infatuation with the dancer was to have important consequences for Bavaria and for Ludwig's two-and-a-half-year-old grandson and namesake who was later to come to the throne as Ludwig II. It is worth therefore telling briefly how the crisis came about.

Ludwig I was the second King of Bavaria. He had been born in 1786, just in time to be made godson to the ill-fated Louis XVI of France, after whom he was named (Ludwig being the German form of Louis). He had come to the throne at the age of thirty-nine in 1825 on the death of his father, Maximilian I.

In his youth a gallant soldier, he was a man of learning and culture with a great love of the art and architecture of Italy and Greece. It was he who turned Munich from a quaint old German city into the 'New Athens' that it came to be called. Munich owes to him the imposing Florentine buildings on the Ludwigstrasse, the church of St Boniface, and the Königsplatz, whose pillared classical buildings were later used as a setting for several political rallies. Though rather hard of hearing, Ludwig I was a man of vibrant personality and strong physical presence.

Ludwig's wife, Therese von Sachsen-Hildburghausen, was a woman of attractive personality and great beauty, but Ludwig had a restless eye, and such was his appreciation of female charms that he commissioned a series of portraits of famous beauties of the day, which now fills a room in the palace of Nymphenburg. At the time Lola Montez came into his life he was sixty-one years old and Lola twenty-eight.

The daughter of an army officer, born in Ireland and brought up partly in India, Lola had already had a stormy life. After a disastrous and short-lived marriage to a ne'er-do-well army lieutenant, Thomas James, she had become a stage dancer. Claiming to be of Andalusian origin, this blue-eyed, dark-haired beauty had danced and strutted her way across Europe, causing riots in Warsaw, tangling with the police in Berlin, having a love affair with Franz Liszt in Dresden and winning the hearts of the literati in Paris.

Arriving in Munich in 1846 she obtained an audience with the King and quickly enthralled him – though both of them later claimed that their relationship had never been physical. Soon he had added her portrait to his Gallery of Beauties and installed her in a magnificent house in Munich, where she held fashionable salons. Under her influence (or so it appeared) Ludwig began to reverse the oppressive policies of the ruling Ultramontane party, under the reactionary Catholic Karl von Abel, who wanted total supremacy of Church over State. To add insult to injury the King proposed to make Lola a naturalized Bavarian. This was too much for von Abel, who wrote to the King threatening to resign, stating bitterly that 'Bavaria believes itself to be governed by a foreign woman, whose reputation is branded in public opinion'.[2] Ludwig reacted by dismissing him and replacing him with the Protestant and more accommodating Ludwig von Maurer, who agreed to Lola's naturalization. Soon afterwards Ludwig made her Countess of Landsfeld and Baroness Rosenthal. By this time Lola had become widely disliked in conservative circles. She was a particular *bête noire* to the majority of students at the University of Munich, who tended to be fiercely Ultramontane and right-wing, though a group of liberal students formed themselves into a band to defend her, calling themselves the Alemannia and wearing smart military uniforms provided at her expense. The fury of the Ultramontanes grew; there were riots, another change of government by the King and more riots. During one demonstration Lola, who had bravely marched out to confront the mob with a handful of her gallant Alemannia, was forced to take refuge in the church of the Theatines after defending herself with a riding whip.

Soon the whole of Munich was in an uproar and the King, presented with an ultimatum, was forced to banish Lola, hoping that this gesture would save him his throne. But it was the year 1848, when Europe was glowing with revolutionary spirit. On 24 February the French King, Louis Philippe, had fallen. Now it was Ludwig's turn. He grew weary of the struggle against bitter opposition and on 21 March declared his abdication in favour of his son, who became Maximilian II. He later regained the affection of the people – in due course they even erected an equestrian statue to him in Munich – and he lived on for another twenty years, probably the most contented of his life, devoting himself to the study of art and the continued embellishment of the Bavarian capital. After his abdication he acquired the splendid castle of Leopoldskron in the hills above Salzburg, later owned by the theatrical producer Max Reinhardt until it was seized by Goering after the Nazis took over Austria in 1938.

These events meant little to Maximilian's son, the two-and-a-half-year-old Prince Ludwig, but children of that age are more perceptive than many people realize, and he would have noticed the change that took place in the household. The family now spent less time in the graceful, gay summer palace of Nymphenburg and more in the imposing Residenz in Munich, with its string of rather sombre courtyards. And his father, austere and remote at the best of times, was to be seen even less frequently at home and was now addressed not as 'Your Royal Highness' but as 'Your Majesty'. The boy might also have noticed that the attitude of servants towards himself had changed subtly. He was now no longer just the Prince, but the Crown Prince, though he did not yet know what a Crown Prince was or in what way he was different from other boys.

The change he would have noticed in his father's status co-incided with a corresponding one in his grandfather's position. By some curious reversal of hierarchy, which he did not yet understand, his father had somehow taken over the importance which had belonged to his grandfather. And the latter was now seen less frequently, spending most of his time at Leopoldskron or one of his other country retreats. This would have been regretted by the boy, who liked the kindly old man with his bad hearing and his deceptively fierce appearance.

The old man, in his turn, felt a bond with his grandson, reinforced by the fact that the boy's birth, at Nymphenburg on 25 August 1845, coincided with the exact date and hour of his own. It was this remarkable coincidence which had prompted him to request that the name Ludwig be added to those the child had already been given: Otto Friedrich Wilhelm. The date was in addition the day of St Louis. So the boy became Ludwig. The name Otto was kept for Ludwig's younger brother and only sibling, born on 27 April 1848, a month after his grandfather's abdication.

At this point we must examine briefly the long-standing rumour that Ludwig's father was not Crown Prince Maximilian. In 1991 this controversy erupted again when the respected Bavarian historian Prof. Karl Bosl gave a lecture at the University of Munich, suggesting that Maximilian was infertile and that, in order to secure the succession, a proxy father was found in the person of the dashing royal adjutant, Baron Ludwig von der Tann. Although this allegation had been around for many decades, Bosl's lecture caused outrage among Ludwig's admirers. Even the Bavarian Social Democratic Party issued a press release attacking Bosl on the curious grounds that 'a de-mythologizing of our King Ludwig II . . . could lead to an unpleasant destabilizing of the Bavarian tribal consciousness'.[3] Other historians have attributed the rumour to the fact that many Bavarians disliked Crown Princess Marie as a Protestant and a Prussian. Another person rumoured to have been the proxy was Joseph Tambosi, an Italian servant in the royal household. The argument for Tambosi is put forward by Rudolf Reiser in his book *Königsmord am Starnbergersee* (Regicide on Lake Starnberg).[4] Reiser argues that Maximilian had contracted a sexual disease in his youth and no longer had intercourse. Consequently, he says, a drastic remedy was adopted: the Crown Princess was made pregnant by Tambosi after being drugged with alcohol. There have been calls for an exhumation of Ludwig's body and a genetic analysis to settle the matter once and for all. In the absence of any such proof, there is little point in speculating further about these matters, and here I shall assume that Maximilian was indeed Ludwig's father.

Ludwig's parents were a strangely assorted pair. His father, thirty-six years old at the time of the birth, was an earnest, pious, somewhat priggish individual. He made much of his devotion to learning and culture, and said that if he had not been a king he would like to have been a university professor. He indulged this whimsy by cultivating the company of writers and academics. In appearance he was of medium height with a moustache, a receding chin and a face that seemed to be three-quarters forehead. He was always of tender health and, like his father and later his son, he was a martyr to headaches. In his way he was a decent and conscientious man and an able and enlightened ruler, but he lacked the strong, open-hearted, effective personality of his father and concealed insecurity of character behind a rigid and unbending devotion to principle. Such men do not make good fathers, and Max was no exception.

Max's wife, whom he had married at the age of thirty-four, was his cousin, Princess Marie, niece of King Friedrich Wilhelm III of Prussia. She was seventeen when she married and an extremely beautiful woman. Max's outspoken father, who like most Bavarians was unsympathetic towards Prussia, at first held up his hands in horror when he heard of the proposed marriage, shouting in dismay, 'Another Prussian!' But he was soon won over to Princess Marie and even had her portrait painted for his Gallery of Beauties. Her beauty was not the kind that goes with a passionate temperament. She preferred the gentle warmth of mutual affection to the red-hot glow of emotion, and she once suggested that the word 'love' should be replaced in poetry by the word 'friendship'. Lacking intellectual and cultural pretensions, she was cast in the active rather than the contemplative mould. She loved open-air pursuits such as stiff mountain walks – a trait inherited by her son Ludwig. She was in fact a rather endearing woman and must have brought a breath of fresh air into her husband's rather stuffy court.

This incongruous couple, the earnest, bookish, Catholic, physically tender Bavarian Prince and the unintellectual, Protestant, robust Prussian Princess, seem despite their dissimilarities to have made a reasonably contented marriage. Neither of them, however, came very close to their son Ludwig. Between Ludwig and his mother there was always tenderness, especially in his childhood and again towards the end of his life, but there never developed any mental or spiritual bond between them. As for his father, Max was too remote and aloof to be loved as a father should be, and later he became a figure to be feared as a harsh disciplinarian. He never provided the kind of firm but affectionate fatherly guidance that might have offset Ludwig's highly strung nature. The royal Cabinet Secretary, Franz von Pfistermeister, recalled in his memoirs:

> The King saw his two sons, Ludwig and Otto, only once or twice during the day, at midday during the second breakfast and in the evening at dinner. He very rarely visited the rooms where they were growing up; when he did he usually just held out his hand in greeting and took his leave as quickly as possible. It needed long and hard efforts to persuade the King to take his eldest son with him on his morning walk in the English Garden between 9 and 10 o'clock. But even so it only happened a few times. The King declared: 'What am I supposed to talk to the young man about? Nothing that I deal with interests him.'[5]

What Ludwig's boyhood world lacked in affection it made up in visual richness. Even as a small child he must have begun to derive pleasure from the beauty around him and to absorb the family's long-standing passion for art and architecture. Nymphenburg, where he was born and spent much of his childhood, must have played an important part in his early aesthetic education. This summer palace, then lying just outside Munich, was begun in 1664 by Adelaide of Savoy, wife of the

Elector Ferdinand Maria, and was added to by successive rulers over the next century. No place embodies more vividly that urge to which the Germans are prone and which they call *Drang nach dem Süden*, the 'yearning for the South' and all that goes with the South – the acanthus leaf, the orange grove and the marble colonnade. It is really a yearning for all that is exotic and colourful and romantic, and in Ludwig's case it was to include a yearning for other colourful worlds: the Orient, the court of Versailles, and the never-never land of the Grail stories.

The English Victorian writer Walter Pater understood this trait better than most non-Germans, and one of his remarkable *Imaginary Portraits* is of a certain Duke Carl von Rosenmold who bears a strong and probably intentional likeness to both Ludwig I and Ludwig II. Both of them nurtured in their different ways a vision of what Pater calls the 'northern Apollo', the 'god of light, coming to Germany from some more favoured world beyond it, over leagues of rainy hill and mountain, making soft day there'.

The spirit of this 'northern Apollo' was present in the ornate rooms of Nymphenburg, with their rococo plasterwork and exuberant murals; it lingered also in the park outside, among the pavilions, statues, fountains and waterways. The very name of the place was originally Italian, Borgo delle Ninfe, the 'Palace of the Nymphs', for it was dedicated to the goddess Flora and her maidens.

From in front and behind the palace run two canals, each about a mile long, the one behind ending in a lovely marble cascade which was one of Ludwig's favourite spots as a child. He also loved the fountains and lakes and must have been fascinated by the pavilions dotted about the grounds: the Chinese Pagodenburg, where perhaps he first acquired his taste for the oriental; the curious Magdalenenklause, a mock hermitage of artificially derelict appearance, with a grotto-cum-chapel, which

foreshadowed the grottoes and retreats that he later built himself; the lovely late Baroque Amalienburg, designed by François
Cuvilliés, a dwarf with an angelic touch in plasterwork and
silver-gilt. Ludwig must have been enchanted by the round
Mirror Room in the Amalienburg, which in snowy weather
became a brilliant igloo of silver, blue and white. He later built
similar rooms himself, though never with quite the delicacy that
Cuvilliés attained. In fact in Nymphenburg and its park we can
see a microcosm of the world that Ludwig subsequently created
for himself.

Other elements of that world were already present in Ludwig's childhood mind. His mother recorded that he 'listened
with delight when I told him Bible stories and showed him
pictures from them, especially the story of the good Samari-
tan . . . He had a special affection for the church of Our Lady in
Munich and enjoyed dressing up as a nun. He liked theatrical
plays, pictures and the like, and listened with pleasure to stories
being read to him. From childhood he liked giving presents to
others from his own money and possessions.'[6] She also observed
that 'early on Ludwig began to take a pleasure in art; he loved
building, especially churches, monasteries and the like'.[7]

Given the family tradition of architectural patronage this
penchant for building was not surprising. His grandfather was
pleased with the development, as he made clear when writing to his son Otto, who had been made King of Greece
in 1832:

> For Christmas 1852 I gave Ludwig a model of the Siegestor [the
> Victory Arch which he had just erected in Munich, based on the
> Arch of Constantine in Rome] . . . he loves building, and I have seen
> him carry out surprisingly good constructions in excellent taste. I
> discern a striking similarity between the future King Ludwig II and
> the politically dead Ludwig I; also in his devotion to his governess
> I find a reminder of my own devotion to my Weyland.[8]

The governess in question was Sibylle Meilhaus, after her marriage Baroness Leonrod, a kind and motherly woman with whom he continued to correspond as an adult. She was perhaps closer to him than anyone else, apart from his brother Otto, during his childhood years. His affection is demonstrated by the poem he wrote to her on his eighth birthday:

> *Dear Meilhaus!*
> *Could I more than wish, could I give,*
> *dearest Meilau, how quietly and pure*
> *would all your days pass by,*
> *how happy this high feast would be!*
> *But as I have nothing better now*
> *take my thankfulness as a gift.*
> *My heart is full of love for you*
> *and hopes that you will love it too.*[9]

Fräulein Meilhaus knew how to treat Ludwig with affection without spoiling him, and she always tried to counter any selfishness in him. Once when they were together in the little town of Füssen near Hohenschwangau he took a cheap blue and silver purse from a shop without paying for it. When she discovered this and scolded him he asked what he had done wrong. 'One day I shall be King,' he said, 'and all that belongs to my people belongs to me.' No doubt she told him firmly that it is wrong even for a king to take what is not his.

A lively picture of Ludwig and his brother as young boys is given in Maria Schultze's biography of Queen Marie. She writes:

They were the darlings of the people and in fact the most charming and beautiful children one could imagine ... Though their faces were similar there was a discernible difference in them: the Crown Prince with dark hair and dark eyes, Prince Otto, on the other hand, blond and fair. The Queen loved to walk with them through the streets of Munich, especially the Maximilianstrasse which was then being built . . . Even as a child Ludwig had a special love for building with toy bricks. He also liked erecting a model of the Holy Sepulchre, decorating it and embellishing it with lights. Prince Otto's favourite toys were lead soldiers . . . One Christmas the Princes were taken to the Max-Joseph children's home where they joined the children in cooking a feast, which was their usual Christmas enjoyment. The two had such fun with all the graters, mortars and baking moulds that the Queen decided to give the children of the home a treat in return. On New Year's day she appeared with a load of delightful knick-knacks and held a lottery with which the Princes helped. One little girl drew only a silly-looking wooden doll and Ludwig demonstrated his good-hearted nature by handing her a dainty scent bottle.[10]

There is another anecdote which illustrates the young Crown Prince's generosity. When Ludwig was about seven years old the family was staying at the Hermitage palace near Bayreuth. As they were having an evening meal together in a room of the palace, Ludwig asked if the sentry on duty outside had eaten since midday, knowing that the man had just come seven miles from the town to do his turn of duty. The King said no, and Ludwig asked if he could give the soldier something to eat. His father told him that a soldier, as long as he was on sentry duty, was not allowed to accept anything from anyone. But the Crown Prince, not to be put off, suggested that he could sneak quietly up to the sentry and put something into his ammunition pouch. This was suitably arranged with the officer in charge, the royal aide-de-camp von der Tann, whereupon each Prince put an entire cake into the sentry's pouch.

They both must have sympathized with the pangs of hunger for, as part of their upbringing, they were given rather meagre rations and often relied on the generosity of servants and kitchen staff to appease their appetites.

Certainly Ludwig grew into a strong physical specimen, and showed no outward ill effects of the near-mortal illness he had suffered when seven months old as a result of having to be suddenly weaned when his wet-nurse died of typhoid fever. Even as a toddler he had strikingly good looks which his mother liked to enhance by dressing him in blue, a colour which always remained his favourite.

The two brothers were on the whole devoted to each other, but there was occasional friction as a result of Ludwig's insistence on priority as the Crown Prince. Otto sometimes showed resentment at this, and on one occasion, for example, threw his gloves into a carriage before Ludwig climbed in. During the summer of 1857, when the family was at Berchtesgaden, there was a serious quarrel. When Otto refused to behave like a 'vassal' Ludwig tied him hand and foot, gagged him and tried to 'execute' him by tying a handkerchief round his neck and twisting it with a stick. Fortunately a court official arrived in time, and when the episode was reported Ludwig received a thrashing from his father. This experience tainted the environs of Berchtesgaden in his mind for the rest of his life; he always preferred the family's other retreats, such as Berg castle and Hohenschwangau.

The tyrannical streak which the 'execution' episode demonstrated was later to become very marked. The failure to check it can be blamed largely on the clumsy way in which Ludwig's whims were handled when he was a child. He was, for example, very antipathetic to physical ugliness, and if a servant with an unattractive face entered the room the boy would turn his eyes to the wall. The King at first attempted to cure his son of this phobia by ordering that two or three singularly ill-favoured servants should be his attendants. When this failed to work and Ludwig's phobia grew, his father capitulated and removed the unattractive servants. After that, care was taken to surround him only with servants whose faces pleased him. Hence the antipathy to ugliness remained with him for the rest of his life and sometimes caused him to be unjust. For instance, later presiding as King over a gathering of the Knights of St George, he noticed that one of the Knights Companion, appearing in the character of herald, was a plain man who looked rather ungainly in his tabard and coat of mail. At the next festival the herald was deprived of his dignity 'by order of the King', and though the order was later rescinded, the man was cautioned to keep out of the King's way on future festive occasions.

Another trait Ludwig showed as a child was his propensity to immerse himself in a dream world. One day he was found by the famous theologian Ignaz von Döllinger, later his religious adviser, sitting alone on a huge sofa in a darkened room where he was being kept because his eyes were troubling him.

'Your Highness should have something read to you,' the kindly Döllinger suggested, 'which would help you to pass these tedious hours.'

'Oh, they are not tedious to me,' the Prince replied. 'I think of lots of things and I am quite happy.'[11]

Already he had a private realm of the imagination into which he could retreat, and already he had begun to discover the symbols which enabled him to enter that realm. Among these the figure of the swan, also a favourite of his father's, was preeminent. He never grew weary of hearing his mother tell him the story of how the swan first came into being.

From the foam of the sea Venus was created, but the other waves complained to Zeus that they had been overlooked, and Zeus the Almighty stretched out his hand, took some of the foam from the offended waves and created from it . . . the swan! Since then the swan has glided regally over the waves which carry him proudly. Wisely gleams his eye, snow white are his feathers. And when he is hit by the hunter he dies slowly and with a divinely beautiful song.[12]

Ludwig often drew pictures of swans and sometimes sealed his letters with a swan and a cross.

Given the fascination which the swan held for him it is not surprising that he looked forward passionately to the times which the family spent at Hohenschwangau, whose name means literally 'High Country of the Swan'. It is a small, battlemented building of pale gold stone, set on a pine-clad slope overlooking the lake known as the Alpsee. Dating from the twelfth century, Hohenschwangau is one of the oldest castles in Bavaria. Max had bought it in 1832 in a derelict condition and had had it restored and the interiors completely rebuilt and redecorated.

Ludwig must have found this rustic little castle, with its small, intimate rooms and its views over the wild scenery, a pleasant change from the well-mannered Nymphenburg and the heavily imposing Residenz. A sign which can still be seen in the entrance hall expresses the spirit of the place: 'Welcome wanderers! Gentle ladies! Put your cares aside! Let your soul give itself over to poetry's gay mood.' At Hohenschwangau it was easy to follow this advice. Ludwig's young soul cried out for poetry, and here it found symbols in plenty that answered to that need – above all his own favourite symbol, the swan. Apart from the real swans on the Alpsee and the Schwanensee ('Swan Lake'), which the Queen sometimes took Ludwig and Otto to feed, there was an abundance of swan images in the castle. They were painted on the walls, there were vases in the shape of them, and if Ludwig wandered into his mother's audience chamber he could run his fingers over a magnificent silver candelabrum with swans as the candle bases.

Ludwig loved the swan not only because of its beauty and regal aloofness but because it was associated in his mind with the other things that Hohenschwangau offered him. As he looked down from the castle windows into the blue-green water of the Alpsee, or up to the wilderness of pine-covered slopes and rocky peaks, his imagination took flight and his loneliness became the exhilarating solitude of a soaring bird. And when he turned away from the windows his eyes would rest on the murals which his father had commissioned the artist Moritz von Schwind to design. He also had his own album of the artist's drawings for these murals. They depicted scenes from stories and legends such as those of Tannhäuser, the Holy Grail and the Grail knight Lohengrin, who travelled in a boat drawn by a swan. Not surprisingly, Ludwig came in his fantasies to identify himself with Lohengrin. Part of him was the knight in shining armour. Another part was the swan itself – aloof, majestic and pure. He knew that one day the swan in him would be able to take flight, but before it could do so it was to spend frustrating years in a gilded cage.

2

The Captive Years

With the departure of Sibylle Meilhaus in 1854 Ludwig lost perhaps the healthiest influence on his formative years. She knew how to stop him from becoming too self-important and at the same time treat him as a human being who needed love and affection. Had she remained close to him throughout his adolescence she might have counterbalanced his tendency to self-absorption and given him the ballast of good-humoured common sense that would have helped him through the critical years ahead. But the plan for Ludwig's education decreed that she must go, and henceforth his teaching was to combine intellectual saturation and emotional starvation.

In many respects this toxic diet was similar to that of Ludwig's near-contemporary, the future Edward VII of England, four years his senior. Both princes had fathers of earnest, Germanic temperament, stiff, restrained, intolerant of human failings and more anxious about their sons' training as future kings than about making them happy and well-adjusted human beings. In both cases the education resulted in unhealthy exaggeration of natural traits. In Edward it brought out a frivolous and tempestuous streak by a process of reaction. In the case of the more reflective Ludwig it kept him trapped in the hothouse world of his own mind, which in the end grew more real to him than the world outside.

Ludwig had already started some formal education at the age of eight, when Dean Reindl began giving him religious instruction and lessons in writing. But his schooling started in earnest on 1 May 1854, when Major-General Theodor Basselet de la Rosée was appointed his overall tutor. This fifty-three-year-old ex-cavalryman, with his strict, old-fashioned, militaristic attitude, must have seemed a formidable figure to Ludwig. Although beneath his starched exterior he was a good-hearted man, there is no denying that his effect was damaging. He went against the sensible tradition in the Bavarian royal house that no member should be styled 'Royal Highness' until the age of eighteen and that even after that the simpler form 'Highness' was to be preferred; instead la Rosée insisted that all servants should treat the Crown Prince with the full deference due to his rank. The Prince in turn was not to greet the servants too warmly. La Rosée also believed that the two boys should associate only with members of the nobility. All this tended to increase Ludwig's natural vanity, a weakness that he himself realized, as is proved by a passage he wrote in an essay in 1857:

> Vanity can also be the consequence of flattery. If one is, from one's youth, surrounded by people who do nothing but flatter, one very easily becomes vain and when one grows older it is very hard to give it up. Very often vanity is the cause of egotism which is very bad for men because one thinks only of oneself and forgets one's neighbours. The vain man might be said to have a poisonous snake gnawing at his heart.[1]

Not many boys of twelve could produce the strikingly morbid metaphor in the last sentence. The passage shows remarkable psychological penetration and self-awareness, and is an early indication of the potential which he possessed and which could have been developed in the right hands.

In addition to pandering to Ludwig's vanity, la Rosée also encouraged a sense of guilt. 'Try unceasingly to train your mind and body,' he wrote to Ludwig in 1855. 'If evil tendencies come up again, suppress them: with a strong will you can achieve anything.'[2] Such injunctions must have contributed to the intense sexual repression from which Ludwig later suffered, and greatly increased the agonies of his struggle with homosexuality.

La Rosée in the same letter urged Ludwig to 'be obedient. Because it was disobedience that brought man to his first misfortune.' But, while wishing Ludwig to 'be obedient', he also wished him to have a strong will. The education of any child with a mind of its own is a balance between these two aims, but la Rosée failed to achieve it. By his domination of his pupil he drove Ludwig further into the world of the imagination. Then, when he realized this tendency, he tried to counteract it in his usual heavy-handed way. 'The Prince . . .', he wrote to the Queen,

is to be kept from brooding; he must not linger over disagreeable impressions, but try to be less sensitive towards them. A sum of pocket-money is to be granted, but the Prince is to give an account of how he spends it. Special care is to be taken to train the Prince's will because the strength of the will can be trained; it is all the more necessary to emphasize this because ours is an age in which the imagination and the mind are fostered, but the will to act and live is neglected.[3]

Most of Ludwig's other tutors were equally unsuitable. His German teacher was Michael Klass, an educational theorist who had published a pamphlet outlining a system for improving the German elementary school system. Klass had some relatively

modern ideas, advocating for instance the production of open-
air plays in schools. But he held fast to an almost medieval view
of society as a kind of divinely organized hierarchy with the King
as God's regent. Ludwig clearly absorbed these ideas, and his
later attempts to live like a king who ruled by divine right must
be put down partly to Klass's influence.

Two of Ludwig's tutors were a cut above the rest. One
was Father Ignaz von Döllinger, a distinguished theologian and
historian who was later excommunicated for opposing the doctrine of infallibility. The other was the great chemist Justus von
Liebig, whose lectures Ludwig later attended at the University
of Munich and for whom he cherished a lifelong regard. Neither of them featured very large in his childhood education,
but both of them later played an important part in his life.
He mentions Liebig in a letter he wrote to his mother from
Nymphenburg when he was nearly ten years old, describing
how he and a young count had been playing in the park:

> Near our little brook the Count and I built a little group of rocks
> and we conducted the hose, which Liebig gave me, through it. If
> we pour some water into the hose it runs out of the rocks and
> looks like a well, and this stands for the water which Moses struck
> out of the rock with the rod of Horeb. The Count cut the tablets
> of stone in wood and I wrote the Commandments on them.[4]

The letter shows that even at that age Ludwig was able, in
a most unusual way, to bring practical ingenuity to the aid of
fantasy. The accomplishment was to stand him in good stead in
the building of his castles.

Ludwig was a person of outstanding intellectual gifts, and it
is one of the great tragedies of history that his education failed
to bring out his full potential. Had Ludwig lived today he would
probably have been given a schooling specially geared to his
needs and abilities. As it was, his teachers merely attempted to

squash him into the mould that was required for a future King. The way in which his education proceeded between 1855 and 1864 is clearly documented in a series of timetables preserved in the Secret Archives.[5]

In 1855, the year when he reached the age of ten, his day would begin at 5.30 or 5.45 a.m., when he would rise and dress. On a Monday his lessons, most of which were separate from Otto's, would then proceed as follows:

6.30 – 7.30	homework and breakfast
7.30 – 8.30	arithmetic
8.30 – 9.30	homework
9.30 – 10.30	German language
11.00 – 12.00	Latin
12.00 – 13.00	riding
13.00 – 15.00	walk and lunch
15.00 – 16.00	history
16.00 – 17.00	French
17.00 – 18.00	visit with the Queen Mother
18.00 – 19.00	piano practice

Other periods during the week were taken up with drawing, physical exercise and religion. The lessons continued right through Saturday, and Sunday morning was taken up with mass and religious instruction. So apart from the evenings, Sunday afternoon was Ludwig's only free period during term time. Riding lessons, however, were a welcome break, as he took keenly to riding and came to think of horses as dear friends. He very quickly became a skilled horseman.

It was decided that from 1856 the education of the Crown Prince should proceed more intensively. A high court official, a cabinet minister and a general each submitted a scheme, and an amalgamation of the three was eventually adopted. Seven years remained until Ludwig was due to go to university, and in that time it was planned that he should cover what the average Bavarian high school pupil would cover in eight years. This programme was similar to the one adopted for Crown Prince Rudolf of Austria, but comparing the two, Ludwig wrote at the age of thirty to Rudolf:

> It was your good fortune that you enjoyed so thoroughly excellent and understanding an upbringing and what is more, that the emperor took such a keen personal interest in your education. In the case of my father it was unfortunately quite different. He always treated me *de haut en bas*, and at best bestowed on me *en passant* a few cold words of favour.[6]

The quotation shows, incidentally, how Ludwig liked to pepper his writing with French, a language in which he early became proficient.

Ludwig must have liked the summer term best, when the family was based at Nymphenburg. Here he could escape in his free moments to roam in the park where he could have at least the illusion of freedom. The Monday timetable for the term beginning 1 June 1856 would start with the usual rise at about 5.30, followed by homework and breakfast. Then, between 7.00 and 10.00, would come mathematics, more homework and German. At 10.00 the Princes would go to spend some time with their mother. Then they would board a carriage and make the journey of half an hour or so into Munich where they would be instructed in Latin, riding and French. At 2.00 p.m. they would set out again for Nymphenburg where they would have lunch followed by a free period. At 4.00 Ludwig would settle down to some homework for Klass. Between 5.00 and 6.00 he and Otto would once again be with the Queen, then between 6.00 and 8.00 there would be swimming, exercising and walking. The evening meal would be at 8.00, after which they would at last be free until bedtime.

In August the programme was eased. Ludwig could stay in bed until 6.15 and linger over breakfast until 8.00. The daily journey to Munich and back continued, but after lunch he was free for the rest of the day.

By the time he was thirteen this heavy programme, combined with his highly strung mind, was beginning to take its toll, and Ludwig was starting to show signs of mental disturbance such as a tendency to have hallucinations. On one occasion his personal doctor, Gietl, recorded that while playing billiards Ludwig thought he heard loud voices talking to him and turned round to look at the invisible speakers. Otto also suffered from similar imaginings. The medical experts, however, assured the Queen that such things would pass as the boys developed.

Part of Ludwig's training in self-discipline was to be given a small monthly allowance and to have to keep a careful record of how he spent it. The allowance began on 1 April 1856 at 12 gulden or florins; see the Appendix on monetary values, p. 309, and the accounts continue from then until the early weeks of 1864. His outgoings consisted mostly of charitable donations, large and small, and also of gifts – knick-knacks of various kinds for his mother, bouquets for her ladies-in-waiting, lead soldiers for Otto. For himself he bought things like chocolate, bread for feeding the deer, swans and fish in the royal parks, and occasionally practical things such as tools, garden seed, copybooks, toothbrushes and nailbrushes. He also had a curious passion for gloves and would buy himself about two pairs every month. By 1860 his allowance had risen to 25 gulden per month and his purchases reflected his developing interests. In September of that year he bought a statuette of William Tell, one of his favourite heroes. By 1862 he was buying many books, such as Rüstow's *Campaign of 1859* and Walter Scott's *Quentin Durward*, and luxuries such as a golden chain, a golden swan-feather pen, and a medallion with swan and diamond cross.

From 1863 he was free to visit the Court Theatre as he wished, and as only full-grown princes were allowed the use of the royal boxes he had to buy tickets for himself and his companions at about 3 florins per seat. But this did not prevent him from making full use of the theatre.

As he galloped through his intensive education the programme became progressively wider in scope. When he reached fifteen it included Bavarian history, English, Greek, geography, drawing and dancing. His piano lessons were stopped in 1861 after five years, as his teacher declared that he had no talent for music and did not like it. But this assessment is not necessarily true. The music teacher was disliked by Ludwig, and it is quite likely that he delivered his verdict out of malice. The Prince acquired little knowledge of Greek and Latin, but otherwise his schooling and his own wide reading left him with a well-stocked mind and wide-ranging abilities. He could read and write French fluently and could read English well enough to tackle *Romeo and Juliet* in the original, as he reported to Baroness Leonrod in 1863 – Shakespeare and Byron were his favourite English authors. He was also good at mathematics and voluntarily pursued the subject. As far as German literature was concerned, he had read all of the great medieval classics such as the *Nibelungenlied*, Gottfried von Strassburg's *Tristan* and Wolfram von Eschenbach's *Parzival*. Goethe and Schiller he was for some reason not allowed to read until towards the end of his schooling, but he quickly made up for lost time, and Schiller became his favourite German dramatist. Most of what he read he retained, much of it by heart, for he had an outstandingly good memory. What he lacked, however, was the ability to focus and coordinate his knowledge. This had never been taught him, and his mind remained like some eccentric private museum, full of exotic and uncatalogued objects. At the age of eighteen he finished off his education by attending a few lectures at the University of Munich, among them those of Liebig on chemistry and Jolly on physics. Jolly remarked that the Prince appeared to comprehend the lectures well but that he was the only student who demanded a special seat, set apart from the others. Already he was beginning to manifest that shyness and reserve that were to become so marked later on.

At the same time he was coming to know the satisfaction of close friendship. His first real friend was his cousin Karl Theodor, who rejoiced in the nickname of Gackl and later became world-famous as an oculist. Writing to Baroness Leonrod in 1863 Ludwig declared:

> Knowing your good heart, which takes such a lively interest in everything I do, I feel I ought to tell you that I have found a true and faithful friend whose only friend I am; it is my cousin Karl, the son of Duke Max. He is hated and misunderstood by almost everybody; but I know him better and know that he has a good heart and soul. Oh, it is so beautiful to have a true and beloved friend to whom one can cling in the storms of life and with whom one can share everything![7]

After the lonely years of Ludwig's childhood we can imagine the effect on him of the discovery of friendship. Gackl, however, was soon supplanted by Prince Paul von Thurn und Taxis, one of the two lieutenants appointed as aides-de-camp to Ludwig when he was eighteen. He was Ludwig's second cousin, and his family, who had an imposing palace in Regensburg, had been hereditary postmasters to the Holy Roman Empire since the early seventeenth century. Two years older than Ludwig, he was handsome, charming, open-hearted and loyal.

The two young men first got to know each other well during a family sojourn at Berchtesgaden in September 1863, when Paul accompanied Ludwig in his capacity as aide-de-camp. Both of them loved the open air, and they went for many mountain walks together, casting aside the usual formalities between Prince and aide. Ludwig always found it easier to unbend when he was away from the stiff conventions of the court. Among country people and peasants he could always be relaxed and informal. In fact Ludwig to some extent idolized the peasants, as is shown by the following incident which Desmond Chapman-Huston relates:

> One day he and Paul were out on a mountain climb and in one of the loveliest valleys of the stately Watzmann they paused to look at a wood mill. Ludwig in particular was attracted by a handsome young woodworker whose good looks were generally admired in the locality. The month was September, the weather mild and perfect and, as is the custom, the lad would be working almost naked – the brief leather shorts concealing but little of his muscular legs, the torso exposed to light, sun and air, the head also bare. One may be sure that Ludwig and Paul talked to him, perhaps sharing with their new-found friend their sandwiches as well as their smiles.
>
> Ludwig never forgot what would have been to any ordinary youth a trifling incident and, later, sought to have his peasant immortalized in a work of art. Peasants and kings were always encountered together in fairy and folk tales – so why not now?[8]

Back in Munich after this idyll, Ludwig walked, for the second time in his life, alone in the city. The first time he had been allowed to do this was soon after his eighteenth birthday. On this second occasion he went to visit Paul at his apartment in the Türkenstrasse. The relaxed intimacy between the two friends is shown clearly in the letter written by Paul to Ludwig from the Taxis country house at Donaustauf on 27 October 1863.

> Most Honoured Crown Prince!
> A thousand heartfelt thanks for the dear letter which reached me from the distant friend. I was very glad to see that there was a little more quietness in the young wild little brain, and that there is the good intention to face the future . . .

Often, very often I think of you, especially in my daily prayers
I remember you and pray to God that He make me worthy of the
confidence which you have given to me . . .[9]

Paul's teasing reference to Ludwig's 'young wild little brain'
shows the confidence which he must have felt in their relationship. But soon that confidence was to receive a jolt. Jealous
tongues had started to wag, attempting to discredit the Prince's
companion, and rumours reached Ludwig's ears that Paul lived
a frivolous life. Having little malice in his own nature, Ludwig
could never get used to it in others and at first he probably took
the rumours about Paul at face value. He came to know better,
and his increasing dislike of the court was due in large measure
to his aversion to the malicious intrigue that went on there. He
must have quickly discounted the criticisms of Paul, for soon all
was well again between the two friends.

The friendship with Paul was to continue until after Ludwig
became King. In view of Ludwig's later homosexual proclivities,
it is important to emphasize that at this stage any leanings he
had in that direction must have been well below the surface.
For one thing it is unlikely that Ludwig understood yet fully, if
at all, what homosexuality was. It would therefore be a mistake
to read too much into his relationship with Paul. Consciously
at least, it was a deep friendship and nothing more.

As for his relationships with women, these were of the con-
fiding rather than the amorous kind, as they tended to be
throughout his life. Apart from his old governess, his main
confidante during his adolescence was his cousin, Anna von
Hessen-Darmstadt, daughter of his maternal aunt and sister-in-
law to Queen Victoria's daughter, Alice, who was married to
Prince Louis of Hessen-Darmstadt. In his letters to Anna, two
years his senior, Ludwig revealed much about his inner life,
his joys, his worries and his friendships. Another woman who

featured large in his life was another cousin, Elisabeth, daughter of Duke Max in Bayern, who was married to the Austrian Emperor Franz Josef. Eight years his senior, the strikingly beautiful Elisabeth became for Ludwig the object of a romantic and highly idealized adoration.

But the person who most profoundly influenced Ludwig's life from his early adolescence onwards was one whom he had not yet met: Richard Wagner. It seems that Ludwig's passion for Wagner was initially planted in his mind at the age of twelve by his governess, who attended a production of *Lohengrin* staged in Munich on 28 February 1858. Her thrilling descriptions of the performance with its theme of the Swan Knight, already so dear to Ludwig, aroused in him an immediate desire to see the opera. This desire was not to be fulfilled until he was fifteen, but the following Christmas one of his tutors, Professor Steininger, gave him a copy of Wagner's ponderous *Opera and Drama*. He also found, on the piano in the town house of his Bohemian uncle, Duke Max in Bayern, copies of Wagner's *Art Work of the Future* and *The Music of the Future*, which he read again and again. According to Wagner's biographer, Ernest Newman, Ludwig 'had studied Wagner's prose writings perhaps more ardently than anyone else in Germany or Austria outside the small circle of the elect'.[10] Newman mentions a list of Wagner's published prose works drawn up by the Munich bookseller, Christian Kaiser, at Ludwig's request in 1863. He also learned the texts of the operas by heart and later, in his correspondence with the composer, was able to break into quotations from them at will.

After pestering his father for three years he was finally allowed to see the performance of *Lohengrin* staged on a February 1861, with Moritz Grill in the title role. And it was this experience which turned his admiration for Wagner into something like religious devotion. Here on the stage before him was the Swan Knight himself, whom Ludwig had seen on the walls of

Hohenschwangau, and here in the background of the story was the Holy Grail. This miraculous vessel, guarded by a divinely-appointed king in a mysterious castle, was another motif that appealed strongly to Ludwig. It was all set in the most haunting words and music, which reached their climax in the third act when Lohengrin reveals that he is the son of the Grail King. He sings of a castle far away called Montsalvat, in the midst of which is a magnificent temple where the Grail is kept and where once a year a dove appears from heaven to renew the Grail's powers.

As Ludwig watched and listened he was overcome with emotion and tears rolled down his cheeks. The effect of the imagery which already held such potency for him, presented in dramatic form and combined with Wagner's wonderful music, burst upon his consciousness like a voice from heaven. The following year Ludwig heard *Tannhäuser* with equally spellbinding effect, and in 1863 there came into his hands a copy of the poem for Wagner's projected *Ring* cycle. The preface to this ended with the question: would there ever come a Prince who could provide the resources necessary to bring this vast work to the stage? And Ludwig answered in his own mind: yes, he would be that Prince. He did not know that the opportunity was to come unexpectedly soon.

3

From Cage to Throne

Whatever his faults as a father, Max was a conscientious king, and this was to prove his undoing. By 1863 a rapid weakening of his health, which had always been uncertain, coincided with a deterioration in the political stability of the German-speaking world which kept him from taking the rest that he needed. Like the rulers of the other smaller Teutonic states, he had reason to be worried by the state of flux in which Germany found herself. The old Reich, the Holy Roman Empire, had been dissolved by Napoleon, but one vestige of it still remained in the form of a kind of Germanic United Nations called the Deutscher Bund, the German Confederation, which met at Frankfurt-am-Main and whose aim was to guarantee the integrity of all German states, regardless of size and power. This Confederation was, however, threatened by two things: first, by the growing movement for national unity, which aimed at a far more close-knit Germany than the loose Confederation allowed for; secondly, by the rivalry between the group's two strongest members, Austria and Prussia. The latter state possessed in Bismarck a politician of formidable force.

Ruthless, unscrupulous, devious and brilliantly clever, he was utterly dedicated to the advancement of Prussia. His policies were to bring about changes in Europe whose effects are still being felt today.

King Max II had refused to take sides with either of the two giants. He advocated a triad concept with a south German grouping under Bavaria's leadership acting as a balancing third force in the Confederation, though this was made difficult by the South's lack of military strength and by the dynastic jealousies between Württemberg and Saxony. When a meeting of the Confederation was called by Austria in August 1863 to discuss changes in the constitution, Max felt obliged to attend.

As it turned out this was one of the most ill-fated gatherings of the century. Had the Confederation been allowed to develop with the wholehearted support of all German states it might have drawn the old empire together again peacefully and enabled it to take on a new lease of life. But that was not Bismarck's plan. He was set upon creating a brand new Reich under Prussian leadership, with the exclusion of Austria which he distrusted. He therefore threatened to resign as Prime Minister if Prussia sent a delegate to Frankfurt. Without Prussia's participation the conference ended abortively.

Meanwhile Bismarck was planning his next move, which was to take advantage of the Schleswig-Holstein crisis. This came about when King Frederick VII of Denmark died in 1863 without direct heirs and was succeeded by Prince Christian IX of Holstein-Glucksberg, thus bringing the duchies of Schleswig and Holstein into Danish territory. This was opposed by the rival claimant, the Duke of Augustenburg, who had the support of Austria and Prussia.

While the crisis was brewing, Max II had at last agreed to take a rest cure and was recovering in Italy from rheumatism of the joints. But in the middle of January 1864 an emissary was sent from Munich to tell him that the Schleswig-Holstein affair had reached serious proportions and that his presence in the capital was urgently needed. Max, who favoured an independent Schleswig-Holstein, heeded the call of duty and returned, despite the fact that he could do nothing to prevent the joint Austro-Prussian occupation of the duchies in February 1864. He might have served his country better by staying in Italy to complete his recovery, for after his return he developed a fever and his condition rapidly worsened.

Bulletins about King Max's health kept being sent to Ludwig, but they were on the whole misleadingly optimistic. On 25 February came the message: 'His Majesty the King is better in every way.' Then on 27 February it was reported: 'The fever of His Majesty the King has completely gone and the catarrh is getting better.'

Ludwig was sufficiently unworried to attend a performance of *Lohengrin* on 21 February with Albert Niemann in the leading role. Niemann, with his fine voice and striking looks, was for Ludwig the ideal Lohengrin. Further performances were ordered, and the singer was invited to a series of audiences with the Prince. Ludwig also sent Niemann bunches of flowers and a pair of jewelled cuff-links with a swan design.

In the eyes of many Munich people this preoccupation with an opera singer at such a time was disrespectful towards his sick father and showed a lack of concern about the worsening Schleswig-Holstein crisis. Ludwig, however, did not grasp, or did not want to grasp, the seriousness of his father's condition. And as for the Schleswig-Holstein affair, it bored him, as he confided to Anna in a letter of 7 March. 'I am sick of this eternal Schleswig-Holstein business . . . *Please don't show this to anybody*!!!'[1]

But he could not ignore reality for long. Early on the morning of 10 March 1864, Max lay dying in the Residenz. At 4.00 a.m.

he received the last sacraments, and at 5.00 the bells of Munich rang out, calling the people to say a final desperate prayer for the salvation of their King. At 8.30 Max saw the two Princes. What passed between father and sons is not recorded, but we can assume that Max gave Ludwig a few last words of advice and wished him well in his coming new responsibilities.

Max's hold on life grew steadily weaker throughout the day, and towards midnight the Archbishop of Munich stood up from the King's bedside where he had been kneeling with members of the family and walked into the crowded anteroom.

'Is the King still alive?' he was asked.

'Yes,' he replied 'he is alive in heaven.'[2]

Everyone in the room started to weep. In the bedroom Ludwig was standing near his father's body when a page first addressed him as 'Your Majesty'. He went suddenly pale. He had known for years that this moment would arrive, but now, when he heard himself addressed as King, he felt the full and awesome realization of his new position.

Two days later, while Max's body lay in state, the new King was installed in a ceremony held in the throne room of the Residenz. After all the great notables of Bavaria had been assembled there, placed in strict order of precedence, Ludwig, dressed in military uniform and accompanied by the high officers of the realm and his personal staff, passed through the ornate state apartments into the throne room itself. If he was nervous Ludwig showed no sign of it. Carrying himself with noble bearing, he mounted the wide, semi-circular steps and, standing before the throne, surveyed the assembly while the officers of the realm and members of the Cabinet took up their positions around him and below him on the steps. When he spoke to take the oath of the constitution several officers present were almost moved to tears by the solemnity and emotion in his voice. As Bavaria had no coronation ceremony as such, when he had taken the oath he was officially King, and it only remained for the Prime Minister, von Schrenk, to read the speech from the throne.

The public's first glimpse of the new King came during the funeral procession for Max, in which Ludwig and Otto walked behind the coffin as it was carried through the crowded streets by a deliberately roundabout route from the chapel of the Residenz to its final resting-place in the church of the Theatines, where sixteen years earlier Lola Montez had taken refuge from the mob.

Ludwig was dressed in the uniform of a colonel of his infantry regiment. He was then rather too thin for his enormous height, and his clothes hung on him as though too big. Nor was he handsome in the conventional sense, with his pale face, prominent ears and sloping shoulders. But these defects in a subtle way increased his impact. The eye was first held fascinated by his rather odd figure; then one became aware of the peculiar radiance that he possessed – in his large, soulful eyes, in the dignity of his bearing and in the serene intensity of his whole presence. The charismatic impression that he made on the people of Munich that day has become legendary. Here is how one observer, Julius Hey, described the occasion:

> The pale young King walked in the middle of the procession beside his chubby younger brother. Ludwig's sad expression naturally aroused the sympathy of everyone and immediately won him the hearts of the citizens, who shared his grief. If only you could have seen him, this pale young man, as he walked with bowed head and faltering step behind the coffin of his beloved father! He had extraordinarily expressive eyes . . . The whole impression given by his appearance was both moving and regal.[3]

The favourable impression made by Ludwig on the crowds was shared by the officials and others who came into close contact with him during the early part of his reign. In fact seldom has a King started with so much promise. Ludwig entered on his new life with exemplary zeal, and when confronted with a decision to make would often ask: 'What would my father have done?' Feeling that he needed to learn thoroughly about the government of his country, he arranged for a different minister to come every day of the week to instruct him. One of them was the Minister of Justice, Eduard von Bomhard, who describes the experience in his memoirs as follows:

> These sessions took place every week on the day allocated. One took one's seat on the sofa beside the King, and it was a pleasure to see the wide open expression in his eyes when some part of the conversation specially interested him. The King's demeanour had a certain degree of natural youthful shyness, which became him, but was at the same time impressively regal. He listened to one's discourse with great attentiveness, often looking searchingly into one's eyes. Afterwards he would talk about general things, but always the loftier questions of the day, never about mundane gossip of court and town . . . He was mentally gifted in the highest degree, but the contents of his mind were stored in a totally disordered fashion.[4]

It is interesting to learn from this description that Ludwig never talked about 'mundane gossip' but only about higher things. It was one of his characteristics that he always kept his mind fixed on a star and hated to have it brought down to earth. This was to be another cause of his isolation. When reality failed to live up to his ideals he shut out reality. A sense of humour would have helped him to keep his feet on the ground, but Ludwig showed only rare traces of humour. There is, for example, hardly a joke or even a mildly funny passage in the entire five volumes of his correspondence with Wagner. Otto, by contrast, had a natural wit and a quicksilver quality which was lacking in his more self-conscious brother.

Ludwig's daily routine would begin with an early breakfast, followed by a visit to his mother. Then, from 8.30 to 9.30 or 10.00 he would confer with his Cabinet Secretary, Franz von Pfistermeister or another member of the secretariat. At 11.00 he would have his daily session with one of the ministers, then a second breakfast followed at 12.00 by an audience. He would dine at 4.00 p.m. then see one of the secretariat again, after which Count Leinfelder would read extracts from the newspapers until it was time to close the official day with tea at 9.00.

Leinfelder was a kind of court archivist and general aide who had also worked for Max II and had been a member of the royal staff since Ludwig's childhood – it was he who had taken Ludwig to that crucial performance of *Lohengrin*. One of Ludwig's first actions after becoming King was to re-appoint the old retainer to the job of making extracts from the newspapers and from relevant literature. During the reading sessions Ludwig was always very considerate to Leinfelder, drawing up a chair for him, peeling him oranges, offering him glasses of wine and asking after the condition of his sick mother.

There is an anecdote concerning Leinfelder which throws an interesting light on Ludwig's character. When Ludwig was about twelve he was asked by an old woman near Hohenschwangau for some money. Reaching into his pocket, he found that he had nothing left of his monthly allowance, so he stopped Leinfelder who was passing at that moment and asked him for the loan of a six-florin piece. Leinfelder obliged, and Ludwig gave the money to the old woman. Ten years later, when Ludwig was King, he reminded Leinfelder of the debt and presented him with a brooch containing a pearl the size of a six-florin coin. The story illustrates Ludwig's natural generosity and also his remarkable memory, especially where kindnesses were concerned.

Leinfelder's devotion to Ludwig is illustrated by a remark he made to Count de la Rosée. Two days after Max's death

Leinfelder had met the Count on the stairs of the Residenz and, expressing his grief, had added that 'our only consolation is that we now have an angel on the throne'. Ludwig's old tutor, having a more sceptical view of the young monarch's character, had merely remarked that Max's death was the greatest tragedy that could ever have happened to Bavaria.[5]

Soon after this la Rosée fell fatally ill, and Ludwig hurried to see him, for despite the frustrations he had suffered at his tutor's hands he had come to respect and perhaps even like the old soldier. There might also have been an element of guilt at not having lived up to la Rosée's expectations of him as a pupil. When he arrived at the house he was at first prevented from entering by a servant girl who did not recognize him – though when she discovered her mistake she went down on her knees to beg forgiveness, which Ludwig no doubt readily gave. He paid his respects to the dying man and next day, after la Rosée's death, spent an hour consoling the bereaved family.

An intimate picture of the young King, at ease in the country and in the company of his mother and brother, is given in a description by Bomhard, writing of his meeting with Ludwig at Hohenschwangau on 27 September 1864 after his appointment as Minister of Justice. The account is also interesting because of the light which it throws on Ludwig's incipient schizophrenic tendencies.

> I was struck by the way in which every now and then, just when his expression and whole demeanour seemed to show contentment, he would suddenly straighten up and – looking around him with a serious, even stern, expression – would reveal something dark in himself that was in complete contrast to the youthful charm of a moment ago. I thought to myself: 'If two different natures are germinating in this young man, as it has seemed to me from the very first conversation with him, may God grant that the good one may be victorious.'

Later they were joined by the Queen and Otto for a meal, after which they sat on a balcony of the castle, a beautiful view in front of them, while Ludwig talked widely and impressively about books, history and state affairs. Then Ludwig and Bomhard boarded a carriage to go for a ride, arranging to rendezvous with the Queen and Otto at a spot some distance from the castle. Bomhard's account continues as follows:

> After an hour's journey we climbed out, and the King sent the carriage and servants back; we were alone in the vastness of the mountains. Suddenly the King declared that he had lost the way . . . A peasant girl, when asked for directions, fled in embarrassment; darkness was falling, and I was very worried. At last we heard the barking of dogs and went towards the sound. Then we saw torchlight approaching us. The anxious Queen had sent people out to look for us. We found her, together with Prince Otto, two ladies-in-waiting and two aides-de-camp, in front of a peasant house, sitting at a table in the open air. I had to sit down between the Queen and Prince Otto. The Queen herself spread butter on bread and served up coffee and beer. Relaxed, convivial conversation followed. I travelled back in a carriage with the King, Queen and Prince under the magnificent starry sky . . . [6]

After further acquaintances with the King, Bomhard wrote: 'He placed great value on feeling that his heart was pure and that his soul was chaste and unsullied . . . He gloried passionately in everything beautiful, great and noble, in the most exalted ideals.' [7]

In the arts Ludwig sought to have his ideals projected into word and image. He loved Schiller, for example, for his loftly conceptions of heroism, and it was through a Schiller play that he first met the actor Ernst Possart, who was to play an important part in his theatrical interests. Possart performed before Ludwig for the first time in October 1864, in the unsympathetic role of the scheming secretary, Wurm, in Schiller's *Kabale und Liebe*.

Ludwig was impressed by Possart's acting in the early part of the play and in the interval sent his aide-de-camp to congratulate the theatre director on having engaged the actor. This compliment, relayed to Possart in his dressing-room, spurred him on to even better acting in the latter part of the play, and after the final curtain the King stood in his box applauding while the audience called out Possart's name. Possart was invited to an audience with Ludwig, and two days later he reported at the Residenz in a very nervous mood. His account of the visit in his autobiography proceeds as follows:

> I was shown into a wide, three-windowed room with light blue wallpaper, in the middle of which was a clump of enormous potted palms. Anxious moments passed; nothing broke the stillness. Suddenly I gave a start when out from the greenery stepped a slim figure, towering above average human height and approaching me slowly and ceremoniously. I was breathless. Raising myself from a deep bow I found this majestic figure close in front of me; I had to tilt my head sharply backwards in order to look him in the face. But my gaze could take in nothing but two powerful, steel-grey eyes,[*] framed in dark eyelashes, which looked penetratingly into my own and held them captive . . . Now the King was speaking to me in a quiet, kindly-sounding tone, but I could not grasp the words – I just looked spellbound at those lofty, shining stars.[8]

Possart was one of the many people from the world of the arts – actors, actresses, poets, painters, architects, composers – with whom Ludwig felt a rapport. But one artist loomed larger in his life than any other single person. This was Richard Wagner, and it is to his curious relationship with the composer that we must now turn our attention.

---

[*] Considering that Ludwig's eyes were thought to be so striking, it is odd that people disagreed about their colour. Some described them as blue.

4

The Coming of the Friend

Gloomy weather hung over Munich in late March, 1864, as though spring were waiting a decent interval after the death of the old King before signalling to the population that they could begin celebrating the advent of the new. In such an atmosphere few people would have noticed the arrival in the town of a middle-aged composer, en route from Vienna to Switzerland to escape his creditors. Six weeks later he was to be back in Munich as an honoured guest, his financial problems at an end, but for the moment he walked through the streets unobtrusively.

Any passer-by who happened to recognize him as Richard Wagner, composer and librettist of *Rienzi, The Flying Dutchman, Tannhäuser* and *Lohengrin*, might have reflected that he looked rather unlike the heroes of any of his operas. He was slight in build and carried himself with a rather hunched bearing, as though his small body had trouble in supporting his head – a head so large that a Regent Street hatter had once had great difficulty in fixing him up with a top hat. His pale face was etched with tightly drawn lines, giving it a somewhat harsh appearance.

Forehead, nose and chin jutted forward aggressively. In this striking face was set a pair of alert, heavy-lidded eyes which, according to one of his biographers, Judith Gautier, were 'as blue as the Lake of Lucerne'.

As he passed a shop window on his walk through Munich these eyes were caught by a photograph of the young King, which made him stop and look. Wagner later wrote that the portrait caused him to be 'stirred by the special emotion that beauty and youth arouse in us'.[1] It was his first glimpse of the man whose life was to become so intimately bound up with his own in one of the stormiest, most incongruous and most fruitful friendships in history – a friendship that was of tremendous importance to the lives of both men.

In order to understand the significance of this friendship it is necessary to appreciate the colossal impact of Wagner, not only on music but on the whole world of the arts as well as on ideas and politics – an impact whose tremors are still being felt today. It is a measure of Wagner's importance that more books and articles are said to have been written about him than about almost any other historical figure. He is also immortalized in the word 'Wagnerian', an epithet which can be used to apply to so many different things, from a musical phrase to a large and noisy mother-in-law. Who was Richard Wagner? What did he stand for? What was the secret of his hold over Ludwig? And what was Ludwig's importance to him? To answer these questions we must know something of his life and work.

Richard Wagner was born in Leipzig, Saxony, in 1813, the youngest in a family with eight children. Ostensibly he was the son of the police actuary, Carl Friedrich Wagner, but it has been argued with some plausibility that his real father was the actor, Ludwig Geyer, who lodged with the family during his seasons in Leipzig. Carl Friedrich died six months after

Richard's birth, and his widow, Johanna, married Geyer the following year, soon afterwards moving to Dresden. Geyer was a talented performer and had a good enough singing voice to be used occasionally for small opera parts. Though he died when Richard was only eight, he must have helped to plant the seeds of Wagner's later development.

Early on the boy showed signs of a highly strung disposition and an imagination that was often painfully vivid. He soon became addicted to the theatrical milieu to which Geyer had introduced him, and almost as soon as he had learned to read he was planning dramas on a Shakespearian scale. While he could still do little more than play the piano with two fingers he was dreaming of continuing the work of Beethoven, whose 7th Symphony intoxicated him when he first heard it. He also loved Weber's *Der Freischütz*, which had set young Germany ablaze after its initial performance in 1821, striking an early blow at the predominance of the Italian operatic tradition in Germany.

Initially his ambitions lay solely in the field of drama, but by his fifteenth year the spell of music had taken as firm a hold on him as that of the theatre; and, with the boldness and determination that characterized his whole life, he began to teach himself composition. By the age of sixteen he was writing piano sonatas, and by seventeen had had his first orchestral piece performed. Meanwhile he was living a wild life, drinking heavily, taking part in riotous student escapades and discovering the magnetic power he had over women.

After a brief appointment as a solo and chorus rehearser at the Würzburg theatre, he entered on a wandering existence that was to continue for most of his life. He became musical director to a theatre troupe and married one of the actresses in it, Minna Planer, a step which he was to regret during most of the quarter century that the disastrous marriage lasted, for Minna was never able to understand the original artist in him. He held a two-year appointment as Kappellmeister at Riga in Russia, fled from his creditors to London, then proceeded to Paris where he lived in extreme poverty and failed to interest the musical world in his creations. He was saved by being made Kapellmeister at the Dresden Court Opera after the performance there of his opera *Rienzi*, which scored a resounding success. But in 1849 he took an active part in a violent insurrection in the town, the purpose of which was to set up a revolutionary government. When the revolt was crushed Wagner fled with a price on his head to Zürich, where he remained for ten years, outlawed from the whole of Germany until 1860 when he was partially amnestied by the King of Saxony. His full amnesty came in 1862.

A second attempt to conquer Paris failed, and in 1863 he settled at Penzing, near Vienna. His debts, however, were mounting ever higher. It was not only his profligate spending that was to blame for this; he was also a victim of the iniquitous system of paying composers at that time. Most of the German theatres secured the rights of limitless performance of a work after paying its creator an initial sum that was often derisory in comparison with what it earned for the theatre. Thus, while Wagner's operas were being produced throughout Germany to public acclaim, he was often without the money to continue composition.

By this time, however, he was a force to be reckoned with in the operatic and musical world. After *Rienzi* and *The Flying Dutchman* he had become more boldly original in his composition. The music of *Tannhäuser* and *Lohengrin* was something strikingly new and had given audiences a foretaste of the even more revolutionary work that was to come. The poem of his *Ring des Nibelungen* was finished and published, and he had written the music for the first two of the *Ring* operas, *Das Rheingold* and *Die Walküre*, and for part of the third, *Siegfried*. He also carried with him the unfinished *Meistersinger* and the completed

Tristan und Isolde which, however, no opera house had yet been able to stage. In addition he had written a number of essays and books setting out his artistic and philosophical ideas. Already there was a 'Wagnerian' school of thought growing up, with its fervent opponents and supporters, one of Wagner's most loyal allies being Franz Liszt, whose daughter Cosima he later married.

An anecdote related by Thomas Mann brings home just how original and epoch-making Wagner's work was. One evening, after a performance of *Tristan und Isolde* in Munich, Mann left the opera house in the company of Bruno Walter, who had conducted the orchestra. They walked in silence for a while, then Walter turned and said: 'You know, that's not just music any more.' What he meant was that Wagner not only fused music and drama in a way that had never been done before, but in so doing stretched the potentialities of music to a point where it became something of a different order.

Wagner realized that this capacity of music could be used not merely to enhance a story by linking it with a series of tunes but to make the listener feel the story in the very depths of his being. His capacity to produce music that would do this was matched by his capacity to create poetry and drama of extraordinary elemental force which explored such eternal themes as religion, power, ambition, adultery, incest and greed. The fact that many people found the presentation of these themes uncomfortable and dangerous, yet were irresistibly drawn along by the power of the music that went with them, is one of the reasons why Wagner's work was, and still is, so controversial.

Another reason lay in the innovations of his musical technique, which – apart from such devices as the *Leitmotif* – relied heavily on what is known as 'chromaticism', that is the use of the intermediate notes in a scale – those that we see as black keys on the piano, given the scale of C major. These notes lie outside the diatonic sequence, so that when we hear them we feel a need to return to the firm ground of the 'white' notes. They create uncertainty and psychological tension in the listener, which can be played upon by the composer.

Western music has seen the increasing use of chromaticism, especially from the nineteenth century onwards. Chopin, Liszt and Berlioz all exploited it (though mainly in a decorative way). But Wagner went further into the chromatic realm than anyone had done before – indeed at times he went almost as far as it is possible to go without using a different musical scale altogether as Schoenberg did. The prelude to *Tristan und Isolde* is a good example of the effectiveness of this technique. The music builds up tension, momentarily releases it, then builds it up again until the listener is floating in an eerie but exhilarating limbo. In other words the music has the effect of inducing a kind of mystical ecstasy. When such music is allied to strong archetypal imagery woven into dramatic form the result is something akin to magical ritual. Thus Wagner enthusiasts tend to approach performances of his work in a spirit of worship – that is in an expectation of something higher than the enjoyment afforded by most music or drama.

Often people with little previous knowledge of music or enthusiasm for it are nevertheless carried away when they come into contact with the powerful ethos and atmosphere of the Wagnerian world. Much of Wagner's early support is said to have come from people of this type, who were less put off by his radical technical innovations than those with more musical knowledge. It has also been claimed that Ludwig was one of these 'non-musical' Wagnerites. Indeed Wagner himself said that Ludwig had no real understanding of music.

However, to talk about 'non-musical' Wagnerites or to call Ludwig one is, I think, to oversimplify matters. As we have seen, each of Wagner's operas forms a totality, in which words, music and action are fused (although the term *Gesamtkunst-werk*, 'total work of art' is used to apply only to the operas after *Lohengrin*). Many people fail to respond at all to Wagner, but anyone who does respond deeply must, given the nature of the work, respond to the whole. Thus when we talk about a 'non-musical' or 'musically uneducated' Wagnerite, what we really mean is someone in whom Wagner's work has awakened a degree of musical response through the power of the totality.

This, I believe, is the way it was with Ludwig. The fact that he abandoned the piano after five years of lessons means very little – Wagner himself was a poor pianist until quite late in life, never becoming more than competent, and his remarks about Ludwig being unmusical are typical of the dismissive way that he often spoke when it came to other people's musical understanding. Although Ludwig was drawn to Wagner initially by the mythology of the Wagnerian world, we know from eyewitness accounts how deeply moved he was by, for example, *Lohengrin*, and it is impossible that the music could have played no part in this.

The essential thing about Ludwig's attitude to Wagner's work is the element of worship that I have mentioned. Ludwig understood perfectly Wagner's concept of his works as serving to lift the audience on to a higher plane. This, for Ludwig, was the function of all the best art, but in Wagner it reached its peak. The Wagnerian ritual and mystique satisfied him so completely that in the end it partially supplanted even his deep Catholicism, so that towards the end of his life he observed the rites of the Church only outwardly.

At the same time Ludwig fully appreciated the practical and technical problems that Wagner faced in launching his new art form, and particularly the unfinished *Ring*, which was clearly going to be even more difficult to stage than any of his earlier

works. In view of the limitations of the German musical world
at the time, Wagner had set himself a colossal undertaking,
and by carrying it through he was to change the whole musical
arena. It is in this, as much as in his originality as a composer,
that his significance lies.

Great innovative thinkers challenge the technical capacities
of their age. Wagner forced the musical technology of his era
to rise to his demands and so pushed the evolution of German
music and musicianship forward. This was no mean achievement when one considers the stagnant condition of the German musical world as Wagner found it. The low social status
of musicians and composers, the derisory salaries for musical
posts, the exploitation of composers by theatres and publishers, the restricted state of music publishing, the low standard
of orchestral performance and interpretation – all these conditions militated against any attempts to extend the frontiers
of music. As a young man Wagner found that most German
orchestras had not the faintest idea of how to give a faithful rendering of a Beethoven symphony. And in opera the problems
were even greater. Because of the long-standing dominance of
the Italian tradition it was extremely difficult to find German
singers of the right quality. As late as 1867, when *Lohengrin*
was being prepared for Munich, there was only one tenor in
the whole of Germany on whom Wagner could rely for the
leading role, namely the fifty-nine-year-old Josef Tichatschek.
Added to this were the physical problems posed by the inad-
equacy of most theatres to cope with works on the scale of
Wagner's operas.

By the end of Wagner's life all this had changed. He had lifted
the status of the composer to that of a seer, raised the standard
of musicianship, brought into being a whole new school of
singing and conducting, built the revolutionary Bayreuth opera

house, and created in Germany an operatic tradition that was the admiration of the world. Furthermore the mythology which he welded together and the ideology which he promulgated played a key role in the launching of a new German nationalism.

But all this would have seemed a remote prospect to the penniless fugitive who passed through Munich in March 1864. Had Ludwig not come into his life it is doubtful whether Wagner would have lived to see these achievements. His impact would have been much slower to take effect and would probably have been smaller. Ludwig was probably the only man in Germany who had a thorough understanding of Wagner's ideas as well as the tremendous financial resources necessary to bring them to fruition.

While Wagner was hurrying through the Bavarian capital, Ludwig, unaware that his hero was passing the doorstep, was already making plans to seek Wagner out. One day he asked his Cabinet Secretary, Franz von Pfistermeister, whether Wagner's name was on the current Munich strangers' list. Pfistermeister replied that there were many Wagners; which one did His Majesty have in mind? Ludwig replied that for him there was only one Wagner: Richard Wagner. And he ordered the Cabinet Secretary to find the composer forthwith.

Pfistermeister must have thought himself singularly ill-suited for such a mission. About forty-four years old at the time, he was a public servant of the old school: somewhat narrow and conservative in outlook and a bit of a plodder, but stout-hearted, dependable, hard-working and conscientious. In appearance he was somewhat schoolmasterish, heavy-faced and bespectacled with a moustache and goatee beard. He probably knew little about the man he was seeking, apart from Wagner's reputation as a revolutionary, and he must have shaken his head over the strange whim of his young master. But he was loyal and eager to please, and so on 14 April this unlikely emissary set out for Vienna.

On arrival he found that Wagner was not at his house in Penzing. After making inquiries he discovered that the composer was in financial difficulties and had sought refuge with his friend Frau Eliza Wille at Mariafeld, near Meilen on Lake Zürich. Pfistermeister did not go straight to Switzerland, but reported back on 20 April to Ludwig in Munich, where the court was in mourning after the death of Princess Augusta, wife of Ludwig's uncle, Prince Luitpold. This delayed resumption of the search until the 30th, when Pfistermeister left Munich for Lindau on Lake Constance where he spent the night. The following day, 1 May, he crossed the lake and travelled to Mariafeld. Once again he was too late. The Master had gone to Stuttgart, where his friend Karl Eckert was Kapellmeister at the Royal Opera.

So to Stuttgart went Pfistermeister. On Monday, 2 May, Wagner was spending the evening with the Eckerts when a card was brought to him bearing the name of a man describing himself as 'Secretary to the King of Bavaria'. Wagner, suspecting a trick on the part of a creditor, sent word that he was not there, but when he returned to his hotel he was told by the landlord that a persistent gentleman from Munich wished to see him on urgent business. He therefore reluctantly made an appointment for the following morning and slept badly that night. At ten o'clock Pfistermeister was shown into Wagner's room. Introducing himself as Cabinet Secretary to His Majesty King Ludwig of Bavaria, he expressed his pleasure at having found Wagner at last, handed him a photograph of the King and a ring of Ludwig's as tokens of regard, and conveyed a verbal message to the effect that Ludwig was the composer's most ardent admirer, that everything Wagner needed would be placed at his disposal in Munich, and that the *Ring* would be produced there.

Wagner was flabbergasted and went off in a high state of excitement to tell the Eckerts the good news. The next day he wrote a letter to the King in the florid, gushing style that was to characterize their whole prolific correspondence:

Dear, gracious King!

These tears of heavenly emotion I send to you to tell you that now the marvel of poetry has come as a divine reality into my poor, love-thirsty life! And that life, to its last poetry and tones, belongs now to you my gracious young King: dispose of it as you would your own property! In the greatest joy, faithful and true, your obedient

Richard Wagner
Stuttgart, 3 May 1864[2]

The same day, Wagner, lacking the necessary cash, settled his hotel bill by handing over a valuable snuff-box which had been presented to him in Russia. He then borrowed the fare for a first-class rail ticket and boarded the five o'clock train for Munich in the company of Pfistermeister. Arriving at 10.30, he took a room at the Hotel Bayerischerhof, then, as now, one of the best in the city. Meanwhile Pfistermeister hurried off to the Residenz where he found Ludwig sitting up in bed. Pfistermeister told him the good news, and Ludwig, with the occasional disregard which he showed when he was excited, kept his tired and hungry Cabinet Secretary standing until midnight while he talked. It was arranged that the King would receive Wagner at two o'clock the following afternoon.

Accordingly Wagner presented himself at the Residenz at the appointed time, dressed in evening suit and white tie. At 2.15 he was ushered into the audience chamber. The Master and his disciple came face to face for the first time. Each was deeply moved: Wagner by the youth, beauty and charisma of the King, Ludwig by the presence of the man he had idolized for so long.

For once both of these garrulous men must have been somewhat at a loss for words, but they soon overcame this and entered into an eager conversation which lasted for an hour and a half. What they talked about is not recorded, but we can surmise that it concerned Wagner's work and the details of his future life in Munich. Afterwards Ludwig asked Pfistermeister to order a portrait and bust of Wagner to go with the portraits of Shakespeare and Beethoven in his study.

The same evening Wagner wrote to Frau Wille: 'You know that the young King of Bavaria sent for me. Today I was presented before him.' And he added prophetically: 'He is, alas, so beautiful, spiritual, soulful and splendid that I fear his life must run away like a fleeting, heavenly dream in this common world.'[3]

There has sometimes been speculation that the relationship between Ludwig and Wagner might have had a homosexual element. But I believe this can be ruled out. There is no evidence that Wagner, in his whole philandering life, ever had homosexual inclinations. As for Ludwig, his later infatuations were all directed towards young and handsome men. Wagner, at the time he met Ludwig, was just approaching his fiftieth birthday – in other words there were thirty-two years between them – and he was not a very attractive-looking man in the conventional sense. We must also remember that Ludwig was particularly averse to physical ugliness in human beings, and his devotion to Wagner must have been in spite of rather than because of Wagner's physical traits. It is true that in their letters they constantly used such words as 'love' and 'devotion', but this kind of language would have been fairly common between two close friends at that time. It was a style which went with the high plane of intensity on which they carried on their relationship. That relationship was, we must conclude, not of a homosexual nature, but was a friendship of a very special kind.

Friendship can be a powerful catalyst. The greatness of many a man of genius has been helped to realization through the nourishment, stimulus and sympathy of a kindred soul. One thinks of Boswell and Johnson, Marx and Engels, Rimbaud and Verlaine, Goethe and Schiller. Such friendships are rare, especially when the friends are as different as Ludwig and Wagner were. Here were two individuals widely separated in age, rank and cast of mind, but both of them egocentric, arrogant and temperamental – an explosive recipe for a relationship. Explode it did on many occasions, but it lasted for nearly twenty years. And again and again, as we explore Ludwig's life, we shall see in it the influence of that friendship.

5

The Second Lola

In 1864 the American Civil War was at its height and Karl Marx was in London busy founding the First International. This was also the year when the Italian criminologist, Cesare Lombroso, published his book *Genius and Madness*, and when Holman Hunt painted *The Shadow of Death* – diverse events that are stuck, perhaps prophetically, into the scrapbook of history on the same page as the accession of Ludwig II to the throne. In two years Germany was to be embroiled in an equally disastrous war between north and south, and half a century later Ludwig's capital was to be the scene of a short-lived Marxist revolution. Genius and madness, some would say, contended for the soul of Ludwig, and even then the as yet invisible shadow of death hung over him.

But the spring of 1864 was for Ludwig like the dawning of a new era. He was at an age when life seems to be charged with infinite possibility. What was more, he had just become a King, and now he had at his side the man whom he worshipped above all others. The day after their first meeting he wrote to Wagner, still addressing his new friend somewhat shyly:

Honoured Sir!

I have asked Court Counsellor Pfistermeister to discuss with you the question of a suitable dwelling. Rest assured that I shall do everything in my power to compensate you for past sufferings. I wish to remove for ever from your shoulders the lowly cares of everyday life and to give you the peace that you long for, so that the mighty wings of your genius can unfold in the pure ether of your joyous art![1]

The immediate necessity was to meet Wagner's financial needs, and initially he was given an annual allowance of 4,000 gulden, or florins. This was a large sum by the standard of the day (see Appendix, p. 309, for a comparison of monetary values), and it was later doubled. When one considers that an advocate at the Bavarian Supreme Court was paid 2,800 florins, and a senior civil servant with eighteen years' service received 3,900 florins, it is easy to understand the resentment which Wagner's favoured treatment aroused. In addition he was given 16,000 florins towards the partial settlement of his debts in Vienna – a further 40,000 came in October to clear the remainder. The total sum which Wagner cost the royal treasury during his entire stay in Munich amounted to about 99,400 florins.

On 9 May Wagner went to Vienna to settle his most urgent debts, and came back four days later bringing his servants Franz and Anna Mrazeck, their baby and his old dog Pohl – throughout his life Wagner had an inordinate fondness for dogs. On his return he established himself and his household at the Villa Pellet on Lake Starnberg, which meanwhile had been rented as his home for the summer at the King's expense. The house was a solid, three-storeyed building somewhat in the style of a large chalet, looking on to the lake and set in a wooded landscape.

Its great advantage from Ludwig's point of view was that it lay only a short distance along the lake from Berg castle, one of Ludwig's favourite retreats, a cosy doll's house of a palace with little turrets and mock battlements. Like Hohenschwangau, it had been completely renovated by Ludwig's father. On the opposite shore of the lake was the castle of Possenhofen, home of Ludwig's great-uncle, Duke Max in Bayern, the father of Elisabeth, Empress of Austria and her younger sister Sophie – two women who were later to play important roles in Ludwig's life.

It was at Berg that Ludwig and Wagner spent a kind of honeymoon during the latter part of May and the early part of June 1864. Wagner described this idyllic interlude in a letter written to Mathilde Maier on 18 May.

> The young King is a quarter of an hour away from me in his little castle of Berg where he is having a short stay and which he visits in the summer from time to time. He has me fetched and brought to him every day . . . I read my works to him, and when anything is unclear he asks eagerly for an explanation and shows deep involvement and great powers of comprehension; his attentiveness is often staggering, and his beautiful features register deep sorrow or great joy depending on how I affect his mood.[2]

The way in which Wagner knew how to speak to Ludwig's innermost convictions is shown by the essay, *On State and Religion*, which the composer wrote at the King's request while the latter was away at the spa town of Kissingen in Bavaria meeting an assemblage of royalty including the Emperor and Empress of Austria, the Tsar and Tsarina of Russia and the heir to the throne of Württemberg and his wife. This essay of Wagner's belies the widely held view that Wagner was a muddled thinker and writer when he strayed outside the field of music and drama. It is a somewhat bizarre but brilliantly argued analysis of the nature of kingship and its relation to religion and art. For the following summary of it I rely on the edition of Wagner's prose works translated by W. A. Ellis.

Wagner begins by emphasizing the exalted mission of the monarch. 'In no State,' he writes, 'is there a loftier law than that which centres its stability in the supreme hereditary power of one particular family . . . in the person of the King the State attains its true ideal.' The role of the King, Wagner goes on to say, is essentially a tragic one, since he is called upon to strive for such irreconcilable ideals as justice and humanity. Because of this it is given to the King, more than to any ordinary citizen, 'to feel that in Man there dwells an infinitely deeper, more capacious need than the State and its ideal can ever satisfy . . . it is *Religion* alone that can bear the King to the stricter dignity of manhood.' The 'religious eye', Wagner argues, perceives that there must be 'another world' above the everyday one with its strife and rivalries. 'For *this* is the essence of true Religion: that, away from the cheating show of the day-tide world, it shines in the night of man's inmost heart, with a light quite other than the world-sun's light, and visible nowhere save from out of that depth.'

The King, then, stands at the point where State and Religion meet. 'Yet an irrecusable urge to turn his back completely on this world must necessarily surge up within his breast, were there not for him – as for the common man . . . a certain distraction, a periodical turning-aside from the world's earnestness which else is ever present in his thoughts.' This 'certain distraction' is, Wagner says, provided by art, and he continues: '. . . in conclusion I therefore point my highly-loved young friend to Art, as the kindly Life-saviour who does not really and wholly lead us out beyond this life, but, within it, lifts us up above it and shews itself as a game of play . . . in his most rapt beholding of this . . . there will return to him the invincible dream-picture of the holiest revelation.'[3]

This essay is more than just a general treatise on monarchy, religion and art. It was clearly written with Ludwig himself in mind and was intended to help him come to terms with his own dilemmas and conflicts by giving him a philosophical viewpoint that would bring the contemplative side of his life into harmony with the requirements of kingship. Wagner saw clearly that, without some powerful unifying vision, these two sides would drift apart. He also knew that such a vision would involve his own work. Inevitably, therefore, Wagner's influence over Ludwig went far beyond the field of the arts. There was a mystical bond between them.

Both of them were essentially lonely men, and each was truly understood only by the other and by one woman – Ludwig by Elisabeth of Austria and Wagner by Cosima von Bülow, the illegitimate daughter of Franz Liszt and a French countess. Twenty-four years younger than Wagner, she eventually became his wife, but at the time when they first became attracted to one another she was married to the conductor and pianist Hans von Bülow, Wagner's close friend and collaborator, a brilliant musician but a delicately strung, arrogant and temperamental man who was to cause Wagner much embarrassment in Munich by his tactless partisanship in the Wagnerian cause.

The blossoming love affair between Wagner and Cosima was intensified while Ludwig was away at Kissingen. Wagner had invited the Bülow family to come and stay at the Villa Pellet, but Hans, who was ill, had to delay his visit until 7 July, and Cosima went on with two of her three children, arriving at the villa on 29 June. During the week before Hans's arrival Cosima conceived Wagner's child, Isolde, who was born on 10 April 1865.

Meanwhile Ludwig was basking in the company of the Empress Elisabeth at Kissingen. He also developed a strong admiration for the Tsarina, formerly Princess Marie of Hesse, twenty-one years his senior, who hoped that he would fall in love with her ten-year-old daughter, Alexandrovna. Ludwig toyed with the idea of a future alliance with the girl, but when he broached the subject with his grandfather the old King was unenthusiastic: 'At your age,' he wrote, 'one is far too young for matrimonial life and, considering that you grew up so very quickly, it is doubtful whether a marriage would be good for your health. If you give your promise to marry you deprive yourself of the liberty of seeing other princesses.'[4] After leaving Kissingen Ludwig had returned briefly to Munich, where Wagner arranged a concert at which Bülow and another pianist, Klindworth, played exerpts from *Tristan und Isolde* and the *Ring*. Then he left for a visit to the Rhine, stopping in Schwalbach for another meeting with the Tsarina. He described the trip in a letter to his old governess, Frau von Leonrod:

'Not until 11 July did I leave Schwalbach where I had gone to see the Empress of Russia again. She is an extremely spirited and likeable woman . . . From Schwalbach I journeyed to the honoured and holy city of Cologne, travelling there by railway from Mainz down the left bank of the majestic Rhine.' No doubt the Rhine music from the *Ring* was still resounding in his mind, adding to the impact of the view from his royal carriage. 'What a wonderful river!' his letter continued. 'What magnificent banks! On either side of this splendid stream rise up imposing mountains which remind one of ancient times. I had with me a book containing legends of the Rhine, and so it was possible for me to transport myself back into the marvels of the Middle Ages. And now the enchanting Cologne! The wonderfully beautiful cathedral with its spires reaching towards the heavens must inspire a feeling of piety in every soul.'[5]

On Ludwig's nineteenth birthday on 25 August Wagner visited him at Hohenschwangau, bringing with him a *March of Homage* which he had written for the occasion. But unfortunately the performance of the march had to be cancelled, owing to the unexpected arrival of the Queen Mother, to whom Wagner was *persona non grata*, and the military band of eighty players, who were staying in readiness at Füssen nearby, had to be sent back to Munich – the work was finally performed in the courtyard of the Residenz on 5 October.

Soon after his visit to Hohenschwangau, Wagner wrote to Ludwig on 2 September,[6] describing how he had left the castle feeling reproachful with himself for being in a despondent mood on that occasion and fearing that he might have appeared ungrateful. With such a noble-minded and generous saviour, he added, there was no excuse for him to be fainthearted, and he was now resolved to apply himself to his task with renewed vigour.

Wagner goes on to say that it has taken him a while to adjust to his new situation, but that he has now gathered himself together and has started to apply his mind to the realization of his work. He continues: 'The difficulties are immense. A single conversation with one of the wretched people who move about like unconscious machines in the ordinary ruts of theatrical and musical routine is often enough to drive me to flight from the world...' He looks forward to the projected performance of *The Flying Dutchman* and believes that it will be within the capacities of the Munich performers. But *Tannhäuser* and *Lohengrin* will be another matter. And as for *Tristan*, he shudders at the thought of the difficulties involved – there had already been an unsuccessful attempt to produce the work in Vienna. He proceeds to attack the artistic schools and musical conservatoires. The time has come, he says, to tackle the problem of the unproductiveness of these institutions with their

'pitiful proletariat' of the arts. He realizes, he says, the need
to tread carefully in this area in view of the strong bourgeois
vested interests that are at stake, but suggests that it would be
a good idea to look into the advantages of organizing artistic
training along lines specially geared to his new art – a suggestion
which was later to turn into his scheme for a new music school
in Munich.

Ludwig's reply two days later was enthusiastic, but struck a
cautious note:

> I grant you that it will be difficult to achieve an improvement in
> this area; most men of our time, preoccupied as they are with
> selfish, money-making aims, have a greatly diminished sense of
> the splendour of true art. I therefore strongly urge you, my dear
> friend, to proceed with your plan in the manner you propose in
> your letter, namely with extreme caution.[7]

Wagner and Ludwig were right to be apprehensive about possible resistance from the artistic 'proletariat' and from 'bourgeois vested interests', for whispers against Wagner were already beginning to be heard, whispers which Wagner did not
help to quell by the increasingly opulent style in which he
lived on the King's money. In the middle of October 1864
he moved into a grand house with a garden in the fashionable
Briennerstrasse. Initially it was rented for him, but in May of
the following year it was bought outright for him by the King.
It was situated within a stone's throw of the former home of
Lola Montez in the Barerstrasse, but any prophetic meaning in
this escaped Wagner, for when Pfistermeister warned him that
his occupation of such a house would attract the envy of the
Müncheners, Wagner declared that he was no Lola Montez. He
would have done well to heed Pfistermeister's warning, for his
enemies were soon to dub him 'the Second Lola', giving him
the nickname of 'Lolotte' or 'Lolus'.

Just after moving into the house Wagner signed a contract with the Court Secretary, Julius von Hofmann (who was in charge of the privy purse), the purpose of which was to give him the security he needed for the completion of the *Ring*. The essential terms of this were that a copy of each of the four operas of the cycle was to be delivered to Hofmann within three years, that the work was to be the property of the King, and that Wagner was to receive over the period a total of 30,000 florins.

With an advance of 15,000 florins in his pocket Wagner proceeded to decorate the Briennerstrasse house in a style appropriate to some millionaire's brothel, for in order to function as an artist Wagner needed luxury as some people need alcohol. Sebastian Röckl, in his book *Ludwig II and Richard Wagner* (1913), gives a vivid description of what Wagner called his 'Grail room' with its acres of pink and yellow satin, its Smyrna carpet and its 'soft, springy couch covered with a white flowered moire'.[8]

But what began to irritate the Müncheners more than Wagner's personal extravagance were the far-reaching innovations that he attempted to make in Munich, with Ludwig's support, in order to accomplish his artistic designs. Wagner had planned a sequence of performances of his works extending over the next nine years, including *Tristan* in May and June 1865 and the *Ring* in August 1867. But two things were necessary for a production of the *Ring*: first, a new type of singer capable of coping with the technical problems posed by the vast work; second, a new opera house embodying a sunken orchestra pit and other improvements which Wagner had long had in mind — the sunken pit is one of the innovations which posterity owes to him.

A corollary of the first requirement was a new school for performers. Wagner outlined his ideas on the school in a *Report to his Majesty King Ludwig II of Bavaria upon a German Music School to be founded in Munich*, a brochure of some fifty pages which he submitted to Ludwig in the early spring of 1865. In it he argued that in both music and drama Germany lacked a style of performance answering to the national spirit. The main objectives of the new school would be to cultivate the right way of rendering the great German music of the past, and in so doing to establish a style that would answer the needs of contemporary German creative artists. As soon as the news of Wagner's scheme became public there was alarm and resentment in many quarters. The music teachers saw their positions threatened, and performers and theatre-goers alike took offence at the suggestion that Wagnerian opera was all that mattered. Small wonder that the scheme was never realized.

As for the plan for a new theatre, this appears to have been first mooted by Ludwig himself in a letter to Wagner of 26 November 1864, in which he wrote: 'I have decided to have a large stone theatre built, so that the production of the *Ring* may be a perfect one. That incomparable work must be presented in a place worthy of it.'[9] Wagner decided that the best architect would be his old Dresden friend Gottfried Semper, now professor of architecture at the Zürich Polytechnic. In December Semper came to Munich, held several conversations with the King and was commissioned to proceed. The site chosen was the Gasteig hill, a green height on the eastern bank of the river Isar, near the place where an unobtrusive statue of Ludwig now stands, the only effigy of him in a public place. In the short term, however, a temporary theatre was to be erected in the Glaspalast, the Munich equivalent of London's Crystal Palace, which suffered the same fate as its counterpart, for it was destroyed by fire in June 1931. The whole scheme fizzled out about three years later owing to obstruction from the politicians and Wagner's eventual loss of interest. Meanwhile Semper had devoted much time and energy to the project, producing plans and a model and making frequent visits to Munich. He had been advised by

Wagner, for reasons of tact, not to press for a formal contract, and it was not until the beginning of 1869 that, with the help of pressure from a lawyer, he received the money due to him for his work. It is something of a stain on the reputation of both Ludwig and Wagner that, having treated Semper in a rather shabby manner, they chose to be aggrieved by his quite legitimate impatience over his fee.

In January 1865, when nothing seemed to stand in the way of the scheme, Wagner had drawn up a revised timetable for future performances of his works, based on the assumption that the theatre would be ready by the summer of 1867.[10] In the meantime, *Tristan und Isolde* was to be performed that summer in the Residenz Theatre, and the following summer in the same venue performances were to be given of *Tannhäuser* and *Lohengrin* with a repetition of *Tristan*. The timetable continued as follows:

August 1867.	*Ring des Nibelungen* in the newly built festival theatre.
August 1868.	*Ring des Nibelungen* repeated.
August 1869.	Small-scale festival: *Die Meistersinger*, perhaps with the addition of *Tannhäuser* and *Lohengrin*.
August 1870.	*Die Sieger* [a projected opera on Buddhist themes which was never written] together with *Die Meistersinger*.
August 1871.	*Tristan und Isolde. Sieger. Meistersinger*.
August 1872.	*Parzival*, with repetitions.
August 1873.	*Ring des Nibelungen*. Preceded by *Tannhäuser, Lohengrin, Tristan*. Followed by: *Meistersinger, Sieger, Parzival*.

In the event the only part of this timetable to be realized on schedule was the 1865 performance of *Tristan*.

It is an interesting thought that if things had turned out slightly differently Munich rather than Bayreuth would have become the Mecca of the Wagner cult. Alterations to the city were to have included a magnificent new street forming a triumphal way from the Residenz down to the Isar and across a splendid new bridge to the theatre. In retrospect, however, Wagner must have been glad that he chose Bayreuth, for that small town came to be dominated by the Wagner establishment in a way that Munich never could have been. Even Ludwig himself never worshipped Wagner to the exclusion of all other art, and he intended the festival theatre and the music school to be merely part of a general refinement and elevation of the cultural life of Munich. Writing to Wagner on 8 November, 1864, he declared:

> My intention is to bring before the Munich public such serious and significant works as those of Shakespeare, Calderón, Goethe, Schiller, Beethoven, Mozart, Gluck, Weber. In doing so I wish to raise audiences to a higher, more concentrated mood and gradually to wean them of the more vulgar, frivolous type of performance.[11]

With his voracious appetite for reading, Ludwig had devoured the works of most of the great dramatists of the past, and now he wanted the public to share the sense of elevation that he had gained from those works. He also appreciated certain modern playwrights, such as Ibsen. If he had been able to accomplish his cultural mission, or even to go on believing that it could be accomplished, his life would have had a meaning and purpose that could perhaps have averted the progressive alienation from the world that led to his untimely end. With Wagner at his side it was easier for him to believe in himself and his mission, but when Wagner was eventually chased out of Munich at the end of 1865 one of the foundation stones of his existence was removed. As Ernest Newman has written in his *Life of Richard Wagner*: 'Had Wagner been permitted by

Fate to spend the remainder of his life in Munich, the King's personal destiny for certain, and possibly the political history of Bavaria, would have been different from what they subsequently were.'[12]

The opposition to Wagner and the frustration of the plans for the music school and the festival theatre can be put down to a number of factors, but basically it was a case of a conflict between two incompatible views of the world. The common dream of Ludwig and Wagner constituted a soaring artistic and philosophical conception that would recognize no values but its own. Against this was set the conservatism of a traditionally-minded public and the interests of a cynical and opportunistic group of courtiers, politicians and journalists. In order to understand the battle that was being played out between Wagner and his opponents it is necessary to know how the court and government operated in Munich at that time.

In Bavaria a rather unusual system existed whereby the King communicated with his government ministers not directly but through what was called the 'Cabinet Secretariat', a group of close advisers and aides who wielded considerable power and influence. What in most English-speaking countries would be called the 'Cabinet' (governing by mandate from the electorate) was in Bavaria known as the 'Council of Ministers'. The institution of the Cabinet Secretariat as it then stood dated back to the reign of Ludwig I who, under the pressure of his duties and preoccupied as he was with the rebuilding of Munich, decided to create a new level of officials. The result was a curious anomaly: a group of officials who were in a sense part of the private staff of the monarch and in another sense an extension of the government. In effect this group constituted a shadowy authority in some ways more powerful than the Council of Ministers itself, and the post of Cabinet Secretary was therefore a crucial one. The existence of such a system made it easier for Ludwig to turn his back on affairs of state and so exacerbated the problem which was to grow increasingly acute throughout his reign.

To make things more complicated, the King had another set of officials called the Court Secretariat. Whereas the Cabinet Secretariat dealt mostly with questions of state, the Court Secretariat administered the privy purse and concerned itself with the King's theatrical and architectural projects and other such matters. As the royal treasurer, the Court Secretary was a key official, and Ludwig came to regard the holder of this post as more important than his Cabinet Secretary.

Who were the personalities who inhabited this labyrinth of power? I have already mentioned the Cabinet Secretary Pfistermeister and the Court Secretary Hofmann. Another key member of the staff was the wily Assistant Cabinet Secretary, Johann von Lutz, who was to play a fateful role in Ludwig's life. In addition there was a host of other official and semi-official courtiers such as the 'reader', Leinfelder, and Count von Holnstein (1835–95), a sinister figure who will also play an important part in this story. Holnstein was *Oberststallmeister* (Chief Master of the Horse) from 1866, a more important position than might be supposed since horses were a key element in the life of the court, and the *Oberststallmeister* was in frequent contact with the King and could use his position to influence matters outside of the stable. It must also be remembered that Ludwig was particularly interested in horses and was a stunningly good rider. On his accession to the throne one of the first thing she did was to order a list of all the riding horses of the royal stable so that he could try them out one by one. Böhm describes Holnstein as 'a man of true Bavarian type and manners, powerful and intelligent enough to accomplish just about anything he wanted'.[13] In the large retinue of 119 people who accompanied the King on his journeys, Holnstein evidently played a key role, being responsible not only for the horses but for other transport arrangements as well. These then were some of the members of Ludwig's personal and Cabinet staff.

As regards the government, the figure who concerns us most at present is Baron Ludwig von der Pfordten (1811–80) whom Ludwig made Foreign Minister and Head of the Council of Ministers (Prime Minister) in December 1864 – the two posts traditionally went together in Bavaria. Pfordten had already served under King Max II from 1849 to 1859. A Bavarian by birth, he had been Professor of Roman Law at Leipzig and, having entered politics, was made Minister for Education in 1848 by King Friedrich August II of Saxony. In May of that year Wagner had tried unsuccessfully to interest Pfordten in a plan to set up a German national theatre in Saxony. Pfordten remembered Wagner with particular distaste for his part in the Dresden uprising of 1849. In fact he was a bitter enemy of Wagner to the end of his life. Everything about Wagner – his music, his political ideas, his personality – was repugnant to Pfordten, and in 1858 he had told the actor Emil Devrient that 'if the princes would only hold together as the democrats do, Wagner's music would not be given anywhere'.[14] He had tried to persuade King Max II not to allow *Tannhäuser* to be performed in Munich, something for which Ludwig had evidently never forgiven him. The young King also disliked Pfordten's professorial habit of lecturing him as though he were a student. Nevertheless, Pfordten was at the time the only practical choice as Prime Minister, and Ludwig bowed to necessity. With such a bitter enemy at the head of the government Wagner would have to watch his step carefully – something that did not come naturally to him.

Another important faction in the fracas surrounding Wagner was the Bavarian press, which was immensely influential and for the most part unscrupulous in its use of power. For example the liberal *Allgemeine Zeitung*, published in Augsburg, played a part in frustrating the plans for the festival theatre by denying that such a scheme was being contemplated, when its editors must have known full well that the King had given it his full backing. During Wagner's stay in Munich the press became increasingly vociferous and savage in its hostility towards him, and played a decisive part in his downfall.

It would be wrong, however, to see Wagner and his supporters as the totally innocent victims of a witch-hunt. They themselves were also partly to blame for what happened, on account of the arrogance and indiscretion of which they were frequently guilty. One example is the notorious remark made by Hans von Bülow while he was conducting rehearsals for the *Tristan* production in May 1865. Bülow wanted the orchestral area to be enlarged, and when the theatre machinist told him that this would mean sacrificing thirty seats in the stalls Bülow snapped out: 'What does it matter whether we have thirty *Schweinehunde* [curs] more or less in the place?'[15] This remark was reported in the *Neueste Nachrichten* five days later, and in the same journal Bülow subsequently published an apology which was courteously accepted by the newspaper. The episode was, however, never forgotten by the enemies of Wagner and Bülow, and it was eagerly seized upon by other newspapers. The *Volksblatt* declared that if Bülow had made such a remark in the Hofbräuhaus, being torn in pieces would be the least thing that would happen to him. The *Neuer Bayerischer Kurier* printed every day for a week the headline: 'Hans Bülow is still here!' And the satirical journal *Punsch* (the Bavarian equivalent of the English *Punch*) published a cartoon showing an audience of howling dogs which was captioned: 'Three rows for Bülow in the stalls.'[16]

As for Wagner himself, there was at first little hostility towards him. The politicians waited and watched to see what would happen, and the press confined itself initially to satirical but good-natured barbs. But as Wagner's relationship with the King grew closer, as his demands on the royal purse rose, and as his love affair with Cosima became an increasingly popular subject for malicious gossip, opposition mounted on all sides. The politicians were alarmed at Wagner's influence and financial extravagance. And the most conservative elements among the Munich population were scandalized that this libertine Protestant with his revolutionary views should have such an apparent hold over their young King. The press, for its part, began to exploit eagerly any opportunity to attack Wagner and was particularly quick to seize upon any signs of a rift between the King and his favourite.

The first such rift occurred in February 1865 and arose over a misunderstanding. The King had presented Wagner with a portrait of himself in oils and had said that he would like to commission one of Wagner from the painter Joseph Bernhardt. Wagner, however, thought it would be better to choose an artist who knew him better, and accordingly he arranged to sit for Friedrich Pecht. The King was delighted with the resulting portrait and sent his heartfelt thanks. When Pfistermeister raised the matter of payment with Wagner, the latter assumed that the change of artist had not altered the King's intention to pay for the picture and he told Pfistermeister to settle the matter with Pecht on the basis of whatever fee had been proposed for Bernhardt. When he learned that Ludwig now preferred to look upon the portrait as a gift from the sitter, Wagner arranged to pay Pecht himself and in due course sent him 500 gulden (of which Pecht graciously returned 100). Meanwhile, however, Pfistermeister had, it seems, mischievously told the King that Wagner was demanding 1,000 gulden for the portrait, and shortly afterwards he or someone else at the court had leaked to the press the story that the King was exceedingly displeased over the affair. Soon the newspapers were full of reports that Wagner was in disgrace. The town already knew that Ludwig had not attended a performance of *The Flying Dutchman* on 5 February, and it was assumed that this was a sign of his displeasure, when the truth of the matter was that after a performance of the *Dutchman* the previous December, with which Wagner had not been satisfied, it had been agreed that, until a model *Tristan* performance could be given in the summer of 1865, the King would not attend any more Wagner operas. But there is no smoke without fire, and it does appear that for a few days Ludwig was annoyed with Wagner, to the extent of refusing him an audience on 6 February. It is possible, however, that this displeasure was due less to the incident of the portrait than to a minor indiscretion on Wagner's part when, in conversation with Pfistermeister, he had referred to the King as 'Mein Junge' (my boy). In any. event, relations were quickly repaired, and Wagner was soon communicating with Ludwig as before. Whatever the cause of the temporary disfavour, it seems that Pfistermeister, whom Wagner still wrongly imagined to be his ally, had deliberately stirred up the trouble. Such upsets continued to occur from time to time in the relationship between Ludwig and Wagner, but they never disturbed the basic affinity which the two men felt for one another.

It is important to be clear about the exact nature of Wagner's influence over Ludwig. Some writers would have it that Wagner was a wily opportunist who, having gained a hold over Ludwig through art, then proceeded to exploit his patron for his own political ends. Others would maintain that Wagner was scrupulously selfless all along in his dealings with the King and never abused his position. The truth lies between the two extremes. Wagner certainly did not 'exploit' Ludwig in the way that many people have imagined. Ludwig was not the sort of man to allow himself to be exploited. He had a proud sense of himself and his office and was quick to resent any infringement of his dignity and independence. Furthermore, his political judgement was shrewd and he was perfectly capable of resisting any attempts to sway it, even when they came from Wagner. In fact Wagner himself confessed to a friend that, whenever he started talking about politics in their conversations, Ludwig would look up at the ceiling and begin to whistle softly to himself. This is not to say that Wagner had no influence over Ludwig. On the contrary, he had a strong influence which extended not only to music but on occasions to politics as well – Ludwig's whistling notwithstanding. But this influence came largely from their shared ideals. I believe that Newman describes their relationship correctly when he writes:

> The simplest reading of the situation . . . would seem to be this – that even as a boy Ludwig had had a romantic vision of himself, as King, leading the German people along ideal paths, and that the Wagner writings simply happened to strike into that vision at the critical time and with tremendous impact.[17]

Wagner, for his part, came to Munich primarily with the intention of furthering his art and creating for himself the sort of life which enabled him to do that. In the beginning he had little desire to meddle in politics, but when he found that the plans which he and Ludwig had laid were being thwarted by obstructive politicians and officials he was drawn willy-nilly into political intrigue. Furthermore, he had become increasingly aware of the vulnerability of the young King. He knew that such purity, innocence and lofty idealism were not the best qualities to withstand the cynical machinations of those who surrounded him. Wagner, in fact, came to feel protective towards Ludwig in a special way. And here we enter an important area in this whole story.

On the evening of 22 February 1865 an old woman named Frau Dangl, an astrologer and soothsayer, called on Wagner. He later described the event to his friend Julius Fröbel, who gave the following account of it in his diary. 'Wagner,' he wrote,

> is imbued with the belief that his relationship with the King, which seems to be a fairly familiar one, places great and high responsibilities on him. In this he is right. But he takes the matter in a quite poetic, almost theatrical way. He told me about the remarkable occurrence involving a mysterious old woman from the Munich populace who came to him one evening and said that she must speak with him about the young King and his destiny. She had already advised Ludwig I and Max II, but they had not heeded her . . . 'Do you believe in the stars?' the old woman asked Wagner in a loud and ceremonious tone. 'In the stars it is written that this young King is called to great deeds. I want my King to have peace, and you, Herr Wagner, must guard him against the misfortunes through which evil men seek to ruin him as they ruined his father and grandfather.' Wagner got into the most excited mood while he was telling me about this event, which appears to have made a deep impression on him.[18]

Fröbel's conclusion is confirmed by the letter that Wagner wrote the day after the incident to Mathilde Maier: 'The fate of this wonderful, unique youth, who is profoundly linked with me by a mystical magic, is entrusted to me, *me* . . . The profound meaning of my duty to the King, which is of significance to a whole people, nay to Germany itself, has been revealed to me by an almost supernatural experience.'[19]

The mystical nature of the bond that Wagner felt to exist between himself and Ludwig is also hinted at in his *Brown Book*, a sort of journal of personal reflections which was never intended for eyes other than his own and Cosima's. In August 1865 he was alone in the mountains, Cosima having gone with Bülow to Budapest, and was feeling lonely and unhappy. 'Oh heaven!' he wrote in his *Brown Book*, 'which of us understands the being by his very side? What do our dearest friends know of us? Unless it [knowledge and understanding] comes from the stars, as with Parzival [his name for Ludwig], no one can learn out of himself who the other is.'[20] And a few days later, reflecting on the divine imperative which he detected in Ludwig, he wrote: 'Only one man have I ever come upon with this divine "must" in his soul – Parzival, my son in the Holy Spirit.'[21]

At that time Wagner had not yet written *Parsifal* (the title of the opera was spelt with 's' and 'f' rather than 'z' and 'v'), which was to be his final work, and some would say his greatest. But he had been carrying the idea around with him for many years. He had read deeply in the literature connected with the Parzival legend, notably Wolfram von Eschenbach's powerful thirteenth-century version of the story, and he had written *Lohengrin* partly as a sort of preparation for the later opera. He must have felt in his heart that *Parsifal* was to be the culmination of his life's work and would contain the purest essence of his art and beliefs. For this reason he allowed the work to mature slowly in his mind over the years and to become part of his being. When he met Ludwig he must have been struck by the similarities between the young King and the figure of Parzival, the 'Pure Fool' (*der reine Tor*, that is, one whose simplicity enables him to attain great goodness and wisdom). Both were strong, brave and handsome, and both were curiously naive and innocent. But, most important of all, both were 'called', as the astrologer Frau Dangl put it, to a high destiny. In the Parzival story the hero is destined by birth to succeed to the Grail kingship, and his footsteps are guided by divine impulse until he finally asks the right question concerning the wound of the 'Fisher King' Amfortas, the previous keeper of the Grail. By asking Amfortas the nature of the wound from which he suffers, Parzival lays claim to the Grail and removes the curse which had kept Amfortas's wound festering and made his kingdom a waste land.

Just as Parzival obeyed the dictates of his God-given birthright, so Ludwig – as Wagner saw it – obeyed the divine 'must' in his soul. Thus when Wagner called Ludwig 'my Parzival' it was more than just a nickname. And when he described the King as 'my son in the Holy Spirit', he meant that in Ludwig he had found someone who would be the real embodiment of all the ideals that he had projected into the figure of Parzival – someone who would be able to fulfil his hopes for the regeneration of the waste land of Germany through art. That Ludwig accepted this view of himself is suggested by the fact that in several of his letters to Wagner he refers to himself as Parzival.

Wagner had some years earlier set down his thoughts on the destiny of Germany, and its relationship to the story of the Nibelung Hoard and other myths, in a remarkable essay entitled *The Wibelungen*. The name, Wagner says, is cognate with 'Nibelungen' and refers to the blood-line of the Frankish kings who, he claims, are the true inheritors of the 'Hoard', by which he appears to mean the possession of supreme worldly power – a power which rightfully belongs to a master-race who came from the east and were descended from what he calls an *Urvater* or 'Original Father', an idea which, according to Wagner, became amalgamated with the story of Christ. All this is more fantasy than historical fact, but Wagner argues the case with eloquence. In a revealing passage he imagines the Emperor Frederick Barbarossa speaking the following words:

> In the German Folk survives the oldest lawful race of Kings in all the world: it issues from a son of God, called by his nearest kinsmen Siegfried, but *Christ* by the remaining nations of the earth; for the welfare of his race, and the peoples of the earth derived therefrom, he wrought a deed most glorious, and for that deed's sake suffered death. The nearest heirs of his great deed, and of the power won thereby, are the 'Nibelungen', to whom the earth belongs in name

and for the happiness of every nation. The Germans are the oldest nation, their blue-blood King is a 'Nibelung', and at their head he claims world-rulership . . . Thus too the Kaiser delegates high-priestly power, originally no less pertaining to him than the earthly might, to the Pope of Rome: the latter has to exercise the Sight-of-God in his name, and to acquaint him with the God's-decree, that he may execute the Heavenly Will in the name of God upon the earth.[22]

After a time, Wagner says, Frederick turned his gaze eastwards.

A force resistless drew him on toward Asia, to the cradle of the nations, to the place where God begat the father of all Men. Wondrous legends had he heard of a lordly country deep in Asia, in farthest India, of an ur-divine Priest-King who governed there a pure and happy people, immortal through the nature of a wonder-working relic called '*The Holy Grail*'.[23]

Frederick was killed while crusading in the Holy Land, but the legend of the Grail took hold and replaced the Hoard as the object of the great quest. Wagner goes on:

Since then, the legend went that once the *Keeper of the Grail* had really brought the holy relic to the Occident; great wonders had he here performed: in the Netherlands, the Nibelungen's ancient seat, a Knight of the Grail had appeared, but vanished when asked forbidden tidings of his origin; – then was the Grail conducted back by its old guardian to . . . distant morning-land; – in a castle on a lofty mount in India it now was kept once more . . . The spiritual ascension of the Hoard into the Grail was accomplished in the German conscience, and the Grail, at least in the meaning lent it by German poets, must rank as the ideal representative or follower of the Nibelungen-Hoard; it, too, had sprung from Asia, from the ur-home of mankind; God had guided it to men as paragon of holiness.

It is of the first importance that its keeper was priest and king alike, that is, a Master (*Oberhaupt*) of all Spiritual Knighthood, such as was introduced from the Orient in the twelfth century.[24]

It must be remembered that Ludwig had eagerly read all of Wagner's published works and must have thoroughly absorbed the ideas put forward in *The Wibelungen*. Much that happened later in his life is explained in terms of this mythology.

6

A Triumph, an Idyll and a Parting

The year 1865 was to be one of the most glorious and also one of the saddest in the lives of both Ludwig and Wagner. It opened full of promise, with plans taking shape for a première of *Tristan and Isolde*, to be held in Munich in the spring. An attempt had already been made to stage this opera in Vienna, but nothing had come of it, mainly because of the lack of a suitable heroic tenor to play the highly demanding role of Tristan. By 1865, however, such a singer had emerged. He was the twenty-nine-year-old Ludwig Schnorr von Carolsfeld, a member of the Dresden opera company. Schnorr was a man whose physical weight and girth were as imposing as his voice, and this had at first prejudiced Wagner against him, but when the composer heard Schnorr perform he was completely won over. The young tenor could both sing and act with great power and sensitivity, and he brought to his Wagnerian performances a deep and intelligent appreciation of the composer's intentions. Furthermore he was a man of genial temperament, singularly lacking in egocentricity and greatly devoted to Wagner and his ideals. In short, he was worth his considerable weight in gold to Wagner. His wife Malvina, some ten years older than her husband, was also a fine singer and was well suited to the part of Isolde.

At the end of February the pair came to Munich for discussions with Wagner, and a test rehearsal was held, as well as a performance of *Tannhäuser* with Schnorr in the title role. Both the King and Wagner were enchanted by Schnorr's singing, and it was arranged with the King of Saxony for the couple to have leave of absence from Dresden for the months of April, May and June. The first performance of *Tristan* was accordingly planned for the middle of May.

After returning briefly to Dresden, Schnorr and Malvina arrived back in Munich on 5 April, and rehearsals began. By a strangely appropriate coincidence, on the day of the first rehearsal, Cosima von Bülow gave birth to Wagner's daughter, Isolde. Her second name, Ludowika, was chosen in honour of the King.

The first performance was fixed for 15 May, and as the day approached Wagner's friends and followers came to Munich from all parts of Europe. The King was beside himself with excitement. On 10 May he wrote to Wagner: 'The joy of my heart gives me no rest: I must write to you. Nearer and nearer draws the blessed day: "Tristan will arise!"' . . . Beloved I shall never abandon you! – Oh, "Tristan", "Tristan" is coming to me. The dreams of my boyhood are to be fulfilled!'[1]

On the 11th a full dress rehearsal of *Tristan* was held before the King and about 600 invited guests. To mark the occasion Ludwig granted an amnesty to those who had been condemned for taking part in the revolution of 1848–9, thereby symbolically removing any guilt that might still have clung to Wagner as a former revolutionary. On the 13th an extra and final rehearsal was held, with no audience.

On the 15th, the day scheduled for the premiere, disaster struck. First came a bad omen for Wagner when in the morning the bailiffs invaded his house and he had to send Cosima to the Court Secretary, Hofmann, with an urgent appeal for 2,400 florins. Then, while Wagner was still recovering from this humiliating experience, Schnorr arrived at the house and tearfully announced that the evening's performance would have to be postponed as Malvina's voice had suddenly become hoarse, the result of taking a steam bath.

That afternoon the postponement was announced, and soon Munich was buzzing with extraordinary rumours about the reasons. Some said that Wagner's appalling music had ruined Malvina's voice. Others declared that Bülow had got wind of a plot to assassinate him. Another theory was that the whole orchestra had gone on strike for more pay. Wagner's enemies in the press gloated boorishly over the disaster, and a small local theatre put on a parody of the opera under the title of *Tristanderl und Süssholde*.

But the set-back, however painful, was only temporary. The Schnorrs went off to the spa town of Bad Reichenhall near the Austrian border to recover, returning to Munich on 6 June. Three final rehearsals were held, and on 10 June, six years after its completion, *Tristan* was finally brought before the public.

It must have been an electrifying occasion. The performance was due to begin at six o'clock, and by ten past, tension was mounting. The audience included ex-King Ludwig I, the King's uncles Luitpold and Adalbert, and Duke Max and his family. Suddenly the young King appeared, dressed in civilian clothes but looking as striking as ever, and took his seat in the royal box. This was the signal for the haggard, quixotic figure of Bülow to raise his baton before the dimly lit orchestra and signal the beginning of the prelude. For the next five hours the audience sat entranced. After each act there was thunderous applause, drowning a small amount of hissing. When the performance ended, Wagner and the Schnorrs appeared on the stage to take a triumphant bow. 'We are all in a dream-state over the extraordinarily complete success,' wrote Billow in a letter a few days later, 'and especially over the public's increasing sympathy. It is the greatest success that a Wagner work has had anywhere.'[2]

As for Ludwig, his rapture made him positively incoherent in the letter he scribbled to Wagner after the performance, even forgetting to sign his name:

> My Unique One! My Holy One!
> How blissful! – Perfect. So overcome with delight! – To drown . . . to sink – unconscious – highest pleasure. –
> Divine work! –
>   Eternally true –
>   to beyond the grave.[3]

Three days later he attended a second performance of the work, but stayed away from a third on 19 June, probably so as to avoid having to share the experience with his uncle Otto, King of Greece, whom he found boring and dull-witted. Instead he hurried away to the country to enjoy his euphoria in solitude.

The happy interlude following the *Tristan* triumph was soon broken by tragedy. The strain of the performances had taken a tremendous toll on Schnorr's physical resources and nervous energy, and during the ordeal he had caught a chill. He returned with Malvina to Dresden on 13 July, their stay having been extended by permission of the King of Saxony. On the 16th he was suddenly attacked by agonizing rheumatism and rapidly sank into a delirious fever. On the 21st he died of an apoplexy of the brain. His last words were: 'Farewell Siegfried! Console my Richard!'[4]

Wagner was shattered. It must have seemed as though a dark angel dogged his footsteps, forever trying to shut out the sun whenever it shone on him. Schnorr's death increased the depression which he began to feel after the elation of the *Tristan* success had worn off.

Meanwhile the King was up in the mountains. On 21 June he wrote to Wagner:

> I am writing this letter on a mountain in a high Alpine region, far from the hustle and bustle of the human crowd . . . Long since the daylight has sunk down and disappeared behind the high chain of mountains; peace reigns in the deep valleys; the ringing of the cow-bells, the song of a cowherd rise upwards to my joyful solitude. The evening star sends its gentle light from afar, showing the wanderer his way out of the valley and once again reminding me of my Dear One and his divine works. In the distance, at the end of the valley, rises the church of Ettal out of the dark green of the pine woods. The Emperor Ludwig the Bavarian is said to have built this church after the plan of the Grail Temple at Montsalvat. There the figure of Lohengrin revives anew in my vision; and there I see in my mind Parzival, the hero of the future, searching for salvation, for the single truth. How my soul longs and thirsts for such works as can re-create those spirits for us . . .[5]

Here again we catch a glimpse of those mythical driving forces that were so important in Ludwig's life. His namesake Ludwig the Bavarian became Holy Roman Emperor in 1328 and was a figure much admired by Ludwig II. As the above letter shows, it was easy for Ludwig to see this earlier Wittelsbach as a kind of Grail King, merging with the figures of Parzival and Lohengrin. In some way he saw himself carrying on this role, perhaps by virtue of some mystical power of the Wittelsbach blood-line, perhaps even through reincarnation. It is significant that two of the men Ludwig admired were both namesakes: Ludwig the Bavarian and Louis XIV of France. The fact that they bore his name might have been to him a divine sign that he and they were really the same individual in different flesh and separated by time. It is also significant that Ludwig linked his two namesakes in another way. The name of the Ettal valley in southern Bavaria, with its 'Grail Temple' attributed to Ludwig the Bavarian, reappeared in Ludwig's code name for one of his castles, Meicost Ettal, an anagram of Louis XIV's famous utterance: *L'état, c'est Moi*.

It would not be surprising if Ludwig believed in reincarnation, as we know that Wagner did so. It is true that Wagner's correspondence with Ludwig rarely touches on such subjects, and during the summer of 1865 his letters to the King were mostly occupied with increasingly vehement attacks on Pfistermeister, advice about political appointments and complaints about how their joint plans were being frustrated by officials. But occasionally he says something more revealing of his profound thoughts. His letter to Ludwig dated 8 August 1865 contains a curious little preface, set apart from the rest of the letter, in which he addresses Ludwig by the intimate pronoun 'Du' before returning to the formal 'Sie', which he normally used, in the main text of the letter. This preface contains the following passage:

> . . . The most beautiful and profound popular myths and the teachings are being lived through by me; and the noble belief in reincarnation is becoming a deeply felt truth. I perceive clearly how I have lived several lives, in myself, in You, in Her, in all those I love; and living thus within them I experience the joys of death, of release, of ceasing to exist. What is this perplexing mystery? It is the mystery of a love that no longer craves but only wants to give, give itself and thus release itself.
>
> Beautiful soul, in whom I live when I have utterly lost myself, how I love myself when I see myself in you . . . in me the one who

has departed lives on, and with him I live in you! The chain is extended, not broken![6]

Wagner must have come into contact with the doctrine of reincarnation through his deep reading in oriental mystical literature. He was profoundly interested in Buddhism and planned to write an opera on Buddhist themes which was to be called *Die Sieger* (The Victors). This project in fact never came to fruition, but Ludwig frequently expressed eagerness to see it finished. For most of his life he was fascinated by the Orient, probably for reasons that went deeper than mere romanticism. He asked to be told of progress on *Die Sieger* in a letter to Wagner on 21 August 1865. He began by expressing disappointment that an impending visit of the King of Prussia would prevent him from celebrating his twentieth birthday in the company of Wagner, then the letter continued:

> ... I long for you. Only when I think of my dear one and his work am I truly happy. How are things with you just now, up there in the joyful wooded heights? ... Dear One, please grant me a request! I beg of you. Tell me something of your plans for 'Die Sieger' and 'Parcival'! I am yearning to hear. Please quench this burning thirst! Oh how null is the world! How wretched and vulgar so many men! Their lives revolve in the narrow circle of everyday banality. Oh, if only I had the world behind me![7]

Did Ludwig perhaps long for annihilation in the belief that he would be reborn into a better, less vulgar world? At any rate, as long as he remained in this world he longed for messages that whispered to him that his life had a meaning beyond the obvious and banal things that being a king meant, messages that came to him when he listened to the words and music of *Lohengrin*, when he glimpsed the 'Grail Temple' in the Ettal valley or when he read about the court of Louis XIV.

After receiving Ludwig's letter of 21 August, Wagner wrote in his *Brown Book* on 26 August: 'How wonderful! The King asks longingly to hear Parzival.'[8] And the following day on the next page of the book he began writing the draft of the libretto for the opera – an example of the way in which Ludwig's enthusiasm stimulated his creative powers.

As a twentieth birthday present Wagner sent Ludwig a handwritten, finished copy of *Rheingold*, eliciting an ecstatic letter of thanks. Cosima also sent him a present: a cushion embroidered by her own hand. In her accompanying letter she explained that the embroidery depicted 'the symbols of the exalted works' which Ludwig had made his own by his generous patronage. The images were those of 'the Dutchman's ship, Tannhäuser's staff, Lohengrin's swan, Siegfried's sword and Tristan's cup . . . all on the green ground of hope'.[9] Each stitch, she wrote, contained a blessing. Ludwig sent her a warm letter of thanks, assuring her that he would always hold her gift in high honour.

He was even more pleased when Cosima sent him in October a collection of Wagner's writings from his Paris period, copied out in her own hand and put together under the title of the *Wagner Book*. He sent her in return a sapphire, 'the colour of Faith – a symbol of the firm faith and unshakeable confidence that inspire me and give me heart to do all that it lies in me to do in order to help build the great, the ETERNAL work'.[10]

As Ludwig's inner life grew more intense his enthusiasm for the conventional role of king waned. And this did not go unnoticed by the public and the court. In September, for example, he offended his generals by refusing their pressing invitations to attend army manoeuvres, causing the following comment in a secret report by the Munich Police Directorate: 'If the King is able to ride for 8–10 hours by night and in fog without endangering his health he should be able to devote a few days to his army.'[11] On 4 September he was absent when his father's coffin was transferred to the church of the Theatines, and in October he offended his grandfather, the ex-King, by refusing an invitation to a family gathering on the 18th on the excuse that he had rheumatism, which did not, however, prevent him from going to the theatre the same evening to see a performance of Schiller's *William Tell*. Already his passion for the theatre had become a subject of comment. A special train conveyed him from Berg castle to Munich and back again for his theatrical evenings, and often his ministers had to confer with him at the door of his box during the intervals.

After the *William Tell* performance Ludwig decided to see for himself the country for which Tell had fought. Ludwig's abiding passion for Switzerland, the land of democracy *par excellence*, might seem at first sight paradoxical for a traditionally minded King. But Ludwig's concept of kingship was a rather special one and was influenced, as I have already said, by Wagner's theories on the subject. What appealed to Wagner, and to Ludwig, was the idea of a monarch or leader in whom power was vested by virtue of the trust placed in him by the people. He was the expression of their collective will, the heroic embodiment of all the accumulated ideals and aspirations of his folk. Whether the leader is chosen because of his blood or for some other reason is not important. What matters is the deeply felt, mystical bond between himself and his people. It was this principle which Ludwig saw at work in the story of Tell, and he admired the bond of confidence which existed between Tell and the people he represented. This was why Ludwig had little use either for politicians of the progressive, liberal kind, or for those of the conservative, monarchist persuasion. Both interposed themselves between the King and his people and interfered with his almost priestly function as leader and hero.

Travelling incognito and with a small retinue, Ludwig arrived in Lucerne on 20 October and booked in at the Hotel

Schweizerhof, where he was given the only three rooms available, on the fourth floor. Later, when it was discovered who he was, the proprietor offered to have the best suite vacated for him. Ludwig, however, good-humouredly declined. Later he moved to the more rustic environs of the Gasthaus Rössli at Brunnen, from which he made a series of excursions to the places associated with Tell, such as the Rütli mountain, where Tell and his men had, according to the legend, sworn to overthrow their Austrian oppressors. He returned home even more passionate about Switzerland than before.

Meanwhile Wagner had begun writing a 'Journal', intended for the political education of Ludwig. In it he bewailed the weakness and corruption of German political and cultural life, and wrote of the need for a hero who could lead and inspire the German people in such a way that they would be able to fulfil their true destiny and potential. Wagner saw Ludwig as being in a position to set an example of such rulership.

Sceptical though he was about Wagner's advice in day-to-day political details, Ludwig was seduced by the vision of himself as a knight in shining armour from a Wagnerian opera – Parzival, Lohengrin and Ludwig the Bavarian rolled into one. As Newman puts it:

> The King . . . was only too happy to visualize himself walking the stage in the rôle for which his mentor had cast him – that of the saviour of German culture, the pair of them marching into the new Jerusalem with all Germany following them, with banners waving, trumpets and trombones blaring, after the manner of a grand operatic procession in the last act.[12]

This is confirmed by the letter which Ludwig sent to Cosima thanking her for sending him a copy of Wagner's Journal. 'Yes!' he wrote, 'we will show the German Folk what it can do when it is well led: I will not weary in my zeal, my ardent enthusiasm, until the "Everlasting Work" is accomplished.'[13]

The only trouble was that the Bavarian politicians were not willing to take part in this operatic fantasy. They decided that Wagner must go, and as the winter approached the plot against the composer gathered momentum. But, ironically, the blow which struck him down was preceded by an interval of idyllic happiness for both Wagner and Ludwig. During the week of 11– 18 November 1865 they stayed at Hohenschwangau together, in a spell of bright, clear, late autumn weather. In this setting Wagner's thoughts turned again to the mystical bonds between them, as he recorded in his *Brown Book*. Hohenschwangau he saw as the 'Grail Castle' where he was 'protected by Parzival's sublime love'. For the first time he realized the full depth and beauty of Ludwig's love for him. 'He is I, in a newer, younger, lovelier re-birth: wholly I, and himself only to be beautiful and powerful.'[14]

During the morning, when the King was occupied with affairs of state, he and Wagner sent each other greetings in prose or verse. But at meals they were alone together, except when they were joined by Ludwig's friend Prince Paul von Thurn und Taxis. On the morning of the 12th three groups of military oboists, brought from Munich for the purpose, along with their conductor, Siebenküs, were posted on the castle turrets. And, as the sun rose over the mountains, they played a series of tunes from *Lohengrin*, the oboes answering each other across the battlements. On the 13th Ludwig and Wagner made an excursion into the Tyrol, and the following day Ludwig sent an enraptured letter to Cosima:

. . . Let us two take a solemn vow to do all it is in human power to do to preserve for Wagner the peace he has won, to banish care

> from him, to take upon ourselves, whenever possible, every grief
> of his, to love him, love him with all the strength that God has put
> into the human soul! . . . O, he is godlike, godlike! My mission is
> to live for him, to suffer for him, if that be necessary for his full
> salvation . . .[15]

It is a measure of Ludwig's innocence of mind that at this time
he had no idea of the true nature of the relationship between
Wagner and Cosima.

After Wagner left Hohenschwangau, Ludwig prolonged his
Wagnerian mood by arranging a kind of *son et lumière* on the
nearby lake, the Alpsee, in which Paul Taxis, dressed as Lohengrin, was drawn across the water in a boat pulled by an artificial
swan. The scene was floodlit and was accompanied by a band
playing the appropriate passages from the opera. Ludwig was so
enchanted that he ordered a second performance the following
evening. All his life Ludwig sought to create moments of this
kind, moments when his inner world sprang into sharp reality.
It is easy to make fun of such performances, but anyone who
knows the Alpsee and has seen *Lohengrin* will realize that this
piece of make-believe must have been an electrifying experience for those who witnessed it. In later years Ludwig himself
used to dress up as Lohengrin, and after his death a costume of
the swan-knight was found among his possessions.

Wagner, now feeling renewed confidence in his relationship
with the King, returned to his role of political mentor, once
more urging Ludwig to appoint a Special Secretary to carry out
royal intentions in artistic matters. His other proposals included
a new musical journal to supplement the work of his projected
new School of Music, and a new political-cum-artistic journal,
with Wagner's friend Julius Fröbel as editor. The post of Special
Secretary should, Wagner suggested, go to Emil Riedel (later
Bavarian Finance Minister). Riedel declined the post, partly

because he did not feel sufficiently familiar with the ways of the court and partly because he wished to devote himself to social questions. But when Pfistermeister heard of these proposals he was alarmed, realizing that Wagner was intriguing to have him removed or to curtail his powers. Furthermore Fröbel was *persona non grata* to Pfistermeister and his associates because his political views did not coincide with theirs.

There now existed in Bavarian political circles a faction which looked towards Prussia as the future leader of Germany. Lutz was a member of this faction and had tried to win Wagner over to the cause by bribery. During the Hohenschwangau visit he made another attempt, revealing to Wagner that the policy of the government was to come to 'an arrangement with Bismarck and the new Prussian tendency' since Austria was considered untrustworthy and the idea of a German parliament was not acceptable.[16] Wagner, however, did not take the bait. He innocently told Lutz that he had nothing to do with politics as such and was not well informed about Bavarian state matters. In a letter to Ludwig of 26 November, however, he warned: 'that your cabinet, in explicit agreement with Herr von Pfordten, is entirely inclined to fall in with Bismarck's wishes, I know from the frank statements of Herr Lutz himself.'[17]

Even if they had succeeded in winning Wagner over, the politicians would probably not have hesitated to throw him overboard when they no longer needed him. As it was, they now decided that he had become too much of a threat and must be removed.

Had Wagner played his cards skilfully he might still have saved the situation. Instead he threw them away by allowing himself to be drawn into a controversy in the press. This had been sparked off by an article published on 13 November in the democratic Nuremberg *Anzeiger*, entitled 'Plain Words to the King of Bavaria and his People on the Subject of the Cabinet

Secretariat', which complained that the King was isolated for seven months in the year from his ministers, 'encompassed only by the entirely unconstitutional institution of the Cabinet Secretariat'.[18] The other democratic newspapers immediately rallied to the support of the *Anzeiger*, and at first the reactionary press was uncertain what response to make, knowing the wide unpopularity of the Cabinet Secretariat. But soon the *Volksbote* found the solution. Pfistermeister and his colleagues might be unpopular, but Wagner was more unpopular still, and an attack on Wagner could be used to serve at the same time as a counter-attack on the democratic press. On 26 November the *Volksbote* published an article in which it was hinted that the cloven hoof of Wagner was in some way behind the *Anzeiger* article of 13 November, and that the attack on the Cabinet Secretariat was really directed against two of its members, Pfistermeister and Hofmann. 'These two men,' it was stated, 'are to be set aside in order that certain hankerings after the exploitation of the royal Treasury may be the more easily satisfied.'[19] The article went on to state how much Wagner had cost Bavaria, and cunningly asserted that the agitation against the Cabinet Secretariat did not arise from constitutional motives but was stirred up in order that 'favourites', i.e. Wagner, 'might secretly make their influence complete and utilize that influence partly for financial ends, partly for those of democracy'.

When Wagner read the article, which he assumed to be by someone in the Cabinet, he went into a blind fury and counter-attacked in a way which played right into the hands of his enemies. In an anonymous, but unmistakably Wagnerian article in the Munich *Neueste Nachrichten* of 29 November, he lashed out at the Pfistermeister clique. These people, he wrote, 'whom I have no need to mention by name since they are the objects of universal and contemptuous indignation in Bavaria' are reduced, in order to save themselves, to representing 'the

King's unshakeable friendship for Wagner' as a danger to the throne. He continued:

> Of one thing you can be quite certain: it is in no way a question of any principle, any party position, being attacked by Wagner: it is purely and simply an affair of the lowest personal interests, and that on the part of a very small number of individuals: and I venture to assure you that with the removal of two or three persons who do not enjoy the smallest respect among the Bavarian people, both the King and the Bavarian people would once and for all be set free from these annoyances.[20]

The last statement of course demonstrated exactly what the *Volksbote* article had maintained, namely that Wagner was eager for the removal of his enemies in the Cabinet. What was more, Wagner compounded his error by pretending to Ludwig that he had not written the article.

Meanwhile, before the appearance of his foolhardy article, Wagner had written to the King sending him a copy of the *Volksbote* article along with an exasperated letter asking Ludwig to promise that no further order relating to their plans should pass through either the Cabinet or the Court Theatre until changes had been made in the staff of those institutions. He also urged the King to form a new Cabinet and to recall as its head Max von Neumayr, formerly Minister of the Interior, who had resigned following riots in Munich in October. Ludwig's reply showed once again that he was capable of being very objective when it came to political advice from Wagner:

> Rest assured, my dear one, that what I am now saying is not the outcome of a momentary superficial emotion . . . No, I am replying to you calmly and after due consideration. I had the best of reasons for dismissing Neumayr and retracting the confidence I had so long reposed in him, and withdrawing my royal favour. It would therefore be quite inconsequent of me were I now to

entrust this man – with whom, I repeat, I have every reason to be dissatisfied, – with the formation of a new Cabinet. Pfistermeister is insignificant and stupid; of that there can be no question. I will not let him remain much longer in the Cabinet; but to dismiss him and the other members of it at the present moment does not seem to me to be advisable: the time for that is not yet. I say this most positively. Believe me, I have my own good grounds for saying it.[21]

He went on to advise Wagner not to pay so much attention to 'press tittle-tattle'. Little did he know what an avalanche had already been set in motion. Two days later Wagner's anonymous article appeared. Ludwig was aghast. No doubt he realized its authorship, and for the first time his idealistic vision of Wagner must have taken a dent. But tactfully he did not reveal that he had seen through the deception when he wrote to Wagner on 3 December. 'That article in the *Neueste Nachrichten*,' he said, 'has contributed not a little to embitter the last days of my sojourn here [at Hohenschwangau]. It was unquestionably written by one of your friends who thought he was doing you a service thereby; unfortunately, so far from helping you, it has injured you.'[22]

Interestingly, even at this stage there was still considerable support for Wagner among the Munich public, and on 1 December he was given a standing ovation when he attended a performance of the Sailors' Chorus from *The Flying Dutchman*. But his enemies in the government, court and church had now scented blood and were in full cry. Pfordten wrote to Ludwig on 1 December telling the King of the considerable resentment against Wagner that now existed in Munich, aroused by the *Nachrichten* article, by the colossal sum of 40,000 florins which had been granted to Wagner in October and by Wagner's general interference in matters unrelated to art. He went on: 'Your Majesty now stands at a fateful parting of the ways: you have to choose between the love and respect of your faithful people and the "friendship" of Richard Wagner.'[23]

By the time Ludwig returned to Munich on 6 December he had come to realize the full gravity of the situation. Back in the Residenz, he immediately asked for reports on the state of public opinion. Then he came to what must have been one of the most painful decisions of his life. 'My dear Minister,' he wrote to Pfordten on 7 December, 'my resolution stands firm. R. Wagner must leave Bavaria. I will show my dear people that its love and confidence are the first things of all to me. You will realize that this has not been easy for me; but I have overcome.'

Meanwhile the decision had been communicated to Wagner on the evening of the 6th by the second Cabinet Secretary, Lutz. Making his way to the Briennerstrasse house in the twilight of the winter afternoon, he found Wagner sitting at tea with Cosima and his friend Peter Cornelius. Lutz, a poor schoolmaster's son from Franconia, must have derived a certain satisfaction from conveying the message which toppled the great Wagner. Cornelius later described the little man's triumphant air as he announced the King's wish that Wagner should without delay leave Munich for a few months. Wagner, thunderstruck, at first refused to believe what he had heard and pointed at the last letter he had received from the King, signed 'unto death, until we cross to the next world, eternally, eternally, your truest friend, Ludwig'. Then, when Lutz made it clear that he was in earnest, Wagner began such a tirade of abuse against Pfistermeister that Lutz had to tell him: 'Restrain yourself, I am here as an official.'[24]

The following day, by way of softening the blow, Ludwig sent a personal letter to the Briennerstrasse:

My dear Friend,

Much as it grieves me, I must ask you to comply with the wish I communicated to you yesterday through my Secretary. Believe

me, I had to act as I did. My love for you will never die, and
I beg you to retain for ever your friendship for me; with a clear
conscience I can say that I am worthy of it. Sundered, who can part
us? I know you feel with me. I know you can measure the whole
depth of my sorrow. I could not do otherwise: be assured of that,
and *never* doubt the fidelity of your best friend. It will certainly not
be forever.

> Until death
> > Your
> > faithful Ludwig.[25]

At a quarter to six on the morning of 10 December, Wagner
left Munich for Switzerland, accompanied only by his Bohemian
servant Franz Mrazeck and his old dog Pohl. He was seen off
at the station by Cosima, Cornelius and two other friends,
Heinrich Porges and his wife. He looked old, pale and tired. As
the train pulled out of Munich he must have known in his heart
that he would never return there to live.

7

Germany in Turmoil

By a cruel stroke of fate, Ludwig's personal distress caused by Wagner's forced departure was closely followed by the second great crisis of his reign, the Austro-Prussian conflict of 1866, known as the Seven Weeks War, in which Bavaria could not avoid becoming embroiled. This war was one of the most important turning points in European history, and Bavaria, like the other German states, was permanently changed by it. Before coming to the events of the war, therefore, it would be useful to obtain a general picture of Bavaria and its position in Germany on the eve of battle.

In 1866 Bavaria celebrated its sixtieth year as a kingdom. During the Napoleonic wars its territory had doubled in size, incorporating Franconia to the north and part of Swabia to the west. When Ludwig came to the throne it had about 4 $^1\!/_2$ million inhabitants. In size and population it was therefore slightly smaller than present-day Scotland, a country with which it is often compared in beauty and national character. In American terms it had roughly the population which the state of

Georgia has today, and an area slightly larger than the state of West Virginia.

By European standards it was a smallish kingdom, but it possessed, as it does today, a great variety of landscape and an abundance of visual riches. Along its southern frontier runs the great chain of the Bavarian Alps, contrasting with the flat agricultural land of Lower Bavaria and the giant stretches of marsh to the south of Munich. There are many beautiful lakes, and the country is criss-crossed by rivers such as the Danube, the Inn, and the Isar (from a Celtic word meaning 'fast-flowing'), which rushes at breakneck speed through Munich and on past the Lower Bavarian capital of Landshut.

Some of its towns, with their red-tiled roofs, half-timbered walls and huddled streets, had changed little since the Middle Ages; others had absorbed a southern influence, boasting Renaissance palaces, exuberant rococo façades and well-proportioned squares. All over the country there were churches built in the joyful Bavarian baroque style of which Johann Baptist Zimmerman was the supreme master. Some religious houses had virtually bankrupted themselves in a frenzy of building, but they had left behind a glorious architectural heritage. It was natural for Bavarian pride to express itself in architecture, and even modest farmers' dwellings were often ornamented with elaborate murals of a kind still common today.

In Ludwig's time Bavaria was predominantly an agricultural country, with about three-quarters of the population employed on the land. Like most rural folk they took a pride in their history and clung tenaciously to the old ways and traditions. They were and still are a rough-edged but jovial people, down-to-earth and easy-going. They worked hard when they needed to, but for the most part they earned a comfortable living from the land, and they enjoyed the good things of life – a hearty song and a glass of wine or beer. Any folk festival was always a popular occasion.

Formerly the country had been almost entirely Catholic but was now about one-third Protestant as a result of the increase in its territory. Moreover, ecclesiastical power, for instance in the control of education, had been greatly reduced by the constitutional changes which had taken place under Bavaria's first king, Maximilian I, and again in 1848. Nevertheless the Catholic Church was still, along with the monarchy, seen as one of the great pillars of Bavarian life. And if the people were loyal to the Church, they were equally loyal to the Wittelsbach dynasty, which they held in great affection.

Although tradition was strong in Bavaria the country had not failed to keep pace with modern developments. In fact, in industrial and technological terms it was well advanced. During the last decade of the reign of Ludwig's father the railways and telegraph lines had been extended. The main towns were gas-lit, and industry was growing. There were machine factories at Nuremberg and Munich, weaving mills in Augsburg and chemical works in Schweinfurt and near Aibling.

The country's political system was commensurately progressive. In the two legislative houses, the Chamber of Peers and the Chamber of Deputies, a balance was held between the conservative-clerical and liberal-democratic factions, neither of which exercised an immoderate influence, though the former looked back with nostalgia to less democratic days and wished to see the power of monarch and Church strengthened again. Press freedom had been granted in 1818 and was eagerly used.

In short, Bavaria was on the whole a happy blend of contrasting elements: Germanic, yet open to southern influences; traditional, yet forward-looking; agrarian, yet with a growing industrial base. Nowhere was this blend more striking than in the capital. Munich had come to prominence comparatively late in history, and not until 1854 did its population top the 100,000 mark. By the time Ludwig came to the throne it had reached about 200,000, still not large for a capital. In a curious way it possessed, as it still does, the character of a village which has suddenly found itself playing the role of an important city. Along with the architectural magnificence, brought to Munich largely by Ludwig I, went a thriving cultural and intellectual life, fuelled by an influx of artists and writers from other parts of Germany and from abroad. Yet side by side with these urbane features there has always existed a strong peasant culture, which can be seen in the abundance of good country food, the fondness for traditional dress, the continual round of folk festivities and the great beer halls such as the famous Hofbräuhaus, where a very different kind of culture can be observed from that offered by the Court (now the National) Theatre only a few streets away.

When the Bavarians looked beyond their borders their sympathies lay with their Austrian neighbours to the south rather than with the Prussians. They disliked and feared that northern race who, on their dusty potato fields and bleak heathlands, had built a formidably efficient and powerful state. The word '*Preuss*' (Prussian) is still used by Bavarians to refer to almost any unwelcome foreigner.

But to the Prussian Chancellor, Bismarck, Bavaria was an important consideration in the plans he was drawing up for the future of Germany. His definition of a Bavarian was someone 'half-way between an Austrian and a human being' – a remark characteristic of his barbed tongue. He wanted to bring Bavaria into the fold of the new Reich while excluding Austria, a country which he distrusted deeply. Throughout Germany the lines were being drawn between the *Grossdeutschen* (Greater-Germanics), that is those who wished to include Austria in any future Germany, and the *Kleindeutschen* (Little-Germanics), those who, with Bismarck, wished to keep Austria out.

Few people at the time can have realized what a formidable figure Bismarck was – a man of torrential force whose re-shaping of Germany was to have the most far-reaching effects on the whole western world. This man of 'blood and iron' was a curious mixture. Behind the dogged, bewhiskered face and steely expression lay a highly strung, even neurotic temperament. He suffered from a multiplicity of psychosomatic disorders and could give extraordinary displays of emotion. Once, after winning a violent argument with King Wilhelm I, he smashed a pitcher against the wall and broke into a fit of uncontrollable sobbing. He was fanatically patriotic and hated the French, yet he wrote French with the elegance of an eighteenth-century Parisian man of letters. Like a master chess player, he had planned far in advance the series of moves that was to lead to the fulfilment of his ultimate aim: the unification of Germany under the dominance of Prussia. The Austro-Prussian annexation of Schleswig-Holstein was the first step. Next it was necessary to provoke a conflict with Austria, and the opportunity soon came. Austria, which administered Holstein, allowed the inhabitants to agitate in favour of the Duke of Augustenburg, whom Austria favoured as claimant to the throne of the two duchies. Bismarck thereupon accused Austria of abetting revolution and asked for an explanation. Austria refused. Diplomatic relations were broken off on 12 June 1866, and soon the two adversaries and their allies were mobilizing for war. Prussia had on her side Italy, Saxe-Coburg-Gotha, Lippe, Oldenbourg and the Hanse towns. Austria's allies were Bavaria, Saxony, Hanover, Württemberg, Baden, Hessen-Darmstadt and Hessen-Nassau.

Bavaria had faced an agonizing decision as to whether to enter the conflict and, if so, on whose side. Militarily the country was ill-prepared for war. The army had been badly neglected for many years and was poorly trained, underpaid and short of men. Many of the politicians, including Pfordten, were sympathetic towards Bismarck, but to advocate siding with Prussia against Austria would have been to commit political suicide in view of the general popular sympathy for the Austrian cause. Pfordten made attempts to urge a conciliatory policy on Bismarck but without success, and in the end he had to admit that there was no alternative to Bavaria's fighting on the Austrian side.

For Ludwig himself the war was a painful business. He had family ties with both the Austrian and Prussian royal families. His mother was a Prussian princess, and his cousin Elisabeth was married to the Austrian Emperor. He would have preferred Bavaria to remain neutral, but that was not possible – those who were not with Bismarck were against him. Although Ludwig was shrewd and well-informed about international affairs, he lacked the commitment and skill that would have been necessary to achieve a political solution to the crisis. He was equally ill-equipped when it came to a military solution. Although he looked very dashing in his uniforms, a less military figure than Ludwig can hardly be imagined. Wagner reported that he hated military life and used to refer to his officers as '*geschorene Igelköpfe*' (clipped hedgehog-heads).[1] On one occasion, seeing a sentry outside the Residenz who looked tired, he ordered a sofa to be brought for the man. Though he was fascinated by medieval chivalry and knightly combat, modern warfare and everything to do with it horrified him. Curiously, however, he once expressed the hope that one day a lethal weapon might be invented which could wipe out whole regiments in a few minutes and thereby shorten the agony.

In the spring of 1866, as war loomed ever closer, he dithered, hoping desperately that a peaceful alternative would offer itself. He had no illusions about Prussia, and when Prince Hohenlohe (later Prime Minister) tried to reassure him that the Prussians wanted only hegemony over north Germany, Ludwig interrupted him with the observation: '*Now*; but later they will ask for more.'[2] Still, he could not bring himself to give the order for mobilization. For fifty years Bavaria had been at peace, and he could not bear to see it broken. Finally, however, on 10 May, he gave in to pressure from his ministers and issued the order. He then retired to Berg castle to hide his head in the sand. Officials who tried to confer with him found, to their exasperation, that he would disappear for hours on end, sometimes to the Roseninsel, a little island in Lake Starnberg where he had a villa. Pfistermeister had a meeting with him on 15 May and afterwards wrote to Privy Councillor Gietl that the King was 'so overwrought that he looked quite miserable'.[3] Moreover he had spoken of abdication on the grounds of mental ill health, and of going to live in Switzerland.

The reason why Ludwig's thoughts were turning to Switzerland lay not only in his love for the country but also in the fact that Wagner had made his home there. After his departure from Munich he and Cosima had settled down in Triebschen, a charming villa on the shore of Lake Lucerne, paying the first year's rent with a gift from Ludwig. Here, supported by the King's continuing allowance, he was to spend the happiest and most tranquil six years of his life, completing *Die Meistersinger* and *Siegfried*, composing *Götterdämmerung* and the *Siegfried Idyll*, and writing some of the most important of his prose works.

Ludwig, in despair at the madness which seemed to prevail all around him, was yearning for the consolation of his friend's company. Abdication in favour of Otto seemed to offer a solution, and on 15 May he sent a telegram to Wagner asking for his advice: 'Increasingly the horizon darkens, the bright sun of peace is in terrible torment. I implore the Friend to send me a speedy answer to the following question: if it is the wish of the Dear One I will gladly renounce the throne and its barren splendour, come to him and never part from him.'[4] Wagner's letter in reply shows that he was capable of giving wise advice:

> ... Renounce, I beseech you, during this half year all concern with art and with our plans ... Turn your attention with the greatest energy to matters of state; give up your comforting solitude in Berg; remain in your Residenz: stay with your people, show yourself to them. If you love me, as I earnestly hope, then hear my plea when I ask you to open Parliament in person on 22 May.[5]

Wagner went on to say that if by the autumn Ludwig still found himself in an intolerable position, then abdication might be the answer.

Ludwig was partly brought to his senses by the letter. Nevertheless he was so eager to see his friend that he ignored the pleas of Wagner and of his ministers to open Parliament and instead set off clandestinely to see Wagner. Having already sent Paul Taxis on ahead, he himself departed on the very day when the crucial opening of Parliament had been due to take place, which also happened to be Wagner's birthday. Early in the morning, in order to allay suspicion, he telegraphed his good wishes to the Friend. Then, after a conference with Lutz, he set out ostensibly for his usual morning ride, accompanied only by a single groom. He made for the station at Bissenhofen and from there caught a train to Lindau on Lake Constance. A steamer took him across to Rorschach, and by the afternoon he was standing at the garden gate of Triebschen dressed in a black coat and broad-brimmed hat like some wandering poet. He announced himself to the servant as 'Walter Stolzing', a character from *Die Meistersinger*. A few moments later Wagner, having understood the message, came down the steps to greet his visitor warmly.

Ludwig stayed for two days at Triebschen, sleeping in Wagner's small study. It was during this visit that he met Cosima for the first time. The details of what he and Wagner talked about are not recorded, but Ludwig left much restored in morale and with a promise that he would abide by the decision of the majority Parliament as to the war.

On his return he finally presided over the opening of Parliament, but by then the news of his visit to Switzerland had leaked out, causing wide indignation. He was given a frosty reception by the crowd on the way to the ceremony, and a few words of abuse were heard as his carriage passed. The press took the opportunity to reopen its attacks on Wagner, and the *Volksbote* published an article hinting in an obvious manner at the true relationship between Wagner and Cosima. This was too much for Bülow. Although he had obviously known for a long time about his wife's infidelity, he did not like to be made a fool of in public and he wrote to the editor of the newspaper demanding either an apology or a duel. He then hurried off to Switzerland to discuss the situation with Cosima and Wagner. At this stage Wagner was in a vulnerable position, and any public revelations about his relationship with Cosima could have been used by his enemies. Bülow and Cosima were equally anxious to keep the truth concealed. As a result of their deliberations a letter was drawn up by Wagner stating that there was no truth in the allegation that Cosima was his mistress. The letter was then sent to Ludwig with a request that he sign it, and it was backed up by an appeal from Cosima stating her anxious wish to keep her husband's name untarnished for the sake of her three children – one of whom was, of course, Wagner's. Ludwig, in his innocence and loyalty to Wagner, signed the letter, which Bülow then published. Later, when the King found out about the deception, he was deeply hurt. The episode is one of the darkest stains on Wagner's reputation.

But such personal problems were being increasingly overshadowed by the general turmoil into which Germany was falling. On 16 June the German Confederation, which included

Bavaria, declared war on Prussia. And still Ludwig refused to
face the situation. On the same day that war was declared,
Hohenlohe wrote in his diary:

> The King sees no one now. He is staying with Taxis and the groom
> Völk on the Roseninsel, and lets off fireworks. Even the members
> of the Upper House, who were to deliver the address to him, were
> not received – a case unprecedented in the constitutional life of
> Bavaria. Not to receive addresses of loyalty, and from the faithful
> senate, that is a bitter pill for the august Chamber! The Munich
> people themselves are again making quite justifiable comments.
> Other people do not trouble their heads about the King's childish
> tricks, since he lets the Ministers and the Chambers govern without
> interfering. His behaviour is, however, imprudent, since it tends
> to make him unpopular.[6]

The following day Ludwig sent a telegram to Wagner saying
that circumstances were forcing him to return to Munich. 'Oh
lamentable time!' he added. 'Oh baneful discord that turns
Germany's will against Germany!'[7] Wagner's letter in reply
was full of much-needed sympathy and encouragement. He
related how a certain Count Enzenberg had written to him
asking him to compose a 'German hymn' – something which
the Count believed Wagner alone was qualified to do. 'I replied
to him,' Wagner continued,

> that such a song cannot be written within months or years and that
> only a moment of the most exalted necessity can inspire it. When
> will this hour arrive? When shall I celebrate the great moment?
> That is a question for Fate! I am no prophet, but – I believe – I
> believe in you, my noble Friend!
>
> Now then: the press told us that you would go with your
> brother to the army. I beg you to do so! Bavaria's King at the head
> of his warriors in the army of the confederation – Listen! Listen to
> me! – such a King would hold the destiny of the world in his hand!
> Fate calls you! She desires that you leave your musty Residenz. Go

out into your land, make a journey through your Bavaria, comfort our Germany . . .

Soon will come the time for the 'German hymn'! But first we have much evil to overcome! Fate calls: to the army! . . .[8]

As Ludwig read the letter the visions which he and Wagner shared sprang suddenly to life again. He had allowed them to become day-dreams and fantasies, acted out in solitude. Now he experienced one of his brief and increasingly infrequent impulses to take these visions out into the real world. Wagner had once written of the 'Hoard' – the supreme worldly power which belonged by rights to the true representative of the ancient Germanic race. Now once again the Hoard was at stake. That was surely what Wagner had meant when he wrote in his letter of Bavaria's King holding 'the destiny of the world in his hand'.

Fired by Wagner's words, Ludwig donned his uniform and sallied forth to pay his respects to the army in the field, spending 26 and 27 July at the military headquarters at Bamberg. He was given a rousing welcome by officers and men, and Paul Taxis, who accompanied him, reported that the tour was a triumphant success. He made a particularly strong impression on a Hessian officer named Fuchs, whose memories of the occasion were later recorded by his grandson, the writer Georg Fuchs. The grandfather recalled sitting having dinner in the officers' mess when suddenly the double doors were flung open and into the room swept a tall young man in a silver and blue military uniform, who cast an arresting pair of dark eyes over the assembled company. He was 'of such unearthly beauty that my heartbeat positively faltered. So carried away was I that a feeling of anxiety crept over me: this divine youth was too beautiful for this world! . . . I asked the Bavarian comrade next to me at the table: "Who is that?" "Our young King," he replied.'[9]

Ludwig was pleased with the success of his visit; but, instead of remaining in the forefront of events, he retreated once more to the Roseninsel and resumed his idyll with Paul Taxis. The burst of conscientiousness created by Wagner's letter had once again evaporated. Soon the military were grumbling again. Ludwig's seventy-one-year-old great-uncle, Prince Karl, who had been made commander-in-chief, complained in a letter to his brother, ex-King Ludwig I, that when he had sent an adjutant to the King with important news the latter had shown no interest. He added prophetically that it would end in Ludwig's being deposed.

Had Ludwig taken a more active part in the war he would undoubtedly have had a healthy effect on the morale of the army and the country, for his proclamation of war, published in the Munich newspaper, the *Neueste Nachrichten*, on 4 July, shows that he cared deeply about the fate of his country:

> Bavarians! We do not stand alone in this difficult struggle. All states true to the Confederation – above all the mighty Austria – are our comrades in arms. Our goals, worthy of the highest sacrifice, are: first, the preservation of Greater Germany as a free and powerful whole, strengthened by the bond between its princes and by the national consciousness of its races; second, the preservation of Bavaria as an independent and worthy member of the great German fatherland. So let us go with courage and determination into the struggle, united in love and trust, strong in our faith that we shall outlive the storm. Let us endure it in the firm confidence that almighty God will give victory to the just cause.

Ludwig's faith in 'the mighty Austria' was misplaced. At the time it looked on the surface as though Austria was strong enough to fight off any challenge from Prussia. But anyone who made a careful comparison of the two countries before the outbreak of war would have had doubts about Austria's chances. Austria was an old and tired country with a fossilized ruling class, presided over by the sad figure of the Emperor Franz Josef, to whom the once proud traditions of the Habsburgs now clung like cobwebs. Its army, which was not based on universal conscription, was numerically superior to that of Prussia, but was plagued by animosity between rival national elements drawn from different parts of the polyglot Habsburg empire. The task of leading the army into the war against Prussia had been given to the sixty-two-year-old Ludwig Benedek, much against his wishes. Benedek pleaded with the Emperor to be given command of the campaign against Prussia's ally, Italy, a country in which he had fought successfully before. But his plea was in vain and he reluctantly accepted command of the northern campaign which focused on Bohemia, a theatre of war which was strange to him. On the eve of battle he wrote to his wife that it would be best if a bullet hit him.

On the Prussian side the picture was entirely different. Prussia was a vigorous, growing nation, young in spirit and forward-looking. There was universal military conscription, with everyone between the ages of seventeen and forty-five obliged to spend two years in regular service and then a period in the reserve. The army, unhampered by internal rivalries, was commanded by Helmuth von Moltke who, though sixty-six years old, had a supple grasp of the latest military methods. Moltke was one of those rare men who combine effectiveness of thought and deed in equal measure. He was a professorial figure with a reputation for knowing much and saying little – indeed it was said of him that 'he could be silent in seven languages'. When he did open his mouth he could talk with authority about the ancient world, history, art and architecture. He was to live to the age of ninety-one and achieve a reputation as a master of German prose. Yet he could leave behind the tranquillity of his study and command an army with the authority and skill of a brilliant strategist. His army had two tremendous

advantages over the Austrians. One was the mobility created by
the advanced Prussian railway system, which enabled units to
be transported rapidly to places where they were not expected.
The other was the new 'needle-gun', the first breech-loader
used in Europe. In many ways it was a crude weapon, and
Prussia was the only great power to have adopted it on a large
scale since it had first been tested in the Danish war of 1864.
In ballistic properties it was inferior to the Austrian rifle, but
it had two immensely significant factors in its favour: it could
be loaded rapidly and also when its user was lying down. In
the hands of the highly trained Prussian soldiers it became a
formidable weapon.

The Prussian and Austrian armies, each approaching a quarter of a million men, finally came face to face at Königgrätz
(Sadowa) in what is now Czechoslovakia. These half million
troops were ostensibly fighting over two insignificant little
duchies on the Danish border. In fact what was at stake, as their
leaders well knew, was the future leadership of central Europe –
or what Wagner would have called 'the Hoard'. At the end of
the day Austria had lost the battle and with it the war. The Prussians could easily have marched on and taken Vienna, as King
Wilhelm now wanted to do. But here was where Bismarck
showed the positive side of his greatness. Realizing that an
occupied and humiliated Austria would in the long run be a
liability, he halted the army and began peace negotiations.

Meanwhile Bavaria was faring badly in the war. The Bavarian
army formed the Seventh Army Corps of the German Confederation, and it was decided that this force should join up
with the Eighth Corps of the Confederation, made up of the
armies of Württemberg, Baden and Hessen. Apart from the
Hessians, the Bavarians were the only members of the south
German combined forces to put up a serious fight, which they
did with great bravery. From the start, however, the campaign

was a fiasco, due partly to the overwhelming odds against them and partly to indecision and errors of judgement on the part of the leadership. Prince Karl and his Chief of Staff, Ludwig Freiherr von der Tann, were ill-qualified to lead a campaign of this kind. Instead of joining with the Austrians to repel the main thrust of the Prussian attack in Bohemia, they took the view that the defence of the Bavarian homeland must come first. Had the Bavarian contingent fought beside the Austrians at Königgrätz, the outcome of that battle and therefore of the whole war might have been entirely different. As it was, the Bavarian army went north to meet the other arm of the Prussian advance and underwent a series of humiliating defeats.

A particularly bloody conflict took place at the spa town of Kissingen on the river Saale, where only two years earlier Ludwig had attended a gathering of royalty. After a fierce struggle, during which the Bavarian commander General von Zoller was killed, the Prussians carried the day.

In the early stages of the war the Munich populace appears to have looked upon the conflict with a fairly detached air. To judge from contemporary articles and advertisements in the *Neueste Nachrichten*, life went on much as normal, except for minor inconveniences such as the fact that telegrams to Frankfurt had to be sent via Stuttgart instead of by the line via Würzburg, which had evidently been cut by the Prussians. Among those who profited from the war were the Munich map-sellers, Mey and Widmayer, who advertised: 'Operations maps of central Germany showing the theatres of war in Saxony, Bohemia, Silesia, the Rhineland, Thuringia and south-west Germany. In colour. Price 30 Krone.' After the defeat at Kissingen, however, a mood of panic swept through the town. People made ready to flee from the Prussian advance, and the most valuable objects in the Residenz and in the libraries and art galleries were packed ready to be sent to safety in Switzerland.

Meanwhile Ludwig was still hiding from the war at Berg or on the Roseninsel, where he and Paul Taxis amused themselves by riding in costume round the island or setting off fireworks, which one evening burned so brightly that the Starnberg fire brigade arrived on the scene. As the news grew worse Ludwig's thoughts turned again to abdication, but once again a letter from Wagner dissuaded him from this course and restored his morale.

After defeat at Kissingen the war had been lost for Bavaria, and on 16 July Ludwig authorized Pfordten to begin peace negotiations. The fears of the Munich population proved in fact to be unfounded, for Bismarck was just as anxious to spare Bavaria from total humiliation as he had been in the case of Austria. His plans of conquest were by no means finished, and he knew that he was going to need the German states as future allies. Moreover he had a soft spot for Ludwig, whom he had once met over dinner at Nymphenburg when Ludwig was Crown Prince. But to begin with Bismarck employed bullying tactics during the protracted peace discussions in Berlin, humiliating Pfordten and pointing out that Bavaria was the only state to emerge from the war with no major ally to stand up for her, Austria having reneged on her agreement with Bavaria and begun separate peace negotiations with the Prussians. Consequently, Bismarck said, Prussia would have to take from Bavaria the territory which was her due and which she could not obtain from the other conquered countries. In the end, however, Bismarck offered a comparatively generous settlement. Bavaria was to cede only a small amount of territory to Prussia and was to pay the comparatively moderate sum of 30 million florins as an indemnity. Attached to this was a secret agreement to the effect that Bavaria would place its armed forces at the disposal of Prussia and under Prussian command in the event of a future war.

In his restrained treatment of the conquered nations, Bismarck was at odds with his King, who continued to maintain an attitude of cold intransigence towards the losers. A letter from his niece, the Bavarian Queen Mother, pleading for lenience was not answered until after the peace negotiations had been completed.

The task of presenting the agreement for King Ludwig's approval fell to the Justice Minister, Bomhard, who arrived at Berg to find Ludwig in a state of aggrieved agitation over the hard-hearted attitude of his Prussian great-uncle. They discussed the peace proposals for several hours. Was this the only way out, Ludwig wanted to know, or was Bomhard only supporting the proposals as a Protestant who might be somewhat sympathetic towards Prussia? Bomhard replied that, opposed though he was to Prussia's policy of annexation, he saw no other solution that would be in the interests of Germany. Ludwig signed the agreement. Had the terms been harsher and more damaging to Bavaria's sovereignty, he would probably have carried out his threat to abdicate. As he put it in a letter to Wagner, he had no desire to be '*ein Schattenkönig ohne Macht*', a 'shadow King without power'.[10]

There was an unexpectedly happy sequel to the war when in November Ludwig, acting on the advice of his ministers and encouraged by Wagner, decided to make a month-long tour of Franconia, in the northern part of the country, which had borne the brunt of the fighting. Travelling through Bayreuth, Bamberg, Kissingen, Aschaffenburg, Würzburg and Nuremberg, he inspected garrisons, looked at war-devastated villages, visited the wounded in hospital and laid wreaths on the graves of dead soldiers. Everywhere he was greeted more like a victor than the King of a defeated nation. Cheering crowds lined his route. There were banquets, balls and torchlight processions arranged in his honour. Nuremberg, the town of *Die Meis-tersinger*, enthralled him most of all, and he even thought briefly of taking up an idea of Wagner's that he should make Nuremberg his capital. But, to the relief of Munich, the idea came to nothing.

8

Sophie

'What I asked you was – do you ask for my hand or not?'
'I do,' the prince answered with a sinking heart.

(Dostoyevsky, *The Idiot*)

L udwig was born when the sun was in Virgo, and in many ways he conformed to the popular image of the sign with its reputation for aloofness and emotional detachment. But when Frau Dangl cast his horoscope she would have discovered that he was also born with the moon in the passionate sign of Scorpio. Psychologically, he must have suffered from a constant tension between these two sides of himself.

A natural reticence, even primness, in sexual matters was exacerbated by his cloistered upbringing. He ascended the throne apparently ignorant of the most basic facts of life, and once inquired of a courtier what a 'natural son' was. On another occasion he asked what the word 'rape' meant, and when it was explained to him he declared with horror that no punishment was too severe for such a crime. After he became King he had ample opportunity for love affairs and no lack of female admirers. But he never could or would break down the barriers that separated him from full heterosexual love. One of these barriers consisted of the latent homosexuality of which he was then probably only dimly aware and which was not at this stage so dominating as to prevent him feeling attraction towards women. What was more of an obstacle was his aloof and self-conscious personality. Except on rare occasions, he could not drop the elaborate façade of kingly dignity which protected his sensitive soul from what he saw as a hostile world. A certain fussy stiffness was nearly always present in his habits and demeanour. Every day he had his hair elaborately curled by his barber into that strange puffed-out style which made his head seem larger than it was. Without his daily coiffure, he declared, he could not enjoy his food. Self-consciousness of this kind is a hindrance to the easy flow of affection that is required in love. Moreover, full sexual love demands a baring of the soul that would have been extremely difficult for a man who had lived for so long behind a mask.

Nevertheless women did play a part in Ludwig's life, especially in his early years as King. There were numerous actresses and singers whom he admired. There was also his cousin, Elisabeth ('Sissi'), Empress of Austria, who was probably closer to him than any other member of the female sex. Yet it was to Elisabeth's sister, Sophie, that Ludwig became engaged in his one brief flirtation with the idea of marriage.

Sophie and Elisabeth were daughters of Ludwig's great-uncle, Duke Max in Bayern, a fun-loving, zither-playing, somewhat bohemian character who had a beautiful house at Possenhofen, across Lake Starnberg from Berg castle. Before and after he became King, Ludwig enjoyed going over to Possenhofen, especially when Elisabeth was there on holiday from Austria. One of the most beautiful women in Europe, she was to lead a tragic life and die at the hands of a mad assassin in Switzerland. Like Ludwig, she was a passionate rider and loved lonely excursions into the country. No doubt he sensed something in her proud, highly strung, unstable temperament that accorded with his own, and when they met he went out of his way to show his devotion to her. After such a meeting in March 1865, Elisabeth wrote to her son, Crown Prince Rudolf:

> Yesterday the King paid me a long visit and had Grandma not eventually arrived he would still be here. He kissed my hand so many times that Aunt Sophie, who was looking through the door, asked me afterwards if I still had it.[1]

Sophie, two years younger than Ludwig, did not have the stirring beauty of her older sister, but by most standards she was very attractive, with a slim figure, blond hair and delicate features. She had the strength and determination of Sissi, but expressed them in a quieter way. Intelligent, tactful and charming, she was altogether a very sympathetic and winning person. Ludwig had known her since childhood. As a boy, he had once written a dramatic adaptation of the Faust story in which he had acted the title role and given Sophie the part of Gretchen. Her great virtue in his eyes was that, unlike most of the Wittelsbach family, she was a strong admirer of Wagner. As they grew older this shared passion drew them together and they began a warm and lively correspondence, aided by Count Holnstein who acted as an intermediary. Often he would spend hours with her while she played the piano and sang the female parts from various Wagner operas.

It seems to have been a combination of factors that in 1867 brought them to the point of becoming engaged. Probably it would never have happened without some pressure on the part of Sophie and her mother, for Ludwig had shown himself very unenthusiastic about the idea of marriage when the Justice

Minister Bomhard had aired the subject with him. 'Is it so urgent for me to marry do you think?' he had asked Bomhard, to which the latter had replied that, for the sake of the country and the royal house, he ought not to postpone the step for too long and should seriously consider a Protestant bride in the interests of sectarian harmony. The King's last words in the conversation, however, were: 'I really have no time to marry, Otto can take care of that.'[2]

But he had reckoned without the determination of Sophie's mother, Ludovika. The Duchess had great marital ambitions for her daughters. Elisabeth was Empress of Austria, and another daughter, Marie, was Queen of Naples. Yet another, Helen, had married a prince of the Thurn und Taxis family (not the aide-de-camp to Ludwig). Now it was Sophie's turn and she had plenty of royal suitors from various parts of Europe.

When the Duchess perceived a close friendship blossoming between her daughter and the King, she saw the chance of another good match and decided to give matters a little push. Calling on the Queen Mother, she declared that her daughter was too good to be trifled with and must know where she stood. She also sent her son Karl Theodor (Ludwig's friend of his adolescent days, known as 'Gackl') to visit Ludwig and ask him about his intentions. Ludwig assured Gackl that he was not disposed to marry, and shortly afterwards, on 19 January 1867, he wrote a curious letter to Sophie in which he said that he must break off their correspondence, adding:

You know the nature of my destiny. I once wrote to you from Berg about my mission in the world. You also know that I do not have many years to live, that I shall leave this earth when the unthinkable happens, when my star no longer shines, when he has gone, the truly beloved Friend; yes, then my time will also be up, for then I shall no longer be able to live. You have always taken such a true, sincere and heartfelt interest in my fate, dear Sophie, that I shall be deeply thankful to you for it for the rest of my life. The main basis of our interchange, as you will confirm, has always been the remarkable, sweeping destiny of R. Wagner.[3]

But within a few days of writing this letter Ludwig had changed his mind. Why he did so is not absolutely clear. It has been suggested that it had something to do with the fact that about this time Paul Taxis and Count Holnstein decided one evening that they would both get married. Ludwig possibly felt a comradely and slightly playful urge to follow suit. There is also a story that Sophie herself precipitated matters. She had evidently made it plain to him that she was growing tired of her mother's efforts to marry her off to young men whom she did not like and that she was counting on Ludwig to rescue her. When he failed to propose she became impatient and one day greeted him coldly when they met in the street. This might have made him realize that if he did not ask her to marry him he would risk losing her friendship altogether. His own account of how the proposal came about was later given in a letter to Cosima after the engagement was over. He blamed Ludovika for misinterpreting his correspondence with Sophie and forcing him to declare that his feelings were not amorous. 'Sophie,' he continued, 'who was in fact in love with me, was infinitely sad when she learned that I did not feel the same way. Moved by her unhappy state and feeling genuine sympathy for her, I allowed myself to be lured into the ill-considered step of becoming engaged.'[4]

Whatever reason or combination of reasons was responsible, things came to a head in a scene that might have been part of a romantic operetta. On 21 January he and Sophie were both at a splendid ball in Munich and danced together far into the night to the music of Johann Strauss, then at the height of his career. Ludwig was carried away, and in the early hours of the morning he announced to his mother that he wished to marry Sophie. The Queen Mother immediately went off to confer with the Duchess, and by 9 o'clock the next morning Sophie had accepted and everything was arranged. On the evening of the same day Ludwig and his mother attended a play at the Court Theatre. Sophie and her parents were also there, and during the interval Ludwig fetched Sophie from her box and led her to his own where she took her seat between him and the Queen Mother. The audience could be in no doubt as to the meaning of this happening. On the same day Ludwig sent a telegram to Wagner telling him the news: 'The faithful Sachs informs Walther joyfully that he has found his Eva, that Siegfried has found his Brünhilde.'[5] Wagner and Cosima were delighted, as was ex-King Ludwig I, who composed a sonnet for the occasion, comparing the engaged couple to Venus and Adonis.

Soon the whole country was talking about the engagement and glasses were being raised to the King's future wife. There were, it is true, a few dissenting voices. Some felt that a match with a foreign princess would have been more advantageous politically, and the Protestant faction were disappointed that Ludwig had chosen a Catholic bride. But most people were pleased and relieved that their King had taken the first step towards securing the succession. The souvenir shops began to do a brisk trade in engravings and medallions of the couple.

But from the start there were hints that all was not as it should be. In the photographs of the pair standing arm in arm, Ludwig looks distant and awkward. Clearly his heart was not in the engagement. The impatience with which he had hurried it through was the reckless impatience of a man who knows he is plunging into something ill-conceived but rushes in a kind of ecstatic foreknowledge of the doom he is bringing upon himself. As soon as he came to his senses and realized the full implications of the course he had embarked upon he began to draw back.

For a time, however, he tried, in his own eccentric manner, to play the part of the ardent fiancé. He sent Sophie numerous letters in which he addressed her as 'Elsa', presumably thinking of Elsa von Brabant in *Lohengrin*, and signed himself 'Heinrich', possibly a reminder of their childhood drama in which he played Heinrich Faust or perhaps a reference to the German monarch, Heinrich IV, who also appears in *Lohengrin*. It is curious, and perhaps revealing, that he did not sign himself 'Lohengrin', which would have been the most obvious thing to do in the context. The striking fact about most of these letters is that they are written in a spirit of make-believe in which Wagner and his world predominate, while any direct expression of love is almost entirely absent. In one of them, for example, he ends with the words:

> So, I greet you with my whole soul my dear Senta, Elisabeth, Isolde, Eva, Brünhilde. Receive the warmest thanks from the bottom of my heart, which beats faithfully for you.[6]

In another he wrote: 'The God of my life, as you know, is Richard Wagner,'[7] a strange thing for a young man to write to his betrothed, and yet it shows a kind of honesty, for he never pretended to her that she was more important to him than Wagner.

Often in the middle of the night he would drive over to Possenhofen from Berg. The young bride and her family would be wakened by the sounds of galloping hooves as his carriage came down the avenue leading to the house. Then all the servants would have to be on their feet, lighting up the house and making it welcoming for the King. Sometimes

Ludwig would suddenly demand to be alone with his fiancée, and for the sake of etiquette a chaperone would be stationed behind a curtain of plants during the conversation. Not that very much ever took place at these meetings, apart from Ludwig's frequent assurances to Sophie that she had beautiful eyes. Physical signs of passion were restricted to a few chaste kisses which he placed on her brow. When she grew tired of this restraint and once kissed him on the mouth he was so shocked that he nearly broke off the engagement there and then.

In public he behaved in a manner equally inconsistent with the role of lover, as is illustrated by an anecdote related by Bomhard concerning a ball given by Prince Hohenlohe at the Foreign Ministry.

> Towards ten o'clock the King came up to me in the middle of the throng of guests and asked me what time it was and whether he would still be able to reach the theatre before the end of a Schiller drama which was playing there. I pointed out to the King that it would be taken amiss if I were seen looking at my watch. Would he, I asked, be so kind as to stand close in front of me. He did so enabling me to pull out my watch and tell him that he would be able to see part of the play. But I added that surely it would not be proper behaviour toward his fiancée if he were to leave the gathering so soon. He took his leave from me politely and shortly afterwards the word went round: 'The King has gone.' I don't know whether he really failed to bid goodbye to his bride, as was said by the astonished guests, but in the light of such happenings I had to conclude that the King did not love her.[8]

Sophie, realizing that all was not well, decided to try to enlist the help of Wagner. When the composer visited Munich in March, Sophie went to see him. As Wagner was *persona non grata* to her parents, the meeting had to take place secretly at the house of her brother, Duke Ludwig, who was married to an

actress. Wagner was charmed by Sophie and shortly afterwards
wrote to Ludwig:

> I was profoundly stirred by your dear chosen one! My gracious
> King! For the first time since your fate was joined to mine I looked
> into a human eye from which blessed but anxious love for your
> Majesty spoke deeply and eloquently to my soul. Oh if only you
> could be united soon, soon.[9]

But Ludwig was in no hurry to be united. At the beginning of
April he was planning a journey to Jerusalem with his mother.
On 3 April he wrote to Sophie: 'Either on Saturday or on
Monday I shall start with Mother for Jerusalem . . . I feel like
Godfrey de Bouillon, I am full of enthusiasm, am enchanted.'[10]
His reference to Godfrey de Bouillon, who became first King of
Jerusalem in 1099, is interesting, since in one of the variants of
the Lohengrin legend Godfrey is said to be the son of the Swan
Knight, Helias.

For some reason, possibly connected with Wagner's visit,
the trip to Jerusalem never took place. Instead, on 31 May
Ludwig set out incognito with Otto for a rather different place of
pilgrimage, the Wartburg castle near Eisenach in Thuringia, an
area that is now part of the German Democratic Republic. This
fortress, which has given its name to an East German motor car,
was made the scene of the legendary 'Singers' War' as depicted
in Wagner's *Tannhäuser*. The castle, with its magnificent hilltop
position, is rich in historical and mythological associations and
evidently had special meaning for Ludwig. It must have appeared
significant to him that the Wartburg was established by a certain
Count Ludwig in the eleventh century. It was said that he
discovered the site while out hunting and that he and eleven
of his men laid claim to it by plunging their swords into the
ground. In later times it was claimed that the ghosts of the
twelve men could sometimes be seen hovering around their

swords like will o' the wisps. Over the centuries the castle became a kind of symbol of German nationalistic feeling, and in the early nineteenth century it was the scene of a torchlight rally at which a gathering of young men pledged themselves to the renewal of their nation. It had gradually been enlarged and altered, and it now boasted some magnificent rooms including the Singers' Hall, where the contest was supposed to have taken place, and the ornate Banqueting Hall. It was the latter room, not the former, which Ludwig later used as the model for the Singers' Hall at Neuschwanstein. When Ludwig arrived, the commandant of the castle, knowing his visitor's identity, was anxious to show him round, but Ludwig insisted on being left to wander alone through the rooms so that he could commune in peace with the spirits that lingered there. The next day he visited the nearby mountain known as the Hörselberg, with its grotto where Venus was said to have lived.

In July Ludwig went on another trip, this time to the Giant International Exhibition which was staged in Paris that year. He took with him a new companion, Richard Hornig, who had recently entered service in the King's stable and was to have a close relationship with Ludwig over many years. Though never as highly placed as Holnstein, the Master of the Horse, he was to hold the important position of Stallmeister (Master of the Horse), running the royal stable of some 500 horses and organizing horse transport for the King, his household and members of the Royal Family. At this time Hornig was about twenty-six years old and had recently completed his military service. He was fair-haired with a lean, wiry build and, like Ludwig, was a magnificent horseman.

Though welcomed unofficially by Napoleon III, Ludwig travelled once again incognito, as the 'Count von Berg'. He spent many hours at the exhibition, where he bought numerous presents for Sophie. He also made a pilgrimage to Versailles and visited the fourteenth-century castle of Pierrefonds which had been recently restored by Viollet-le-Duc. Like the Wartburg, this castle had been built by a namesake, Louis, Duke of Orléans. Napoleon III received him courteously, and Ludwig refrained from showing that he regarded Napoleon as a parvenu monarch. They must have seemed a curiously contrasting pair: the tall, blue-blooded King and the little bourgeois emperor with his pointed moustaches, who spoke fluent German with an Augsburg accent – a result of spending part of his boyhood there. Napoleon is reported to have warned Ludwig not to become too deeply involved with Prussia. Otherwise there is no record of what they discussed. A month later the Emperor and Empress passed through Bavaria on their way to a conference in Salzburg. Ludwig presented his fiancée to them, and the Empress Eugénie, brushing protocol aside, embraced the girl warmly.

But there was little warmth in Ludwig's behaviour to Sophie. At a performance of *Tannhäuser* on 1 August they sat in separate boxes, and Ludwig spent only five minutes with Sophie during the interval. His horror at the prospect of marriage was growing. He wept when he talked about it with his mother, and he confessed to the Court Secretary, Lorenz von Düfflipp, that he would rather jump into the Alpsee than marry. Perhaps his misgivings arose partly from a growing consciousness of his latent homosexuality. Possibly also he was beginning to suspect that he carried within him the seeds of madness, for occasionally he would be glimpsed looking into a mirror, shaking his head at himself and muttering in French: 'Really, there are times when I wouldn't swear that you are not mad.'[11]

The wedding had at first been arranged for August 1867. Then it had been postponed until 12 October, the day on which Ludwig I and Max II had both been married. So far Sophie's parents had been patient, but when the wedding was postponed for a second time their patience was lost. On about 3 or 4 October Duke Max sent Ludwig a letter asking the King either to fix a definite date for the wedding towards the end of November or to withdraw his request for Sophie's hand.

At first Ludwig was incensed that a subject should address him in such a manner, and Düfflipp had to remind him that the Duke was writing not as a subject but as a father. Then he realized that here was his chance of escape. He ordered that Duke Max be informed of his decision to cancel the engagement and also wrote a brief note to Sophie to the effect that her father was tearing them apart. On 7 October at Hohenschwangau, he sat down to write her a proper letter of explanation. He explained how he had felt himself pressured into asking for her hand and that he had prevaricated over the wedding arrangements not because he wished to deceive her but because he needed time to think things over.

'Now that I have had time to reflect,' he went on,

> and to take counsel with myself, I see that my true and sincere brotherly love for you remains as always deeply rooted in my soul, but it is not the kind of love that is required for union in marriage.
>
> I owed you this explanation, dear Elsa; I ask for the continuation of your friendship. If you release me from my word and we part from one another let us, I beg you, do this without rancour or bitterness . . .[12]

It was an honest letter, and no one reading it could doubt that he did the right thing in severing the engagement. But the family was outraged, and it was some time before Elisabeth could bring herself to forgive his behaviour. As for Sophie, once she had recovered from the initial shock, she took the blow with her usual self-possession.

Perhaps the most damaging result of the whole affair was the adverse effect it had on Ludwig's reputation with the public.

This is apparent from a dispatch on the subject sent by the British envoy, Sir Henry Howard, to the Foreign Secretary, Lord Stanley, on 13 October 1867. Howard writes:

> It is evident that His Majesty was not animated with those real feelings of affection towards the Princess which he might have been supposed to entertain considering that she was his own selection . . .
>
> The extraordinary conduct of His Majesty, who appears to have received a very faulty education, may, I think rather be attributed to his disinclination to give up the seclusion in which he has hitherto indulged and descend from his ideal world into the practical and useful paths of married life. A Bavarian gentleman, in conversation with me yesterday, observed that he feared there might be some partial derangement in His Majesty's mind, that this might be an excuse for his recent conduct, but would be a misfortune for the country.
>
> Seldom, in my recollection, has any event in a Royal Family caused a greater or more deplorable public scandal . . .[13]

The following year, after all the fuss had died down, Sophie married Prince Ferdinand d'Orléans, duc d'Alençon, a grandson of King Louis-Philippe, with whom she lived in modest contentment for thirty years until her death in a fire at a charity bazaar in Paris. Heroically, she refused to be carried out until some young girls in the building had been rescued. By then it was too late. She perished in the flames.

An ironic souvenir of the abortive engagement was provided by the magnificent wedding coach ordered by Ludwig, which was not in fact finished until long after the wedding had been cancelled. It rests today in the coach museum at Nymphenburg palace.

9

Lilla . . . and Others

Sophie was not the only woman whose heart suffered on account of Ludwig. He was also pursued by a number of women from the world of the theatre and the arts, and of these the one who succeeded in coming closest to him was a Hungarian actress named Lilla von Bulyowsky, whom he first met in May 1866 when she was playing the title role in Schiller's play, *Maria Stuart*. The martyred Queen of Scotland was one of Ludwig's great heroines, and so moved was he by Lilla's performance that afterwards he ordered the church of the Holy Trinity to be opened specially so that he could pray for her soul. He was also eager to know the actress who had played the part so convincingly.

Lilla was an attractive, dark-haired woman of about thirty-three with a lively and spirited personality. Evidently she had at some stage been married. At any rate her letters reveal that she had at least one child at the time she knew Ludwig. Thus began a curious friendship that was to last for six years and was to be the nearest thing to a love affair that Ludwig ever experienced with a woman. Soon he was writing her enthusiastic letters addressed to 'die geliebte Freundin' (the beloved Friend) and full of quotations from *Romeo and Juliet, Maria Stuart* and other dramas.

Ludwig's biographer, Gottfried von Böhm, knew Lilla well, and he gives the following description of the actress and her relationship with the King.[1]

> What distinguished her from most actresses I knew was the fact that she always remained a real woman of the world. She was not without small faults: somewhat avaricious, somewhat snobbish, somewhat petty, but amusing, even scintillating, and a kind devoted friend. As she was a very pretty woman with many admirers and occasionally adopted a rather free manner, nobody credited her with much virtue, but I would wager my right arm that not many had ever been shown the inside of her charming blue bedroom in the Maximilianstrasse in which, opposite the four-poster bed, hung a big photograph of the young King in the regalia of the order of St George.
>
> According to the information that she gave me in December 1870 and later, and which became increasingly more intimate and detailed, it appears that she was one of the objects of Ludwig II's youthful passion.
>
> There gradually developed between them a relationship that was not without its ebb and flow. One moment she would receive an invitation to visit Hohenschwangau in the middle of winter . . . the next she would be told that she must leave Munich within 34 hours – to which she replied that she knew her rights. One moment the King would be lying passionately at her feet, the next he would forbid her to come near him . . .

Lilla visited Ludwig on a number of occasions at various of his residences, and she described to Böhm a stay at Hohenschwangau when Ludwig showed her his bedroom, decorated with erotic pictures which, she claimed, rather shocked her, even though she was no prude. 'I have a protection against them,' the King said, showing her a little altar on which stood a picture of Lilla as Mary Queen of Scots. Then they had sat down on the edge of the bed and began to recite Goethe's play, *Egmont*. When they came to a kissing scene Lilla evidently became prim and they parted without anything more happening. On this or a similar occasion Ludwig apparently told her that he had never possessed a woman and that he often thought of her during the night and covered his pillow with kisses. After this confession he laid his head on her bosom, and she, without answering, laid it gently aside. Lilla, according to her own account, had gone no further because she did not wish to risk the damage to her reputation and general calumny that would result if it became known that she had seduced a young man. She also claimed that on the same visit Ludwig had actually chased her through the rooms of the castle. Reading Böhm's account one has the impression that Lilla accepted the King's adoration as she might have accepted a bouquet of flowers thrown to her on the stage, but that her main concern was for her career as an actress.

All this does not quite tally with the evidence of her letters to Ludwig. They are not the letters of a *grande dame* warding off the attentions of an adolescent, but of a woman passionately in love. From these it would appear that it was she, not he, who was anxious for greater intimacy between them. No woman likes to admit that she has pursued a man unsuccessfully, especially a younger man, and this would explain why she was anxious to pretend that the passion was on his side rather than hers. As for the suggestion that she was more concerned about her acting career than her relationship with Ludwig, it is true that many of the letters deal with her theatrical ambitions, and cynics might say that she tried to use Ludwig merely to further those ambitions; but this is not borne out by the letters.

Like anyone else who enjoyed the King's favour, Lilla had to contend with jealous and malicious people anxious to discredit her. A letter she wrote to Ludwig on 10 January 1867 shows how vulnerable she felt herself to be in this respect.

Your Majesty, never condemn me without a hearing, for I have no need to reproach myself with anything ignoble or base in my life. Slander reaches the highest levels, and even your Majesty has not been immune to its poisoned arrows, why should they spare a defenceless woman who has the misfortune to be not altogether without allure and moreover an artist who often does not even have any idea of the accusation being made against her and who cannot speak to her King nor indeed even write to him. Oh, the situation is hard – desperate. I have no reason to believe that anyone has yet slandered me to Your Majesty, but an inner voice makes me tremble, especially for the future.

I also hope I am right in believing that the deductions from my salary and pension which I have had to put up with in the conditions of my contract were not initiated by Your Majesty . . . I am not complaining. It is only that I need to preserve the belief that Your Majesty is far removed from all such pettiness, whose source is perhaps to be found in the excessive zeal of Your Majesty's subordinates.[2]

Poor Lilla. She did not receive much in return for her adoration, certainly not where her career was concerned. In an undated letter, written some time during the summer of 1867, she complained: 'For about four to six weeks I have not been allowed to appear, whereas Madame Dahn plays two or three times a week. And I put up with this. Why? So that I can live in the same town in which King Ludwig II resides. God bless him, God protect him and make him happy.'

The news of Ludwig's engagement came as a particularly painful blow, as is shown by the anguished letter that she wrote to him on 4 August 1867: 'From 1 September to 15 December I shall be on holiday – a cheerless and terrible time for me; when I return Ludwig II will be married.'

Ludwig continued to see Lilla during his engagement, and he poured out to her his misgivings about marrying Sophie. Perhaps she even helped – as the Queen Mother believed – to sway his mind against the marriage. At any rate she was overjoyed when he broke the engagement off, as she said in her letter to him of 4 October 1867: 'I believe I have reached the happiest day of my life, but I am afraid that I am dreaming and would rather die in my dream than wake up to reality. What makes me so happy, Majesty, is your news that you can breathe freely again and that deep peace fills your soul . . .'

Similar declarations followed thick and fast, but it was not until 10 June 1868 that Lilla revealed the full extent of her devotion to Ludwig:

> For once I will be open and throw aside my mask, even if in doing so I damage myself in the eyes of my King. From the moment I saw and greeted Your Majesty as Crown Prince in the English Garden I felt for the first time in my life what the word 'love' really means. (It was in the month of May 1863.) From this time onward my only goal was to receive an engagement in Munich and to be able to see my ideal occasionally. I *lied* when I said to your Majesty and several times wrote: 'I need a refuge'. What I needed was only the nearness of King Ludwig II.

She then gives a list of generous offers from various theatres in other cities and from private patrons, all of which she turned down so that she could be in or near Munich. The letter goes on to describe how she shut herself away for five or six months writing novellas and travel descriptions until 3 or 4 o'clock in the morning in order to support herself in Munich while she waited for an assignment, which she finally obtained. She continues:

> Your Majesty knows the rest. From that time dates your high protection, your enthusiasm for Maria Stuart, my happiness. I never

visit a ball or a large gathering and even avoid the theatre. I mingle with no one from the world of dandies. I live only for my ideal, my art and my work. Your Majesty may give millions to Richard Wagner or other artists . . . pearls and diamonds to 'Elsa' . . . the Crown and the royal hand to some boring Princess . . . I will envy none of them if only Your Majesty will preserve a good memory of me in your noble heart. If every three months I receive a small letter, even of only two or three lines, if perhaps once a year I am given a short audience where there is a chance of an eager look from those beautiful eyes, a benevolent smile from that enchanting mouth, a few heartfelt words and perhaps a friendly handshake – then I will be content, in fact I will be overjoyed.

Alas, even these modest consolations were eventually to be denied her; soon after her stay at Hohenschwangau she was summoned by the Queen Mother, who told her that the King would never marry as long as she remained in Bavaria and extracted from her a promise that she would not renew her contract when it expired after a year and a half. Lilla kept her word. Although Ludwig had never returned her love, he had in his own way been extremely fond of this temperamental actress who had brought a breath of fresh air into his life. When she said goodbye to him in 1872 he stamped his foot angrily and exclaimed: 'That stupid goose is to blame for this.'[3]

No woman ever quite took Lilla's place, but Ludwig did strike up friendships with a number of other women, mostly from the world of the stage and the arts. One of them was the soprano Josefine Scheffsky, who was later to take the part of Sieglinde when the complete *Ring* was performed for the first time at Bayreuth. She sang like an angel but had a physique of typically Wagnerian proportions, and it is said that the fastidious King preferred to have her hefty figure concealed behind a screen of plants when he listened to her sing.

She was one of the people who were privileged to be taken to Ludwig's Winter Garden. This extraordinary Aladdin's Cave, which I shall describe in more detail in a later chapter, was built in a sort of huge greenhouse on top of the Munich Residenz and contained a variety of exotic plants and trappings and an artificial lake. There is a story that Josefine (or possibly some other female visitor) fell from a boat into this lake, no doubt hoping that the King would rescue her. Ludwig, however, merely rang for a servant and had her fished out.

In character she appears to have been self-seeking, tactless, dishonest and fond of gossip. It was perhaps because of this last quality that the King for a time had a soft spot for her, since he himself had an ear for gossip – this is true of many monarchs and highly placed people, since gossip provides them with the kind of information that does not always filter through official channels. Ludwig evidently knew how to take her stories with a pinch of salt. He related with a smile to the singer Franz Nachbaur how Josefine had claimed to have been made pregnant by the Cabinet official, August von Eisenhart. She went too far, however, when she tried to discredit the director of the Court Theatre, Baron Karl von Perfall, and the Court Secretary, Ludwig von Bürkel, in the King's eyes. She also tried to cheat Ludwig in a rather foolish and unpleasant manner. It was the accepted practice for friends of the King to present him with presents in return for those they received from him. They were then allowed to collect a reimbursement by presenting a bill to the royal treasury. Josefine gave Ludwig an oriental rug and then handed in a bill for five times the true price. Whether because of this or her other misdemeanours, she was blacklisted by Ludwig and forbidden to appear in the Court Theatre.

A relationship which Ludwig found rather more fulfilling was his friendship with the actress Marie Dahn-Hausmann, who was fifteen years his senior and happily married to the actor Friedrich Dahn. He had first seen her in the role of Thekla in Schiller's *Wallenstein* when he was Crown Prince, but it was evidently not until 1875 that they became friends, when Ludwig invited the actress and her husband to the recently acquired island of Herrenchiemsee where he was to build the last of his palaces. Over the next few years they exchanged a correspondence in which Ludwig expressed himself very openly. For example, on 25 April 1876 he wrote to her:

> That my heart is not dead to all feelings I always realize when I see you, honoured lady, speak to you and read your letters, from which flows a beneficent warmth, a magic which is yours alone. Be firmly, eternally and unshakably convinced that, even though I write seldom, my true feelings for you will never change. I will always sincerely rejoice when you are joyful and be sad when you are oppressed by cares and sorrow. Our souls are, I believe, akin in this respect: our hatred of the base and the unjust, and that makes me happy.[4]

And it was in another letter to Marie, written on 27 April 1876, that he wrote his famous words: 'Ein ewiges Rütsel will ich bleiben mir und anderen' (I wish to remain an eternal enigma to myself and to others).[5]

Ludwig's most eccentric female friend was the sculptress Elisabeth Ney, a great-niece of Marshal Ney, the Napoleonic military commander. Born in Munich, the daughter of a sculptor, she was an adventuress cast somewhat in the mould of Lola Montez, beautiful, widely travelled, unconventional, and admired by many men including the writer Gottfried Keller and the philosopher Schopenhauer. She had caused a great sensation at the Paris Exhibition of 1867 with her busts of Bismarck and Garibaldi and her *Sleeping Fawn*. She had also been received by Napoleon III.

Now she was determined to win the favour of Ludwig II and began to bombard him with flattering letters which at first went unanswered. At length, however, the King was persuaded to take an interest in her, perhaps prompted by the chemist Liebig, one of her friends, who was frequently at the Residenz organizing chemical experiments for Ludwig. In 1868 he consented to sit for her on condition that she took no measurements of him and did not speak to him. One day he arrived for a sitting looking bad-tempered, and she, not wishing to portray him in this mood, asked if she could read to him from Goethe's play, *Iphigenie*. As she read Goethe's resonant words the King's expression brightened and he was soon in good spirits. At later sittings more of *Iphigenie* was read – some reports say that these readings were carried out by the Cabinet Secretary of the time, Friedrich von Lipowsky. Curiously enough, before he had even met the sculptress, Ludwig had commissioned one of his architects to design a house for her in Schwabing where, dressed in oriental robes, she received members of the artistic coterie of Munich.

In 1870 she went with her husband to Texas, where she engaged in an abortive scheme for a utopian settlement. There is now a museum named after her in Austin. Her statue of Ludwig, originally in clay, was later copied in marble by Friedrich Ochs of Berlin, and this copy survives. The statue is the only full-length one of the King made from life. It shows him in the costume of the Order of St Hubert, his left hand on the hilt of his sword, his eyes looking into the distance with a rapt expression as though he were still listening to the words of *Iphigenie*.

A number of other women were at various times favoured by Ludwig. There was the actress Mathilde Mallinger, of whom he commissioned a bust, and there was the Spanish Infanta, Maria de la Paz, wife of his cousin, Prince Ludwig Ferdinand. His correspondence also contains the names of such actresses and singers as Hermine Bland, Hermine Claar-Delia, Klara Heese and Rosa Herzfeld-Link.

His admiration for women of the stage is revealing. Always he saw the ideal rather than the flesh-and-blood human being. His idealistic attitude to women is best summed up in a letter that he wrote to Pfordten:

> You can be sure that I do not underestimate their worth. With most young people sensuality is mingled with their attraction towards the opposite sex. This I condemn.[6]

10

Wagnerian Strains

The time has come to return to the subject of Richard Wagner, who, since his departure to Triebschen, had been out of sight but far from out of mind as far as his patron was concerned. Ludwig's devotion to the Wagnerian aims and ideals never wavered, but his relations with the man himself were more turbulent, and the years 1867 to 1870 in particular were marked by a series of dramatic fluctuations in their friendship. After Wagner had left Munich the two men had continued to correspond warmly, but in the summer of 1867 there came a clash.

In February of that year Ludwig wrote to Wagner asking if another performance of *Lohengrin* could be arranged. Today, when modern sound recording enables us to listen to music at the flick of a switch, even when we are driving a car, it is easy to forget what a treasured experience it was in Ludwig's day to hear a favourite orchestral or operatic work performed. Three years had passed since *Lohengrin* had last been staged in Munich, and now the King was longing to see and hear again the opera which, as he put it to Wagner, had been 'the seed of such unimagined joys'.[1] A production was accordingly planned for June.

The choice of a suitable tenor to play the title role presented a great problem, and Wagner decided that the only possible candidate was the sixty-year-old Josef Tichatschek, his old Dresden comrade who had been the first to sing the part of *Tannhäuser*. In appearance Tichatschek did not make a very convincing Knight of the Swan, for, apart from his age, he was rather fat and not very heroic-looking. Nor did he have the high intelligence of Schnorr von Carolsfeld. He did, however, possess a superb voice, and Wagner was convinced that he would give a fine performance.

But Wagner had underestimated the King's fastidiousness. Like a sexual fantasist, Ludwig had to have a perfect scenario without any jarring features, otherwise the magic of the performance failed to work. When he attended the final rehearsal on 11 June he was bitterly disappointed. Newman describes his reactions as follows:

> Through his opera glasses he saw not the poetic Knight of the Grail of his boyhood's dreams but a sagging face painted and plastered into a simulacrum of youth, and an ancient body maintaining its uncertain equilibrium in the boat only by clinging to a pole let into the deck for that charitable purpose. He saw nothing he could call acting, only a succession of 'grimaces', as he complained afterwards.[2]

In a bad temper he went back to Berg, declaring that this 'knight of the sorrowful countenance', as he called Tichatschek, could come back next year to wash his feet, but he never wanted to see the man on the stage again. Nor did he like the performance of Frau Bertram-Meyer as Ortrud who, he said, 'swept across the stage like a fury'[3]. He ordered that both of them be replaced.

1. Ludwig II's grandfather, Ludwig I, painted by Franz von Lenbach.

2. Ludwig's parents, King Maximilian II and Queen Marie.

3. Ludwig and his brother Otto.

4. A childhood drawing by Ludwig, evincing his early love of swans.

5. Neuschwanstein: As with all his enterprises, Ludwig closely supervised the building and decoration of his 'Grail Castle', shown in its fairy-tale setting in the Bavarian Alps.

6. Neuschwanstein: The Singers' Hall, evoking the world of *Tannhäuser* and the Parzival legend.

7. Linderhof palace, the smallest of the three built by Ludwig.

8. Herrenchiemsee palace: The Hall of Mirrors, longer than its counterpart at Versailles.

9. Richard Wagner knocking on the door of the royal treasury: A cartoon from the Munich satirical newspaper *Punsch*.

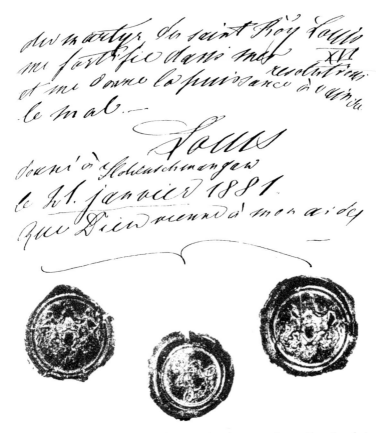

10. An entry, written in French, in Ludwig's secret diary. Translated, it reads: 'May the martyrdom of the holy King Louis XVI fortify me and give me strength to conquer evil – Louis; given at Hohenschwangau, 21 January 1881. May God come to my aid.'

11. A cartoon showing Ludwig as the Swan Knight, Lohengrin. The moon has Wagner's profile.

12. Ludwig photographed near the end of his life, showing the physical deterioration of his later years.

13. An artist's impression of Ludwig struggling with Dr Gudden in the shallows of Lake Starnberg.

14. The funeral procession approaching the church of St Michael in Munich on 19 June 1886.

15. The unrealized Falkenstein castle, as conceived in 1883 by the stage designer, Christian Jank.

Wagner, who had been so moved by his old friend's performance that he had embraced him on the stage, stormed back to Triebschen in high dudgeon, leaving Bülow to find the new singers and take over the supervision of the performance.

Miraculously, it took only five days for Bülow to coach the new singers in their roles, and the first performance took place in the presence of the King on 16 June, with the young tenor Heinrich Vogl as Lohengrin and Therese Thoma as Ortrud. These two, who were enemies in the story, became husband and wife the following year. After the performance Ludwig wrote a letter to Vogl expressing his appreciation.

In August came a production of *Tannhäuser* which Wagner, despite Ludwig's entreaties, refused to attend. The King was not present at the first performance on 1 August because the court was in mourning over the recent death of King Otto of Greece, but he attended a performance on the 3rd to which only a small, select audience was invited.

For some time Wagner continued to feel bruised by Ludwig's behaviour over the *Lohengrin* production, but soon the pair were again exchanging their usual fulsome letters. On 12 July, shortly before his visit to France, Ludwig wrote to the composer:

> It is possible that in about eight days I shall go to Paris for the Exhibition, although it goes against every fibre of my being to visit this modern Babylon, which I abhor. I hate Paris, which I hold to be the throne of materialism, of vulgar sensuality and godless frivolity. I recognize more and more the urgent necessity of erecting, as a counterbalance to this modern Sodom and Gomorrah, a seat of spiritual rulership, where everything noble and beautiful would have its abode; and you, my warmly beloved Friend, I venerate as the priest of this pure cult, the King of the ideal realm that we wish to found in this world of malice and hate.[4]

This letter is further proof that Wagner's work meant much more to Ludwig than just music and opera. In his reply Wagner urged Ludwig to go to Paris and not to judge it too harshly, but Ludwig's visit did nothing to alter his view of the French capital. After his return he wrote to Düfflipp on 1 August asking him to tell Wagner 'that my journey was of the greatest use and that I now see more clearly than ever the urgent necessity of a counterbalance to that barren, inartistic mode of living as it manifests itself so abhorrently in Paris. In Germany we must raise the banner of pure and holy art so that it flies from the battlements, summoning German youth to rally around it.'[5]

For a few months the correspondence between King and composer continued harmoniously, but by the end of 1867 another serious breach had opened up. The reason for this lay partly in a series of articles which Wagner wrote for the *Süddeutsche Presse*, a new journal, supported initially by government funds, which had replaced the official organ, the *Bayerische Zeitung*, at the beginning of October and had as its editor Wagner's friend Julius Fröbel. In these articles Wagner held forth on the theme of the essential superiority of the German nation and the need for a rebirth of the German spirit. Such a rebirth, he wrote, would 'found a new and truly German civilization, extending its benefits even beyond our frontiers'. This, he argued, had been 'the universal mission of the German folk since its entry into history'.[6] He called for an end to the estrangement between the rulers and their people, praising the two preceding Kings of Bavaria and hinting that the present one would set an example to the other German monarchs. He also declared that the theatre was 'the spiritual seed and kernel of all national-poetic and national-ethical culture' and that no genuine folk culture was possible until the lofty role of the theatre had been fully recognized.[7]

At first the King was enthusiastic about the articles, but after eight of them had appeared he began to be disturbed by the direction they were taking. Wagner had once again been unable to resist the temptation to pontificate about political matters and had wandered off his original theme into delivering criticisms of Church and State and lecturing his readers on the functions of the monarchy. Ludwig decided that Wagner had gone too far, and after thirteen articles had appeared a government official called at the office of the *Süddeutsche Presse* with an order from the King that publication of the articles be suspended.

It is possible, however, that Ludwig would not have taken this action had he not already been displeased with Wagner because of the fact that the composer's relationship with Cosima was becoming increasingly apparent. This was due largely to Malvina Schnorr von Carolsfeld, who, since the death of her husband, had been behaving in a very odd manner. In November of the previous year, 1866, she had gone to Triebschen with her pupil, Isidore von Reutter, to make some curious revelations to Wagner. It appeared that Isidore had held a series of conversations with the spirit of Ludwig Schnorr, who had delivered an important message, namely that Malvina was destined to become Wagner's wife while Isidore was to marry none other than the King himself. What Ludwig thought of this notion, if he heard of it, is not known, but Wagner was incensed and forbade Isidore to enter his house again. Malvina, disappointed, angry and jealous of Cosima, stormed back to Munich and denounced Wagner and Cosima in a letter to one of Ludwig's adjutants, Hauptmann von Sauer. As soon as Ludwig had seen the letter he sent it to Cosima, telling her that he found its contents 'outrageous' but adding: '. . . as your sincere and eternally faithful friend I regard it as my duty to send it to you'.[8]

While on the subject of Malvina, it is worth quoting an account which she sent to Ludwig describing a curiously revealing dream that she had experienced:

Dream. I came out of a beautiful wood into a meadow, in the middle of which stood a large, handsome lion surrounded by tigers and hyenas which were tearing at him murderously while the noble animal only surveyed them contemptuously. With a cry of rage I fell upon the lion so that the cowardly killers drew back and, after a second cry, fled hastily . . .[9]

On the following two nights the dream repeated itself exactly, except that the third time it ended with the lion turning into King Ludwig II. When Ludwig sent the account on to Cosima he described it as 'a strange mixture of clarity and confusion, truth and fiction'.[10] He must surely have recognized the dream as a striking allegory of himself, and perhaps somewhere in his mind he had the foreboding that one day the tigers and hyenas would destroy him.

Wagner repeatedly poured scorn on Malvina and her revelations about him and Cosima, but by late 1867 it had become increasingly difficult for him to keep up the pretence. Düfflipp, for one, knew that Wagner was lying and did not conceal this from the King. On 13 December Ludwig wrote to Düfflipp:

I am surprised that you believe the situation as regards Wagner, Frau von Bülow and Frau Schnorr is not quite kosher: if it should turn out that the miserable rumour is true – which I was never able to bring myself to believe – should it after all really be a case of adultery – then alas![11]

By now the cat was well and truly out of the bag; yet still Wagner avoided making a clean breast of the matter, and still he and the King kept up the charade, though relations between them were now strained.

Between 30 November 1867 and 9 March 1868 no letters passed between Ludwig and Wagner, but finally Ludwig broke the silence. In his letter of 9 March he wrote that he could no longer bear being without news of his friend. He asked about

Wagner's work and suggested that he might visit Triebschen during the course of the summer or that Wagner might come to Hohenschwangau in the late autumn so that they could re-live the glorious November days that they had spent there together three years earlier. Quoting *Die Walküre*, he said that Wagner was 'the spring which I have longed for in the frosty depths of winter'.[12]

Wagner wrote back eloquently playing the injured party. He would always be thankful, he said, for what Ludwig had done for him, but he went on to say that Ludwig was wrecking his own salvation and being drawn into a 'whirlpool of self-destruction' while Wagner's voice went unheard. 'I know,' he continued, 'that I am only welcome to you when I am silent. So why do you disturb the silence and wake the old hopeful echoes in me . . .?' He also complained that Ludwig was not able to perceive the world and its phenomena through the eyes of the Friend. 'So I see the enemy,' he added, 'burying the roots of your worth and your power.'[13]

In his penitent reply to this, Ludwig expressed his regret that he had given any credence to the scandalous press reports about Wagner and went on to say:

The tree [presumably meaning their common work and ideals] shall stand for ever. I shall trample on the head of the serpent, for I am what I was from the beginning – God has chosen me . . . Oh my Friend, once the world seemed rosy to me and men seemed noble; since then I have suffered unspeakably bitter experiences . . . fully justified was my feeling of hate and misanthropy; only in myself, and above all in the pursuit of our ideal, was I able to find comfort and uplift; I shut myself away in myself, for I was gripped by abhorrence and shame in the face of the world. Now that phase is past; it was a process of purification, an episode in my life; I am strengthened, I will forget and forgive the dreadful things that were done to me and will throw myself bravely into life, devote myself to my solemn duties . . . for I clearly recognize my great task and will, believe me, fulfil it faithfully and conscientiously.[14]

Wagner, reassured, wrote back to the effect that Ludwig had redeemed himself by this letter. Men of the future would, he said, regard Ludwig II as 'the most astonishing revelation of the divine in the history of the world'. This judgement, he added, 'you have written yourself in this letter'.[15]

During the next few months Wagner made several journeys to and from Munich. In April he was there at the same time as the Crown Prince Friedrich of Prussia, for whom a gala performance of *Lohengrin* was given. Ludwig was in bed and unable either to attend the opera or to see Wagner. But the composer did spend his fifty-fifth birthday (22 May) with the King on the Roseninsel. A few days later he sent Ludwig a book on Buddhism, Eugène Bournouf's *Introduction à l'histoire du Bouddhisme indien*, in which he had marked the passage which had first inspired the idea of writing *Die Sieger*. Ludwig wrote back thanking him and adding: 'Oh, how I look forward to this Indian legend and its artistic representation by you.' He signed himself 'Parcival'.[16]

By this time preparations were in progress for a performance of *Die Meistersinger*, which Wagner had finished the previous year. A fine cast had been assembled, including Franz Nachbaur as Walther and Mathilde Mallinger as Eva. Bülow was conductor of the orchestra. Wagner took overall charge of the production, and the rehearsals went well, despite some friction between Wagner and the theatrical management, and despite the temperamental behaviour of Bülow, who was still loyal to Wagner's music but becoming increasingly hostile towards the man. It was now clear to both men that they would soon have to drop the pretence that Cosima was still faithful to Hans.

Die Meistersinger, with its tuneful music and light-hearted plot, was a far cry from the tense, elegiac world of *Tristan*. But in its own way it was just as much of a landmark: a comic opera combining exuberance and gaiety with a serious message, and full of haunting music in which Wagner fell back on old-established forms yet still spoke with an original voice. Germany had seen nothing like it before.

The final rehearsal, which was to all intents and purposes a first performance, was held on 19 June in the presence of the King, who was enchanted. It was almost like the triumphant summer of *Tristan* all over again. He wrote to Wagner afterwards saying: 'I was so moved and carried away that it was impossible for me to join in with the profane expression of praise through hand-clapping.' This time he signed himself 'Walther', the name of the opera's hero.[17]

On the 21st the official première was held, once again with the King attending and with friends and enemies of Wagner from all over Europe in the audience. At Ludwig's invitation Wagner was seated in the royal box, and after the second and third acts, at the King's request, he bowed his acknowledgements to the applauding audience, a gesture that was regarded by some of the aristocracy present as a shocking breach of etiquette. One astonished journalist commented as follows:

Wagner, the branded, exiled heretic, whom not much more than two years ago even the King's grace could not shield from the malignity of the upper and lower rabble of our art-metropolis, now rehabilitated in inexpressible fashion in the selfsame royal box in which, till then, only royalties and their descendants had ever been seen![18]

Five more performances of *Die Meistersinger* were held, but without Wagner, who had gone back to Triebschen on 24 June. It was to be eight years before he and Ludwig were to meet again.

The opera had been a great success for him, yet he returned home with the intention of never again taking any practical part in a Munich production. He wrote to the King that henceforth he would live only to create. Probably the difficulties he had encountered with the theatre management had made him more convinced than ever that he needed his own theatre where he could be complete master.

It seems likely that the matter of Cosima was also on Wagner's mind. He knew that it was bound to come to a head soon and that when it did it would cause trouble between himself and the King and make things even more difficult for him in Munich. In this he was right. On 12 July Ludwig wrote to Cosima, who was then in Munich, that the accusations about her and Wagner were being bandied about again. Wagner, when he heard about this, wrote to Ludwig on 16 July once again expressing indignation over the charges and saying that Cosima would have to leave Munich. Ludwig was clearly no longer deceived, though he still half pretended to be. On 25 July, shortly before departing to join the Russian Tsar and Tsarina at Kissingen, he wrote to Wagner urging him to try and persuade Cosima not to leave Munich as this would only encourage the evil tongues. He added: 'The memory of the *Meistersinger* days makes me joyful; it will give me strength to endure the dreadful, prosaic turmoil of the coming days at Kissingen.'[19]

The visit to Kissingen was made at the urging of Prince Hohenlohe, who considered that friendly relations with Russia would help to mitigate the insecure position in which Bavaria found herself in the wake of the war with Prussia. Ludwig was in Kissingen from 2–10 August and probably enjoyed his stay more than he had anticipated. On her return journey the Tsarina passed through Munich, and Ludwig invited her to stay at Berg and arranged a magnificent celebration for her, with a great firework display and a dinner on the Roseninsel which the Tsarina declared to have been the most poetic of her life.

For Ludwig's twenty-third birthday on 25 August Wagner sent him a finely bound printed score of *Die Meistersinger*, together with a dedicatory poem of four stanzas in which he praised the relationship between them. The King wrote on 14 September belatedly thanking him for this and adding that the tunes of the opera had alleviated the banality of recent weeks, when he had been obliged to visit his mother at Hohenschwangau and the Austrian emperor at Possenhofen where Sophie and her fiancé were also present – a fact which did not mitigate the boredom of the visit for him as he now found Sophie rather tedious company and her future husband equally so.

After this there was a long gap in communications between Ludwig and Wagner. Apart from a telegram sending good wishes at New Year, Wagner heard nothing from the King until 10 February 1869. After leaving several of Wagner's letters unanswered, Ludwig once more relented and wrote to the Friend thanking him for a gift of the original score of *Rienzi* and part of *Die Meistersinger* arranged for piano. He told Wagner that his faith in the prospect of fulfilling their common ideal gave him strength to carry out his royal duties, and he asked for news of the composer's health and of his progress with work on the *Ring*.

It was the *Ring* that was soon to be the subject of a new disagreement between the composer and his patron. By the terms of Ludwig's financial settlement to Wagner, the *Ring* was to be the property of the King. The first part, *Das Rheingold*, had been completed in 1854, and Ludwig now wanted it to be performed in Munich. Wagner reluctantly agreed, and preparations began for a production scheduled to take place in the Court Theatre at the end of August. Bülow had resigned as Kapellmeister, partly because of bad health and partly because of the ignominy he was suffering as a result of Cosima's desertion. Ludwig had given him three months' leave, hoping that he would recover and reconsider the position – in fact his resignation was to be final. Meanwhile Wagner's gifted disciple and amanuensis Hans Richter was appointed as conductor. Wagner was kept informed about the preparations, and the conductor, singers, designers and stage technicians went to Triebschen during the course of the summer to consult with the master.

During rehearsals there was a lot of friction between Richter and the theatre management. The Theatre Administrator, Karl von Perfall, and his colleagues resented the young conductor's high-handed attitude, and matters came to a head after the final rehearsal on 27 August, at which the King was present. Because the stage effects were somewhat unsatisfactory, Richter sent a telegram to Wagner saying that the première, scheduled for 29 August, must be postponed, and Wagner immediately wired to the King asking him 'to order the postponement of the public performance of *Das Rheingold* to a time when the as yet unsolved difficulties of the production can be better considered'.[20] He suggested that in the meantime some earlier work of his be performed instead. This was sent on the eve of the scheduled first performance. Meanwhile Richter was flatly refusing to conduct with the stage effects in their present state, telling Perfall that he took his orders only from Wagner. This was in fact a calculated ploy, which was part of a discreditable plot that he and Wagner had been laying for some time with the aim of removing opposition in the theatre. The result of Richter's behaviour was that he was dismissed by Perfall with the support of Düfflipp. Wagner now hoped that, faced with having to support either himself or Perfall, Ludwig would choose to dismiss Perfall and reinstate Richter, thus achieving Wagner's aim. But the plan misfired badly. Wagner should have known from the

Tichatschek affair that Ludwig was capable of acting with steely determination in order to have his own way. The King had set his heart on having the *Rheingold* production as soon as possible and was not going to allow anyone to sabotage it.Furthermore, he was infuriated by Wagner's attempts to twist his arm using Richter as a lever. He fully supported the dismissal of Richter, and wrote to Düfflipp deploring the behaviour of 'Wagner and the theatre rabble'. The production, he said, was to be pressed on with urgently, 'for if these abominable intrigues of Wagner are permitted the whole rabble will become more and more shameless and presumptuous and in the end will get quite out of control; so the evil must be pulled up by the roots'.[21] Wagner came to Munich still hoping to dictate terms, but the King refused to see him and he got nowhere with Düfflipp and Perfall in demanding Richter's reinstatement.

Meanwhile Ludwig had written to his former Cabinet Secretary, Pfistermeister, telling him: 'The wretched development of the *Rheingold* affair, which has now grown intolerable to me, has reached its climax in R. Wagner's coming to Munich entirely against my will. It would serve him perfectly right if there is a nasty demonstration against him, now that the Bülow scandal is *au comble. J'en ai assez.*'[22] Wagner went back to Triebschen and sent a telegram to Ludwig in a last attempt to persuade him to countermand the performance. The message was not answered, and the production went ahead, a new conductor having been found in the person of Franz Wüllner, a sound if not outstanding musician who appears to have acquitted himself well. The scenic problems had been overcome, and altogether the production was well received. The first performance was given on 22 September and two more followed, on the 24th and 26th.

Once again the breach was followed by a long gap in Ludwig's letters to Wagner, and once again the King relented and held out an olive branch. In his letter to Wagner of 22 October (the first since 24 June) he showed the anguish of his loneliness and disillusion:

> If I may say so, I think you imagine my position to be easier than it is. To be so completely absolutely alone in this bleak, cheerless world, alone with my own thoughts, misunderstood, mistrusted, this is no small thing. In the first days of my ascension to the throne it was, in a way, by the charm of my novelty that I appealed to the people. But alas for those who have to do with the mass, and well for those who, like yourself, can operate through individuals. Believe me, I have come to know men. I went towards them with genuine love and felt myself repulsed; and wounds like these heal slowly, so slowly![23]

Soon they were back on the old footing again, but Ludwig was very disappointed to hear that Wagner was thinking of abandoning the work on *Die Sieger*. On 15 June 1870 he wrote:

> In a riveting work about India, Brahmanism and Buddhism I found, to my joy and delight, that so simple and yet so stirring and deeply moving tale which you wanted to use as the material for *Die Sieger*. It would grieve me greatly if, as you once told me, you had completely abandoned this work ... India and Buddhism have for me something indescribably alluring, something that awakens longing and heavenly joy.[24]

By this time there was a new bone of contention, for Ludwig was determined that the second part of the *Ring*, *Die Walküre*, should be produced in Munich in the summer of 1870. Wagner, still smarting from his defeat over *Rheingold*, was against the idea. Eventually, realizing the King's determination, he agreed to cooperate if he were given complete control and the production were postponed until 1871. These conditions were unacceptable, and so once more the production went ahead without the blessing of the master. Again Wüllner was the conductor, and the opera was given a successful première on 26 June. Ludwig stayed away from this, but attended a second performance which followed a repetition of *Das Rheingold* so that he could see the two works in the right order. Ludwig had ignored a last-minute letter from Wagner pleading that at least the public be excluded from the performance and expressing his 'deep pain caused by this unheard-of treatment of my works'.[25] Another silence fell between them. But in July came the Franco-Prussian War and Ludwig's decision to mobilize on the side of Prussia. In such an atmosphere personal resentments inevitably faded somewhat, and for Ludwig's twenty-fifth birthday Wagner was moved to send him a poem of homage, praising his action. He also presented the King with an orchestral sketch for the prelude and first act of *Götterdämmerung*.

Whether by coincidence or design, it was on Ludwig's birthday that the wedding between Wagner and Cosima took place in Lucerne, Cosima having been divorced by Bülow. Ludwig, although he had been deeply shocked by the whole affair, sent them a telegram saying that he was with them in spirit.

11

A Crucial Decade: 1866–76

Although Ludwig had lost his early enthusiasm for the practical affairs of kingship, for a long time he continued to take his duties more seriously than he has often been given credit for. During the penultimate decade of his life, from 1866 to 1876, he struggled to preserve an effective and honourable role for the monarchy and for Bavaria at a time when he was faced with great problems, both international and domestic, ranging from the controversy over papal infallibility to the momentous events of the Franco-Prussian War and the unification of Germany.

The aftermath of the Seven Weeks War of 1866 swept many people out of positions of power and brought new ones in. Pfistermeister was dismissed as Cabinet Secretary and replaced by Max von Neumayr under Wagner's prompting. Neumayr resigned soon afterwards and was replaced by Lutz. Hofmann was supplanted as Court Secretary by Lorenz von Düfflipp, a loyal and quietly able man who was to serve Ludwig for eleven years.

On 31 December 1866 Prince Chlodwig zu Hohenlohe-Schillingfürst was appointed head of the government and

Foreign Minister in place of the unfortunate Pfordten, whom the public unjustly blamed for the outcome of the war. Hohenlohe was ostensibly an unlikely choice, since he belonged to the liberal-democratic faction in Bavaria which saw the Prussian ascendancy as the dawn of a new progressive era – a view that was very foreign to Ludwig. But Hohenlohe's candidature was strongly supported by Wagner, and Count Holnstein smoothed the way by acting as an intermediary between the Prince and the King. Eventually Ludwig was persuaded that Hohenlohe was the best man to steer Bavaria through the difficult years ahead.

The Seven Weeks War, in destroying the German Confederation, had removed the last remnants of the old Holy Roman Empire and left Bavaria ostensibly more independent than ever, since she was no longer part of any group of countries. In fact this independence was illusory, for Bavaria would never be able to stand alone in the coming power struggles. The Treaty of Prague, which ended the Seven Weeks War, had established a close confederation of north German states under Prussia's leadership, while leaving the way open for the formation of a similar, but looser confederation of the southern German states – that is to say Bavaria, Württemberg, Baden and those parts of Hessen not united with north Germany. Bavaria was now placed in a quandary. Should she seek closer ties with Prussia and north Germany or with Austria? Alternatively, should she press for the formation of a Southern Confederation?

Although Hohenlohe was pro-Prussian he realized that any ties with Prussia would have to be formed gradually. He therefore agreed, albeit reluctantly, to the King's request that negotiations be opened with Württemberg, Baden and Hessen towards the formation of closer links. In April 1867 these negotiations were interrupted by a sudden crisis. France announced that it proposed to acquire the Duchy of Luxembourg, and

Bismarck opposed the move. For a moment it looked at though there might be war, and Bismarck wanted to know what stand Bavaria would take in this event. Ludwig conveyed the message through Hohenlohe that if a war came his country would honour the mutual defence agreement which it had made with Prussia at the end of the Seven Weeks War. In fact the French withdrew their plan and war was averted for the time being, but anyone with his ear to the ground knew that it would come sooner or later. In order to cement the German states together Bismarck needed a common enemy, and that enemy was clearly going to be France. The Prussian general staff had already drawn up plans for the invasion of France along the lines laid down years earlier by the military theorist Karl von Clausewitz, and these plans were kept up to date year by year as fresh circumstances arose.

Meanwhile the German states were moving closer together. In July an agreement was signed in Berlin setting up a Customs Union (*Zollverein*) with its own legislative assembly, the Customs Parliament. Ludwig disliked the idea of this assembly, but eventually Bavaria was forced to agree to it.

On 4 August 1867, soon after Ludwig's return from Paris, he summoned Hohenlohe to Berg castle to discuss various political matters. During his talk with the King, Hohenlohe recommended that the Cabinet Secretary, Lutz, be given the government post of Minister of Justice. At first Ludwig said that he could not dispense with Lutz, but at a later date he gave way. Lutz was appointed Minister of Justice on 16 September 1867, and simultaneously the former Commissioner of Police, Lipowski, became Cabinet Secretary.

In the meantime efforts were still being made to formulate a plan for a Southern Confederation. Proponents of this confederation were now divided into two main groups. First, there were those who saw any such confederation as a step towards a closer union with the north in order to form a bulwark against aggression from France. Friedrich, Grand Duke of Baden, came into this category. In his view the *Zollverein* had been a step in the right direction, but he wanted even stronger links between north and south, an ambition which was shared by the Prussian Crown Prince. The second group saw the situation in a quite different light. They did not want any closer ties with the north than those that already existed, and they regarded the Southern Confederation as a means of reassuring the French by creating a power block in Germany that was independent of Prussia. This view was supported by the Austrian Chancellor, Count von Beust, who, as he told Hohenlohe, took the view that 'there was a general impression that Prussia desired to incorporate the whole of Germany with itself, and it was imperative that the French should be disabused of this idea by a South German Confederation or Union'.[1]

Ludwig tended towards the latter view. His priorities were to preserve peace and to safeguard the sovereignty of Bavaria and the dignity of the monarchy. Hohenlohe, on the other hand, was in favour of a middle course. He saw the trend towards union with the north as inevitable and desirable. At the same time he thought that the southern states could somehow avoid alarming the French and that Bavaria, by voluntarily seeking an alliance with Prussia, could lay down conditions for the preservation of its sovereignty and the independence of its throne.

On 29 August 1867, Friedrich, Grand Duke of Baden, suggested a quadripartite meeting between himself, the King of Prussia, the King of Württemberg and the King of Bavaria, on the island of Mainau in Lake Constance, for the purpose of discussing relations between the respective states and the question of links between north and south. Ludwig, knowing that the Grand Duke of Baden was in favour of closer ties with Prussia, declined the invitation to attend the meeting, despite the fact that Hohenlohe urged him strongly to accept. Ludwig's refusal was undoubtedly a tactical error. As ruler of the largest of the southern states he was their natural leader, and if he had taken a more active part in discussions between them at this time it is just possible that he could have used his influence to bring about a compromise that would have satisfied aspirations to German unification and at the same time mollified the French. As it was, although he was well aware of the critical importance of a southern union, he thought he could leave everything to Hohenlohe. On 23 November 1867, the Prince sent a report to the King expressing the fear that 'if a feasible form of union is not suggested, it may be foreseen that the idea of joining the North German Confederation unconditionally will gain more and more adherents'. If this happened the autonomy of Bavaria would be seriously threatened. He went on to say that the procrastinating attitude of the south German states in the matter of union was causing anxiety to both Austria and France and that 'in these countries the stipulations of the Peace of Prague will only be regarded as fulfilled when the contemplated union of the South German States is within the range of practical politics'. Hohenlohe continued: '. . . the moment may now have come when these States might consider an alliance from which might at least follow concerted military organization and concerted deliberations as to an identical political attitude.'[2] He asked the King for further authority to explore this possibility.

Ludwig's comment in the margin of Hohenlohe's report was this:

I am much concerned about the independence of my Crown and the autonomy of my country. It was for this reason that I asked you for a statement on the political situation. Your account somewhat reassures me, as I gather that you will succeed in averting pressing dangers by forming a South German coalition. I am glad to express my thanks and my recognition of your efforts, and I agree to the steps which you propose. As this matter has my constant attention, your reports are very acceptable.[3]

Hohenlohe was now thinking in terms of forming what he called a 'United States of Southern Germany'. If this plan had come to fruition it is possible that France's fears would have been stilled, that the Franco-Prussian War would never have taken place and that the subsequent tensions which led to the First and Second World Wars would never have happened. In the light of history, therefore, the southern states were presented at this juncture with a great opportunity. In the event they failed to seize it, for negotiations collapsed, and on 10 April 1868, in reply to an inquiry from the King, Hohenlohe wrote a long explanation of why the plan for a South German Confederation had come to nothing.

Ludwig must bear part of the blame for the missing of this opportunity because of his inability or unwillingness to taking a leading part in the negotiations, but the fault also lay partly with Hohenlohe. Though a man of basically good intentions, he tried to please too many people at once, and Ludwig would have been better served at this stage of his reign by a politician with a clear, unequivocal policy. Böhm writes of Hohenlohe that he was 'a good diplomat, but no statesman and lacking in any productive ideas of his own. He always knew the short-cuts and side alleys, but was not able to follow a straight path with a firm step.'[4]

During this ominous period Ludwig must often have said to himself, like Margaret of Parma in Goethe's *Egmont*: 'I foresee much, yet cannot alter it.' Some great force of transformation seemed to hold the whole of Germany in its thrall. Whether the sun was rising or setting over Germany was a matter of opinion. After all, in German the word *Dämmerung* means both 'dawn' and 'twilight'. Ludwig, like many Germans, must have sensed both hope and foreboding. He must also have felt his loneliness more than ever – a loneliness which was increased by the loss of his grandfather on 29 February 1868. The ex-King Ludwig I died at his villa in Nice and was brought back to Munich to be buried in the church of Saint Boniface, one of the buildings which he had commissioned. Ludwig mourned the death of the old man, whom he had loved and admired, even though he had not always listened to his advice. It must have seemed like the severing of yet another link with the old Bavaria.

Everywhere the familiar pillars were trembling. Even in the Church all was far from well. In 1846 great hope had been placed in the new Pope, Pius IX, with his reputation for enlightenment and liberalism. But these hopes were soon dashed, for Pius turned to dictatorial and reactionary ways, curtailed freedom and democracy in the Church State and encouraged a new papal cult. In the face of bitter opposition this cult was formally promulgated in the doctrine of papal infallibility, which emerged from the First Vatican Council (1868–70). One of the opponents of the doctrine was Ludwig's old religious adviser Ignaz von Döllinger, now a famous theologian and prominent figure in Munich public life. He spoke out bravely against the infallibility dogma and was excommunicated by the Archbishop of Munich. Ludwig tried in vain to dissuade the Archbishop from this course. After the excommunication he urged Döllinger to continue to perform his religious functions. The theologian, however, refused on the grounds that such a defiance of Pope and Church would have serious consequences.

One effect of the infallibility controversy was to widen the gulf between the ultramontane and liberal factions. For years a reasonable consensus had prevailed. Now everything was changing. In Bavaria, as in the Church, a reactionary wind was blowing, and the position of the Hohenlohe government was becoming increasingly precarious. The conservative elements had formed themselves into a group which they called the Patriotic Party, and in the elections of May 1869 this party had greatly increased its strength in the assembly. For the time being, however, Hohenlohe remained in power. On 28 September the Prince had a meeting with Ludwig at which he urged the King to fulfil his ceremonial obligations by officially opening the new assembly. Ludwig had shown before that he hated such occasions, and once again he tried to wriggle out of the task. Hohenlohe describes the conversation as follows: 'We talked backwards and forwards about this, he always trying to get me to say that it was unnecessary, until he was at last convinced that there was no help for it. He wrinkled his forehead all over, but that availed him nothing, and finally he let it be known that "he would consider it".'[5]

As it happened Ludwig was given a respite, for the assembly, having failed to produce a decisive voice, was dissolved and new elections held. These turned out even worse for the government than before, with the Patriotic Party gaining a majority of seats. Hohenlohe tendered his resignation, but Ludwig refused to accept it, and for a while the Prince tried to carry on. On 17 January 1870 Ludwig finally brought himself to open the assembly. When he overcame his insularity he could always make a good impression on an audience, and on this occasion he gave a forceful and eloquent speech.

It soon became apparent that Hohenlohe could not continue in office. In February Ludwig accepted his resignation and appointed in his place Count Bray-Steinburg, who had been Bavarian envoy in Vienna. Bray was of a more patriotically Bavarian turn of mind than Hohenlohe, and his sympathies lay more with Austria than with Prussia. Nevertheless he was in favour of honouring the defence agreement with the Prussians, an agreement which was soon to be invoked, for France and Prussia were moving closer to war as the year 1870 advanced.

Before describing Bavaria's part in the Franco-Prussian War it would be useful to outline briefly the events leading up to this war. Both France and Prussia had for some time been spoiling for a fight: the former because Napoleon III was being pressed by nationalistic elements eager to humiliate Prussia, the latter because Bismarck saw a war with France as being the best way of uniting Germany. It was important for Bismarck that France be seen as the aggressor, and he cunningly waited for an opportunity to goad the French into making the first move. The opportunity came when a dispute arose over the Spanish crown. The succession had been offered to Prince Leopold of Hohenzollern, a Roman Catholic relative of the Prussian King. The French were opposed to this, as they felt that a Hohenzollern on the Spanish throne would make the dynasty too powerful. In the event Leopold refused the offer, but France was not satisfied with this and insisted that no Hohenzollern should ever accept the Spanish crown in the future. This demand was presented by the French ambassador, Count Benedetti, to Wilhelm I at Ems in the Rhineland. The Prussian King politely refused the demand and then sent a telegram to Bismarck explaining what had happened. At this stage a face-saving formula might still have been found, but that was not what Bismarck wanted, and he cleverly condensed the telegram in such a way as to make it as offensive as possible to the French. It was this infamous 'Ems dispatch' that put an end to any hopes of peace. When the condensed version was published in France on 14 July it aroused great fury, and the French declared war on 19 July, thereby falling neatly into Bismarck's trap.

While the storm clouds were gathering Ludwig was at Linderhof, where he was enjoying the surroundings of his new palace in the belief that Prince Leopold's renunciation of the Spanish throne had put an end to the matter. He was planning a pleasant outing to one of his hunting lodges when the Court

Secretary Düfflipp arrived on 14 July and impressed upon him the urgency of the situation. Reluctantly Ludwig cancelled his expedition and went on the next day to Berg to confer with the Cabinet Secretary, Eisenhart (who had replaced Lipowski). Eisenhart was summoned at 11 o'clock in the evening and found Ludwig in the large Balcony Room of the castle. Darkness had descended on the lake outside, and Ludwig was pacing up and down the room with its dark blue walls and paintings of scenes from *Tannhäuser, Lohengrin, Tristan* and *Die Meistersinger*. Occasionally he threw himself into a chair then resumed his pacing. The unfortunate Eisenhart, however, was kept standing throughout the entire audience, which lasted until half past three in the morning. Ludwig's normally considerate behaviour was liable to lapse when he was under stress. 'Is there no way,' he asked Eisenhart repeatedly, 'no possibility of avoiding war?'[6] The Cabinet Secretary pointed out that Bray-Steinburg's efforts to mediate between France and Prussia had failed. Now war was certain, and Bavaria must decide what position to take. To side with France would be fraught with danger and go against all instincts of loyalty to fellow Germans, to say nothing of breaking the mutual defence agreement with Prussia. To remain neutral was a possibility if a French victory could be foreseen, but in the event of a Prussian victory Bavaria's independence would probably be crushed. It was a gamble not worth taking. There was really only one honourable and realistic option: to abide by the military agreement and enter the war on the side of Prussia.

Having reached this painful decision Ludwig retired to bed, where he was woken at five o'clock in the morning with the news of the arrival of Count Berchem, an official in the Foreign Ministry, bringing a letter from Bray and the resolution of the government in favour of mobilization. Eisenhart brought the dispatch to Ludwig in his bedroom and read out Bray's letter. Briefly they discussed the main arguments again. Then Ludwig ordered mobilization with the words *'bis dat qui cito dat'* (he who gives quickly gives doubly).[7]

Bray and the War Minister Pranckh were summoned to an audience later in the day, and afterwards Pranckh commented that he had never seen the King so content. Ludwig, after the heart-searching over his decision, was indeed in a happy mood. To the congratulations of his aide-de-camp von Sauer, he replied: 'Yes, I have the feeling of having done a good deed.'[8]

It only remained for Parliament to vote sufficient money for the war from public funds. There was considerable opposition to this, particularly from certain members of the Patriotic Party, but in the end the war budget was passed with a comfortable majority.

The Munich public was now at fever pitch and awaiting the outbreak of war impatiently but with mixed feelings. Most of them had little or no love for the Prussians and did not understand the real issues over which the war was being fought. But, faced with a challenge from the French, they felt the German blood in them stirring. They also knew of their King's decision and, in the heat of the moment, sensed an upsurge of loyalty to him.

On Sunday 17 July a vast crowd gathered in the Odeon-splatz by the Residenz. Suddenly the white-bearded figure of an ancient Munich worthy named Raila appeared on the steps of the Feldherrnhalle near the statue of General Tilly. The old man stood there, visible over the sea of heads, under the great arches of the monument. It was one of those moments when a prophet appears out of the mob as though conjured up by its collective tension. At the sight of this apparition there was a sudden silence and Raila's voice cried out: 'His Majesty, the German-spirited King Ludwig II, long may he live!'[9] The cry was taken up again and again and swelled to a crescendo when the King himself appeared briefly at a window of the Residenz to acknowledge the cheers. The Bavarian national anthem was sung. Ludwig appeared again. For once he was enjoying being in the public eye. That evening, instead of going to a performance of *Die Walküre*, he worked until two o'clock in the morning with his ministers.

Why was Ludwig in such good spirits on the eve of this war? Werner Richter, in his biography of the King, speculates as follows:

> At this time the King, who was still young, began once more to hope, and this explains the elated mood in which he found himself. Already there were clear indications in the air that this war, if it turned out well, could end only in a new unification of Germany, a unification for which no form was conceivable other than the time-honoured imperial one. And this supreme and historic office, unforgotten and charged with a mystical radiance, would surely thereby be made accessible also to Ludwig's ancient dynasty, the Wittelsbachs, from whom more than one emperor had been drawn. Had not Wagner called him the 'potent embodiment of the German folk-spirit'? And had not Cornelius, after his first meeting with the King, silently dubbed him Emperor of Germany?[10]

Whether or not such thoughts were in Ludwig's conscious mind when he issued the mobilization order, there is no doubt that it must have given him a feeling of excitement to be taking part in the rebirth of the empire. Ludwig's patriotism was not confined to Bavaria. He was very conscious of the bonds that united all the German lands, and he shared Wagner's vision of a Germany filled with a new vitality and sense of common purpose. At the same time he saw the dangers to Bavaria's sovereignty that would come from any closer federal structure. Furthermore he must have thought it a pity that the impulse to unification had come from Bavaria's traditional rival. It irked him to see the Bavarian army placed under the command of the Prussian Crown Prince, Friedrich, though at least its two corps were still commanded by Bavarian generals, von der Tann and Hartmann, whereas the other South German contingents were given Prussian commanders.

Ludwig did not inspect his troops, but he did greet the Prussian Grown Prince when the latter came on 27 July to take command. For the first time the citizens of Munich saw the blue-and-white Bavarian flag flying side by side with the black, white and red of the North German Confederation. Hohenlohe describes the Crown Prince's arrival as follows:

> The Schützenstrasse, the square in front of the station and the neighbouring squares were all full of people. Scarcely had we taken up our position before the Sterngarten, when in the station gateway appeared the escort of cuirassiers followed by the carriage in which was seated the King, with the Crown Prince of Prussia and Prince Otto. The public gave them a good welcome and cried 'Hurrah!' but not too warmly. The lower classes, workmen and so on, were principally represented, and these in Munich are not particularly enthusiastic about the war, nor very inclined to shout '*Hoch!*' to a Prussian Prince.[11]

There was, however, a warmer reaction from the theatre-going public when the King and his Prussian cousin attended a performance that evening of Schiller's *Wallenstein's Camp*.

Later that night the Crown Prince went on to Stuttgart and, as he was about to climb into the carriage that would take him to the station, a letter from Ludwig was handed to him. It expressed the hope that the Prussian King would show his appreciation of Bavaria's faithfulness by respecting the sovereignty of the Bavarian nation when the war was over. The Crown Prince was irritated by the document, which he noticed was written in 'a coarse, ugly hand, with the lines all crooked'.[12] Nevertheless he passed the document on to his father. The latter was all for refusing Ludwig's request, but Bismarck, after another of his arguments with the old King, convinced him that if he did so Ludwig would probably withdraw his troops as would be his right.

Since the war of 1866 there had been a hasty enlargement and reorganization of the Bavarian army, and by the outbreak of the Franco-Prussian War there had not been time to issue new uniforms to all the troops, so that many of them looked a sorry sight in comparison to the Prussians. Morale was further lowered by lack of confidence in the Bavarian leadership. General von der Tann had proved an ineffectual commander in 1866, and Hartmann was seventy-five years old. Nevertheless the reforms had turned the army into a much more effective force, and there is no doubt that the Bavarians made an important contribution to the Prussian victory.

The course of the war can be summarized briefly. As soon as hostilities began, the well-prepared and well-oiled Prussian war machine rolled into action, once again under the able command of Moltke. The Prussians moved forward while the French dithered around on the frontier looking for an ideal position. Most of the early fighting took place in and around Alsace-Lorraine and the Ardennes. The French succeeded in occupying Saarbrücken, but were heavily defeated at Weissenburg on 4 August and at Wörth on the 6th. In both of these actions the Bavarians played a key role. After this there was a succession of Prussian victories. One French army, under Marshal Bazaine, was besieged at Metz and eventually surrendered after holding out for nearly two months. Another army, under Marshal MacMahon, which had been sent to relieve Metz, was intercepted and heavily defeated at Sedan on the river Meuse on 1 September. The following day Napoleon III himself surrendered with 83,000 men. It was the end of Napoleon's career. He was kept prisoner by the Germans until the end of the war and eventually went to England, where he ended his life in the prosaic surroundings of Chislehurst, Kent. With the declaration of a republic after Napoleon's capture a new phase of the war began. The Germans laid siege to Paris and encountered brave resistance. Léon Gambetta, the republican leader, escaped from the city by balloon and went to Tours. From there he rallied the French forces to fight with renewed vigour. But it was now too late to reverse the position. Paris surrendered early in 1871, and the war ended with the Treaty of Frankfurt, signed on 10 May of that year.

The news of the glorious part played by the Bavarians at Weissenburg and Wörth sent a thrill of pride through the country, but Ludwig could summon up little enthusiasm. Even the great victory at Sedan left him unmoved, and he refused to remain in Munich for the official celebration of it on 3 September. His mood of elation when he signed the mobilization order had now vanished. He feared that each Prussian victory brought German unification and the end of Bavaria's independence a step nearer. Once again he found the waters of the Alpsee beckoning him.

Ludwig's reading of the situation was correct, for with the German armies at the gates of Paris the time had come for the step which Bismarck had been planning for so long, namely for Prussia to stake her claim to the leadership of a united Germany. To his headquarters at Versailles Bismarck decided to call representatives of the German states to discuss the formation of the empire. Thus it was that the palace of Louis XIV became the birthplace of the new German Reich. The Chancellor persuaded first Baden, then Hessen and eventually Württemberg to agree in principle to joining with the north. In view of these developments the Bavarian government realized that, if their country wished to avoid total isolation, it must negotiate with Bismarck. Accordingly a Bavarian delegation departed for Versailles, consisting of Bray, Pranckh and Lutz. The outcome of these negotiations was a fiasco for Bavaria or a triumph for Germany, whichever way one cares to look at it.

When the conference opened Bavaria's bargaining position was strong, since the war still hung in the balance. Metz had not yet surrendered, and the new French republic was fighting with renewed vigour. But this advantage was not seized, and with the fall of Metz on 14 October the bargaining advantage was reduced. Bismarck now became more pressing for Bavaria's union with the north. Bray replied by suggesting, in accordance with Ludwig's thinking, an arrangement whereby the Imperial Crown would be worn alternately by the Hohenzollerns and the Wittelsbachs. Under this arrangement the Prussian King would have the title of Emperor, but he and the Bavarian King would represent the empire jointly. This was, of course, unacceptable to Bismarck, but he did not turn it down immediately. Instead he played for time, calculating that the bargaining position would change further in his favour. Meanwhile the liberals in Bavaria were becoming impatient for faster progress.

At this time Ludwig was at Hohenschwangau in the company of Otto, his mood of despair heightened by the autumn storms that swept around the castle. Once again he thought of abdicating in Otto's favour, but when he looked at his brother he must have seen the signs of the madness that was tightening its grip on the mind of the Prince and was soon to overcome him totally. Momentarily overcoming his listlessness, he sent a telegram to Versailles reminding the delegation of his territorial wishes and asking for details of the points still at issue.

By now the tide was flowing fast in Bismarck's favour. On 19 November Baden and Hessen signed the unification agreement, and at the same time word came from Stuttgart that Württemberg was ready to do likewise. Bray was now presented with a stark choice of alternatives. If he signed the agreement without further delay Bavaria would be allowed to retain independent diplomatic representation, a separate army in peace-time, her own railway, post and telegraph administration, control of beer taxes and the right to grant citizenship. At the same time Bismarck unofficially held out the prospect of an extension of territory, either in Alsace or by the return of land taken by Prussia in 1866, but he made no firm commitment to this effect. Delay in signing the agreement could mean the loss of the privileges that Bismarck was prepared to grant to Bavaria and would entail the risk of the country being forced later to enter the Reich on much less favourable terms. On 23 November Bray signed the agreement, subject to the King's approval, writing bitterly to his wife: 'This is the beginning of the new Germany and, if our plans are approved, the end of the old Bavaria. It would be useless to deceive oneself about this.'[13]

There remained, however, one bargaining counter still in Bavaria's hands which could have been used to press for an increase in territory. Bismarck wished to put a finishing touch on the new empire by having the Prussian monarch proclaimed Emperor of Germany, and, in order to give an appearance of legality to this step, he wanted Ludwig II, as King of the largest German state outside Prussia, to write a letter to King Wilhelm inviting him to assume the imperial title. Bismarck hoped to talk Ludwig into this move, and for this reason he had sent repeated invitations to the King to visit Versailles, even offering to accommodate him in the Grand Trianon in the hope that this would appeal to his passion for the *ancien régime*. Ludwig, however, had declined all of these invitations and was tired of Bismarck's pestering. Bray now wired to Ludwig telling him that the Prussian King would assume the imperial crown willy nilly but that Ludwig could avoid going to Versailles if he wrote the desired letter. Bray did not for one moment imagine that Ludwig would go ahead and send the letter without further consultation with himself.

By now Ludwig was becoming more sympathetic towards closer ties with the north. This was partly due to the advice given by his confessor Trost and his friend the philosophy professor Johannes Huber. But he still hesitated before taking the irrevocable step that writing the letter would entail. It was one of the most difficult decisions of his life, possibly the last decision that he would make as a truly sovereign King. It was at this moment that he sought advice from his old *éminence grise* and go-between, Count von Holnstein, the able Master of the Horse, who had come to play an increasingly influential role at the court. Holnstein was ordered to go to Versailles, ostensibly to make the stabling arrangements for a possible visit by Ludwig, but in fact to determine whether the offer of the imperial crown was unavoidable and how far Bismarck would go in bringing pressure on Bavaria. The choice of Holnstein as emissary was a fateful one.

Considering that the Count was neither a diplomat nor a politician he succeeded remarkably quickly in gaining an interview with Bismarck, taxed as the Chancellor was with overwork and lack of sleep. Bismarck immediately recognized in Holnstein a man of powerful and supple intelligence, not overburdened by scruple – in fact, a man cast in his own mould. As for Holnstein, he must have decided then or earlier that a Prussian wind was blowing and that he must bend with it. His policy paid off in the end, for he ultimately became a close friend of Bismarck. At the Chancellor's drinking evenings the beer that was served came from breweries owned by Holnstein, and Bismarck's much-loved bulldog, Sultl, was a gift from the Count.

The meeting with Bismarck began with a few drinks. Then Holnstein, in his broad Bavarian accent, suggested bluntly to Bismarck that he draft out himself the letter that he wanted Ludwig to write to King Wilhelm, the *Kaiserbrief* as it came to be called. The Chancellor's eyes lit up at this idea, and he immediately sat down and, picking up some pieces of rough paper, wrote out two documents: one was the draft of the *Kaiserbrief*; the other was a personal letter to Ludwig. Here Bismarck showed his extraordinary brilliance in dealing with people. He worded the *Kaiserbrief* in such a way that by signing it Ludwig would also be giving approval to the treaty signed by Bray. Then, in his letter to Ludwig, he cleverly sugared the pill by saying that the concessions contained in the treaty could be made with dignity if they were extended to an Emperor of Germany but not if they were offered to a mere King of Prussia. He then assumed a flattering tone by referring to the feudal ties which his own family felt towards the house of Wittelsbach because in the Middle Ages the Wittelsbachs had ruled for several decades over Brandenburg, Bismarck's home territory.

Two hours after the meeting Holnstein was on his way back to Munich, where he arrived at the same time as the returning ministers. But he did not confer with them. Instead he hurried straight on to Hohenschwangau. The rain was beating down on the castle, and Ludwig was in bed with a painful toothache. Holnstein, after virtually forcing his way into the presence of the King, read Bismarck's two letters, repeating at Ludwig's request the passage in which the Chancellor referred to feudal ties. Holnstein saw that he had a golden opportunity. Ludwig was ill and alone in the castle except for his servants. As luck would have it the Cabinet Secretary Eisenhart had just departed for Munich. The wily Count saw that he must press home his advantage. He declared that he had to set off again for Versailles that evening at 6.30 sharp and that the King must make a decision by then. If he failed to do so, the Count said, pressure within Bavaria in favour of Prussian hegemony could lead to Ludwig's being deposed by the army and having to flee to Switzerland. This was an empty threat, but Ludwig was in an uncharacteristically susceptible mood. Sick, weary and confused, he eventually gave way in the face of Holnstein's persistence and called for pen and paper. But he still kept his wits about him, for he did not copy out Bismarck's draft of the *Kaiserbrief* word for word. Instead he re-wrote it so as to give greater emphasis to the role of the princes of the individual states in the new Reich. Then he asked Holnstein to show the letter to Eisenhart and only to send it off if the Cabinet Secretary found it acceptable. Incredibly, he did not ask that it be shown to Bray.

Holnstein hurried off to Munich, where he found Eisenhart attending a performance at the Residenz theatre. Calling the Cabinet Secretary out of his box, the Count handed him the letter. Eisenhart was flabbergasted and flattered that the final decision on such a crucial matter had been entrusted to him. He found nothing wrong with the letter but, to be on the safe side, decided to show it to Lutz, the Minister of Justice, who examined it, as he later said, from a legal and not from a political point of view and found it in order. The fact that neither Holnstein nor Lutz wished to show the letter to Bray indicates the Prussian sympathies of both men. The next morning Holnstein hurried gleefully off to Versailles, requisitioning a train in his haste. On arrival he handed the letter to a delighted Bismarck.

When Bray heard the news he was devastated. Ludwig had thrown away the last bargaining advantage that Bavaria possessed, and thereby lost all hope of any increase in territory. Ludwig himself soon realized the foolishness of what he had done and attempted to recall Holnstein, but it was too late.

It still remained for the Bavarian parliament to ratify the treaty, and after a heated debate the assembly voted in favour of ratification, with the necessary two-thirds majority being exceeded by only two votes. As it turned out, however, the debate was irrelevant. The vote was taken on 21 January, and on 18 January the birth of the new empire had already been formally proclaimed at Versailles. Bavaria was represented at the ceremony by Prince Otto, who wrote back to his brother: 'Oh Ludwig, I cannot describe to you how infinitely sad and painful it was to me.'[14] Nevertheless Bavaria did not come out of the whole affair entirely empty-handed. Instead of territorial gain the country received financial compensation between 1872 and 1875 amounting to 1579 million florins.

Ludwig did not reappear in Munich until the beginning of February, when the capitulation of Paris was celebrated by large crowds. There was more celebration when the Bavarian troops returned to their capital on 16 July. Much as he detested the task, Ludwig had to greet the troops, painfully conscious that they were no longer under his command. At the head of a huge and splendid cavalcade he rode down the Ludwigstrasse. The sunshine, the cheers of the crowd and the martial music served only to deepen his depression. At the Odeonsplatz his cousin the Hohenzollern Crown Prince Friedrich Wilhelm was waiting to greet him.

In the evening the cousins sat together in the royal box at the Residenz theatre for a performance of Paul Heyse's play, *Peace*. After the play they symbolically embraced one another and did their best to conceal their mutual antipathy. The next day they went together to the Roseninsel, and here there took place a scene of open friction between them. The exact cause of this is uncertain, but it probably arose over Ludwig's invitation to the Crown Prince to become head of a Bavarian regiment of lancers. Instead of expressing his thanks at the honour, Friedrich Wilhelm replied that he would have to ask his father's permission and that in any case he doubted whether the tight lancer's uniform would fit him. At the end of the day Ludwig was in such a bad mood that he decided not to attend the celebration banquet that evening in the Glass Palace. Eisenhart begged

Ludwig to change his mind, but in vain. The banquet, which was to have been the high point of the victory celebrations, was held without the King and in an atmosphere of anti-climax. Early the next morning Ludwig departed for the mountains.

Even after the Versailles agreement and the *Kaiserbrief*, Ludwig did not entirely despair of salvaging a dignified role for Bavaria, and in the years following the Franco-Prussian War he tried to give his government a stronger Bavarian character. Bray resigned in 1871, and in his place Ludwig appointed Count Friedrich von Hegnenberg-Dux, who died after a year in office and was replaced by Baron Rudolf von Gasser, who in turn was soon replaced by Baron Adolph von Pfretzschner, the former Finance Minister. Pfretzschner's term of office was also short, and in 1875 Ludwig offered the government to a man with the evocative name of Baron von und zu Franckenstein, who had been one of the objectors to the Versailles agreement. Franckenstein, however, withdrew before taking office. By 1876 it had become clear to Ludwig that it was impossible to form a ministry of the colouring that he desired, and this realization accelerated his withdrawal from government affairs. From about 1872, however, the real power in the government was Lutz, even though he was not officially made Prime Minister until 1880.

Lutz was the most able and effective Bavarian politician of Ludwig's reign, and he dominated the country's affairs for more than a quarter of a century.[15] Born in 1826, the son of a poor Franconian schoolmaster, he had risen to eminence through his ability as a lawyer. He was a short, stocky man with a bald head, a bristling moustache and small, gold-rimmed glasses. Altogether he resembled more a village postmaster or railway official than a politician. But his mundane appearance concealed a capacious brain and a steely will. As a young man he had for a time been attached to a commission set up to examine the possible formation of a common German legal code for trading. This, together with a sojourn in Hamburg, had given him a sympathy for the idea of German unification under Prussian leadership. His influence during the crucial negotiations of 1870 undoubtedly helped to smooth the way for Bavaria's entry into the Reich. At the same time he did not turn his back on Bavaria's interests, and bargained to secure favourable terms for his country. After the formation of the Reich his energies were focused on carrying out in Bavaria the policies of Bismarck's *Kulturkampf*, that is to say the struggle to limit the power of the Catholic Church. Although born a Catholic, Lutz had little sympathy with the Church. His first and second wives were both Protestants, and his children were brought up in the Protestant faith. Lutz's regime was marked by a series of battles with the Church over his attempts to curtail ecclesiastical influence in secular affairs.

Ludwig's religious attitude was one of personal piety but not slavish adherence to the Church as such. Everywhere he went he took with him a portable altar which was set up in the room where he slept, and until the mid 1870s he regularly attended mass. Although to some extent the mythology of Wagner became a substitute religion for him, he retained to the end the habits of an ingrained Catholicism. On the last Good Friday of his life he walked, dressed in black, up the Calvary hill near Füssen and prayed at all fourteen stations of the cross. At the same time he was opposed to clerical interference in government. Although on occasion he restrained Lutz from going too far in his *Kulturkampf*, he favoured limitation of the Church's influence in State affairs. This was one of the reasons why he was at odds with the ultra-conservative, clerical faction in Bavarian politics as much as with the extreme progressive faction.

What Ludwig wanted was a government that would uphold the traditional status of the monarchy without having too clerical a tinge, and only Lutz was able to command this middle ground. Thus Ludwig found himself obliged to support this man whose temperament was so different from his own, whose chief recreation was hunting and who understood little of cultural things. Another thing made Ludwig dependent on the astute little lawyer. Lutz knew how to leave the King alone and to make sure that he was bothered as little as possible with affairs of state. This was something that Ludwig valued increasingly as he became more and more of a recluse.

As he approached the last decade of his life Ludwig presented a rather different figure from the dazzling young man who had ascended the throne twelve years earlier. He had put on weight to such an extent that few horses could carry him. His face had filled out and was now darkened by a moustache and pointed beard. His teeth had begun to fall out, so that when he opened his mouth ugly gaps were revealed. To a man who had always been self-conscious about his looks this deterioration must have been painful.

What was equally distressing to him was the thought that there might be latent in him the madness that was overtaking Otto. In January 1871 he had written to Frau von Leonrod from Hohenschwangau:

> It is really painful to see Otto in such a suffering state which seems to become worse and worse daily. In some respects he is more excitable and nervous than Aunt Alexandra – and that is saying a great deal. He often does not go to bed for forty-eight hours; he did not take off his boots for eight weeks, behaves like a madman, makes terrible faces, barks like a dog, and at times says the most indecorous things; and then again he is quite normal for a while.[16]

A year later Otto's condition had become so bad that his doctors advised that he be kept under observation. Ludwig wrote to his brother on 23 January 1872 saying that in view of the lack of improvement in Otto's state of health he was obliged to endorse the measures advised by the doctors. Otto was to take up residence at Nymphenburg with his usual suite and with the court physician, Dr Brattler. He was to comply at all times with the instructions of the doctors who had been invested by Ludwig with the necessary authority. After he had been taken to Nymphenburg Otto sent a bitter and outraged Letter to Ludwig. 'You have no right,' he wrote, 'seeing that I have done no wrong, to treat me thus. I have submitted to duress, and I am a prisoner; my treatment has been disgraceful!'[17]

With Otto sinking rapidly into madness, Ludwig saw yet another human contact recede. The following year he clutched briefly at a friendship with his rather shallow aide-de-camp Varicourt – a relationship which I shall discuss in Chapter 15. This left him disappointed and as lonely as ever.

Human beings might fail him, but the ideals of his inner world still shone as brightly as ever, and in 1874 he decided to pay a second visit to the country of his hero, Louis XIV. His ministers tried to dissuade him as there was considerable anti-German feeling in France in the aftermath of the Franco-Prussian War, but Ludwig was not to be put off. He arrived in Paris on 21 August, accompanied by Holnstein, a government official called Schomberger and four servants. His host was the former Bavarian Prime Minister Prince Hohenlohe, now German Ambassador to France. During his stay the King spent a long time at Versailles, where the fountains were turned on at great expense in honour of his twenty-ninth birthday. 'The public,' Hohenlohe recorded, 'behaved with decorum, but a few Versailles *gamins* were arrested for amusing themselves by imitating the King's gait behind his back.'[18] He also toured the sights of Paris, especially those associated with the Kings of France, and attended several theatre performances. Once again he travelled under the incognito of the 'Count von Berg', but his visit very soon became public knowledge. In the press he was given a mixed reception. One newspaper, *le XIXe Siècle*, declared that he was 'nothing but a satellite of the star that shines in Berlin', but the *Figaro* commented in a more kindly tone that 'the King of Bavaria has never accompanied his soldiers except on the piano'.[19] His French police escort, Charles Fontaine, recorded the King's extraordinary walk and also remarked that during his entire stay he wore the same clothes: a blue frock coat and trousers and a shirt with three enormous gold fleurs-de-lis as buttons.[20]

A year later Ludwig made a third and last visit to France, this time travelling only as far as Reims where he spent a long time admiring the cathedral where most of the Kings of France had been crowned. On his return he wrote to his mother that he had 'sought out all the places that had any association with monarchy', but added that 'unfortunately so much was destroyed at the time of the great French Revolution'.[21]

Meanwhile Ludwig had found a new friend, a twenty-four-year-old army officer named Count Alfred Dürckheim-Montmartin, who was acting as aide-de-camp to Prince Otto. Dürckheim was a hot-blooded young man of hefty build and ruddy complexion, with a bluff manner and a reputation as a ladies' man. He had little of the courtier about him, and Ludwig sometimes found his manners somewhat coarse, but in the long run he proved one of the most faithful friends that the King ever had and was among the very few who were ready to stand by their monarch at the end.

Their friendship first blossomed during a stay at Hohen-schwangau in September 1874. From there they made excursions to Linderhof, then under construction, and to the

Schachen hunting lodge. Afterwards Dürckheim wrote an enthusiastic letter of thanks, and Ludwig wrote back from Berg on 25 September:

> My dear Count,
>
> Yesterday evening your letter and photograph arrived in my hands. Both pleased me very much, and I hasten to thank you for them. Be assured that the memory of the hours in your company and the days at Linderhof and on the Schachen are unforgettable to me also. The day that you left the Schachen I was so melancholy that I could not find peace and was unable to eat anything at midday at the place with the splendid view over the Höllenthal where we spent such lively hours.[22]

Some two weeks later, on 7 October, Ludwig wrote again from Berg after being obliged to attend the October Beer Festival much against his will. In the same letter he mentions his attempts to get Dürckheim promoted.

> On Sunday, as the weather was fine, I had to submit to the numerous unpleasantnesses of the unholy Oktoberfest . . . for no merciful dispensation stood in the way. Seldom have I shaken so much from fury and wrath as this evening. On the day after my return from Hohenschwangau I sent the order for your promotion to the War Minister. Naturally I believed that, as an obedient subject, he would have immediately carried it out. Imagine, my dear Count, my indignation when this evening I received my directive *sent back*!! by that impudent, self-willed blackguard along with a lengthy dissertation. The despicable swine requests me, would you believe, to withdraw my order as your promotion would make a very bad impression in the army . . . As if the will and confidence of the monarch were not in themselves decisive. Naturally I shall send a secretary tomorrow with a command that should bring the rebel to heel. If he persists, as he might do in his unbelievable pig-headedness, then another War Minister must be found, for, like Pilate, what I have written I have written. I am writing all this to give you proof that I have reason enough to hate the century in

which it is possible for the will of the sovereign to be treated with such uncouth impudence by a mere executive officer.

Ludwig then goes on to refer to Dürckheim's request to enter his service:

I am pleased by your wish and yet I feel obliged to tell you the following: I feel strongly that you could lose your temper very easily, as is also the case with me. I am easily moved to strong anger. It is a painful thought to me that, if we were in frequent contact with each other, anger might arise between us and separate us for ever.[23]

Nevertheless Ludwig did appoint Dürckheim as his aide-de-camp, although not until over eight years later, on 30 March 1883. For the time being Dürckheim remained with Otto, whose condition continued to worsen. In 1876 Otto was gazetted out of the army after an honourable career in which he had reached the rank of Major-General. In 1878 he was finally declared insane and was to spend the rest of his life a virtual prisoner in the royal castle of Fürstenried. The man who pronounced the verdict on the Prince was a distinguished alienist named Dr Bernhard von Gudden, who was later to make a similar judgement about Ludwig himself and thereby contribute to the chain of events that ended in his own death as well as that of the King.

In the spring of 1876 Ludwig emerged briefly from his shell and presided over a series of court ceremonies and receptions in the Munich Residenz. But he now found it increasingly boring to go through the official motions required of him. How much more exciting to be, not merely the King of Bavaria, but the Sun King or the Grail King. To enter fully into these roles in his imagination he needed the appropriate settings, and these he was now busy creating. The building phase of his life had begun.

12

Fantasies in Stone

In most great palaces we see an attempt to impress the world with power and magnificence, and this is no doubt what archaeologists of the future will see when they discover the palaces built by Ludwig II. But they will be wrong. Ludwig built not to prove anything to the world but chiefly to give substance to his dreams and his image of himself. In his architectural creations, therefore, we find a reflection of his whole inner life. Heinrich Kreisel, in his book on Ludwig's castles,[1] divides the buildings into three groups which he sees as corresponding to three prime symbols of Ludwig's universe: the Grail, the Sun and the Moon. Under the first heading come Neuschwanstein and the similar Falkenstein which was never built, both of them evoking the world of medieval knighthood. The second group comprises the royal apartments in the Munich Residenz, Herrenchiemsee, Linderhof, a projected theatre in the grounds of Linderhof, and an unfinished building, the Hubertus pavilion, later destroyed. Into the third category come the buildings in oriental style, namely the Schachen hunting lodge, with its Turkish interior, the Moorish Kiosk at Linderhof, and the Morocco House nearby.

Ludwig began planning his building programme in 1868, and it was the 'Grail' castle that was the first to take shape in his mind. Inspired by recent performances of *Lohengrin* and *Tannhäuser*, he wanted a castle that would incorporate motifs from both of these operas and in general atmosphere be Monsalvat and the Wartburg rolled into one. An ideal spot was a hilltop dramatically situated about half an hour's walk from Hohenschwangau, where the ruins of the old Hohenschwangau castle stood. The building that Ludwig erected on the spot was known as New Hohenschwangau until after his death, when it was re-named Neuschwanstein. On 13 May 1868 Ludwig wrote to Wagner outlining his scheme for the new building:

> I intend to rebuild the old castle ruins of Hohenschwangau by the Pöllat gorge in the genuine style of the old German knightly fortresses, and I must confess to you that I very much look forward to living there in three years' time; it will have a number of comfortable and homelike guest rooms affording splendid views of the magnificent Säuling [the mountain which towers almost vertically on the southern side of the castle], as well as towards the mountains of Tyrol and far out over the plain . . . the spot is one of the most beautiful that one could ever find, sacred and out of reach, a worthy temple for the divine Friend . . . There will also be reminders of *Tannhäuser* (Singers' Hall with a view of the castle in the background) and of *Lohengrin* (courtyard, open passageway, approach to chapel); in every respect this castle will be more beautiful and more agreeable to live in than the lower Hohenschwangau, which is desecrated every year by the prosaic presence of my mother; the desecrated gods will avenge themselves and linger with us on the steep heights amidst the celestial breezes.[2]

The extent to which Ludwig conceived this castle in Wagnerian terms is shown not only in the visual motifs that he wanted to include but also in his choice of vocabulary in the letter to Wagner. When he describes the spot as 'sacred and out of reach' (*heilig und unnahbar*), he is echoing the words of Lohengrin describing the Grail castle in the third act of the opera:

> *In a far country, out of reach of your footsteps*
> *Lies a castle whose name is Monsalvat.*
> *A bright temple stands in its midst*
> *More costly than anything known on earth.*
> *Therein a vessel of wondrous, blessed power*
> *Is guarded as a thing of the highest sacredness.*

Ludwig's need for a Grail castle stemmed from his vision of himself as a Grail King – a Parzival as Wagner himself had called him. Hans Rall and Michael Petzet throw some interesting light on this in their short book on Ludwig:

In the autumn of 1866 he sought a religious and psychological sanction for his – theoretically still sovereign – status as King of Bavaria by the inclusion in the prescribed form of the Mass of a daily prayer for the ruler throughout his kingdom – analogous to that said in Austria for the Emperor by virtue of the traditions of the old Empire, but also, since 1857, in France for Napoleon III. Thus, in the hour of defeat the young King of Bavaria sought liturgical parity with the Emperors in Paris and Vienna – with the support of no less a person than the famous church historian and theologian Ignaz von Döllinger. The Curia, however, was not amenable to Ludwig's wishes. In the fateful month of July 1866, when Ludwig commenced a new volume of his diary, he was no doubt already thinking of the manifestation of his royal status in terms of a religious – and patently visible – symbolism. On the cover we see a fortified castle resembling that later erected at Neuschwanstein, while the end-papers depict a crown over a sceptre and an orb, each surmounted by crosses, the whole being crowned by a bowl inscribed in Church Slavonic and appropriate lettering with the words: 'This vessel be my aid, O Lord . . .'[3]

Plans for the castle began to be drawn up in 1868. The general visual conception of it was provided by Christian Jank, a stage designer at the Court Theatre, who produced a number of highly romantic sketches of the projected building, no doubt in close consultation with Ludwig. The architect employed to carry out the technical planning was Eduard Riedel, who had worked on the restoration of Berg castle for King Max II. The initial plan was for a comparatively modest three-storeyed fortress in the late Gothic style, but subsequently the design metamorphosed into a five-storeyed construction largely in the Romanesque style. The building process, which involved blasting away part of the summit of the hill to form a platform, began in 1869 and continued spasmodically until after Ludwig's death. Riedel retired in 1874 and was succeeded by Georg Dollmann, who in turn was succeeded by Julius Hofmann in 1884.

Parts of Neuschwanstein had already been 'rehearsed', as it were, in the stage sets for various Wagner performances. For example the courtyard was based on Angelo Quaglio's design for a courtyard in the 1867 production of *Lohengrin*. Another stage set, by Heinrich Döll, for the 1867 production of *Tannhäuser*, showing the Wartburg seen from a valley below, was the inspiration for the general prospect presented by Neuschwanstein from a distance. By such curiously indirect stages was the world of *Lohengrin* and *Tannhäuser* transmuted into stone and mortar.

Few people who visit Neuschwanstein today can fail to find it a startling sight. Seen from the plain below it appears surprisingly small, and only as one approaches it by the steep, winding road up the hillside does the full dramatic effect of the building come across. Apart from the red gatehouse it is built of white stone. With its Romanesque windows, its battlements and spiky turrets, it has the look of a castle by Walt Disney out of Arthur Rackham. Architectural purists solemnly shake their heads over its 'bad taste', but the truth is that, like everything else Ludwig built, it has a mad beauty that goes beyond taste, good or bad. It has become something of a visual cliché because of having been shown on countless travel posters, but in fact it is a building of genuine originality, successfully blending many styles into a coherent whole. Seen afresh in its incomparable setting, it has extraordinary impact. And to walk through its rooms, with their luxuriant carving and painted murals, is to feel magic of a very potent kind.

Neuschwanstein is a place of contrasts. To the north it commands a view over the wide, lush plain through which winds the river Lech, a country of rich farmland, dotted with Baroque churches and well-kept, whitewashed villages where in summer the balconies are hung with red geraniums. The castle's southern windows, on the other hand, overlook a brooding, Wagnerian landscape of dark, fir-clad slopes and sharp, rocky peaks often shrouded in mist. The contrast reflects the dichotomy between the light and dark sides of Ludwig's own nature. And inside, the castle embodies another contrast in the King. In some ways he was a figure from the distant past, in other ways astonishingly modern. Neuschwanstein may have looked medieval, but it was centrally heated by a hot-air system very advanced for its time, and the kitchen was scientifically designed with such features as special ducts under the floor carrying smoke from the oven to the chimney. Whether or not Ludwig ultimately became insane, it is surely a sign of eminent sanity to create for oneself an environment which evokes the beauty of the past and yet has the advantages of contemporary technology.

When he came to the interior decorations of the castle, Ludwig enlisted the help of a literary historian with the curious name of Dr Hyazinth Holland (1827–1918), a teacher of

history, literature and fine art at the Therese Ascher Institute, a
Munich school for girls. One of the great intellectual worthies
of the city, he was to live long enough to write an autobiography
entitled *Memoirs of a Ninety-year-old Citizen of Munich*.[4] In this
book Holland writes:

> I had to advise on the building of Neuschwanstein. This was no
> easy task, for the feverish impatience of the King pressed ever
> forwards and allowed no single plan to come to proper matu-
> rity . . . I suggested, following the model of the Wartburg, that the
> German (and Bavarian) myths should be represented in sculpture
> and decorative painting. This idea seemed to appeal to the King.

One of Holland's suggestions involved pillars dedicated to
different gods, with the image of the deity at the top and an
appropriate symbol at the base. For example, one of these
pillars was to represent the Yggdrasil, the 'World-Ash-Tree'
from Nordic mythology. Evidently the sculptors and architects
grumbled that this idea was going to involve them in a great
deal of difficult work. 'Their complaints', Holland goes on,

> were all the more justified as the King had only a very unclear
> conception of the limits of art. For the World-Ash he wanted
> a real tree instead of a pillar clad in artificial bark. All counter-
> suggestions were to no avail. At last it occurred to one of the artists
> to mention that at the entrance to the Doge's palace [in Venice]
> there stood a pillar representing a tree. At this he finally gave his
> consent. My idea was carried out.

During the building work Ludwig was continually demanding
alterations, and Holland claims that signs of madness were
already apparent.

> For example, he suddenly decided that he wanted to have a wa-
> terfall tumbling down one of the staircases. Dollmann had great
> difficulty in dissuading him from this crazy plan . . . The decoration

of the Throne Room was entirely the King's conception. He dictated all the instructions to an ordinary servant, who scribbled down the unfamiliar-sounding names, such as Feirefiss [from *Parzival*], in a handwriting that was often hard to decipher. Everything was gone into by Ludwig in the most minute detail.

Holland describes how, when the painter Heckel showed Ludwig a series of sketches for murals, the King displayed the 'accursed Wittelsbach tendency to ask continual questions and find fault with this or that feature'. At length Heckel grew irritated and eventually exclaimed: 'Your Majesty, I think we understand these things better.' From then on 'the King shrank from personal contact with the artists, and they were no longer allowed to show him their paintings'.

The two most splendid rooms in the castle are the Singers' Hall and the Throne Room. The former is situated right at the top of the main building and commands magnificent views on three sides. It is a feast of sumptuous detail: Romanesque arches, vast chandeliers and a great panelled red and gold roof with carved figures of angels and dragons holding up the side beams. Every inch of wall is covered with pictures or intricate patterns. Episodes from the Grail story predominate and are taken from Wolfram von Eschenbach's *Parzival* and not from Wagner's version. Among the most pleasing features are two engaging little figures carved in wood and supporting the lintel of the doorway from the side passage. They depict two characters from *Parzival*: Kyot, the man who is said by Wolfram to have originally recorded the Grail story, and Flegetanis, the heathen astrologer who learned the secrets of the Grail from the stars. As Wolfram puts it: 'Flegetanis the heathen saw with his own eyes in the constellations things he was shy to talk about, hidden mysteries. He said there was a thing called the Grail whose name he had read clearly in the constellations.'[5] This room is not just

a decorative extravagance. It was clearly intended by Ludwig as
a place for the contemplation of the Grail mysteries in a spirit
of awe. Holland's remarks in his notes for the decorations show
that he shared Ludwig's exalted conception of the Grail:

> The Grail saga is an idea which springs from the innermost spirit
> of Christendom. Under its warm sun in the glorious middle ages
> there ripened that potent wine which inspired both French and
> German poets to their most beautiful creations.
>
> The actual kernel of the saga, however, is rooted and germi-
> nates in the ancient religious notions of the heathen world which
> continue in a discernible chain through the centuries. They ring
> out clearly in the Eleusinian mysteries of the Greeks and more
> quietly in the veiled traditions of the Egyptians; they emerge in a
> very pure form in the holy books of the Jews and appear in the
> splendid cults of the ancient Persians and in the cognate myths of
> the Germanic peoples.[6]

In addition to the depictions of Flegetanis, Kyot and other
figures from the Parzival story, Holland also wanted to include
Zoroaster, Orpheus, the 'veiled image of Sais' and 'the ancient
Egyptian Hermes cult and the beaker of Horns'. Among his
notes are drawings of swastikas of both the Indian and western
designs – an interesting and graphic example of the way in which
Holland links Germanic mythology with the concept of ancient
wisdom inherited from the Orient.

In the event only the Grail motifs and related themes were
included in the decorations for the Singers' Hall, but through
Holland's notes we catch a glimpse of the surprisingly deep
recesses of Ludwig's inner world. We see that the aesthetic
features of his castles are only the tip of a large iceberg. The real
purpose of his buildings was to provide temples which would
reinforce his conception of himself as a divinely sanctioned
king, one of a chain of rulers who knew the inner mysteries of
Christianity and drew power therefrom.

This comes across powerfully when one enters the Throne Room, which is the heart of the castle and which has never contained a throne. The focal point of the chamber, and therefore of the whole building, is an empty platform set in a great alcove and approached by a flight of white marble steps. This alcove is usually seen as the place where the throne was to stand, but I would like to speculate that it had a different function. We have seen how important the legend of the Holy Grail was to Ludwig and how the Grail is the key motif at Neuschwanstein. This alcove was, I believe, the place for the absent Grail – absent because to place an actual vessel there would be banal, and after all the Grail has never been found. I find there is something highly potent in the notion of this absent or invisible Grail at the heart of Neuschwanstein. On the gold background of the alcove behind the platform is a pattern of lions, the symbol of Bavaria, and higher up is a row of figures representing six holy kings: Stephen of Hungary; Henry VI, King of Germany and Holy Roman Emperor; Casimir of Poland; Louis IX of France (Saint Louis); Edward of England (presumably Edward the Confessor); and Ferdinand of Spain. Between the figures are palm trees representing peace, and looking down on them are Christ, the Virgin Mary and a group of angels. The plans for the room state that these kings 'through their perfection in Christian virtues stand as exemplary models and intercessors at the throne of the Eternal One'.

The domed ceiling of the room is painted blue with a pattern of stars and a great sun in the centre. The floor is set with an oval mosaic depicting trees and animals of different kinds. No doubt this symbolism is intended to show that the King stands, as it were, between heaven and earth, ruling over the latter in the name of the former. Opposite the alcove is a mural showing St Michael fighting the dragon, a motif which is repeated in a statue high up on the north wall of the castle and also in a mural on the eastern wall. Like the lion, the theme of Michael (or his *alter ego* St George) was a ubiquitous one in Bavaria, and Ludwig was fond of using it. There was also a special reason for featuring the motif at Neuschwanstein. Among the plans for the castle is a reference to the story that 'St Michael struck a jewel from the crown of Lucifer, and according to legend this stone fell to earth and became the Grail'.

This castle, which was also built in homage to Wagner, was in fact never visited by the composer. The King himself stayed there for the first time in the summer of 1884, and it was there that he was taken into medical custody after being declared insane. Within a few weeks of his death the building was opened to the public. How ironic that a place which was intended as an inviolable shrine, 'sacred and out of reach', should now be exposed to the gaze of a constant stream of tourists.

In the same year in which the building of Neuschwanstein was begun, Ludwig was already planning another castle. On 7 January 1869 he wrote to Frau von Leonrod:

> Near the Linderhof, not far from Ettal, I am going to build a little palace with a formal garden in the Renaissance style; the whole will breathe the magnificence and imposing grandeur of the Royal Palace of Versailles. Oh, how necessary it is to create for oneself such poetic places of refuge where one can forget for. a little while the dreadful times in which we live.[7]

Linderhof, whose architect was Georg Dollmann, was originally to be called Meicost Ettal which, as I mentioned earlier, is an anagram of Louis XIV's famous utterance, *L'état c'est moi*, and also refers to the Ettal valley with its magnificent Baroque church belonging to the monastery of Ettal. Eventually, however, the site of the new Versailles was changed to an island in the Chiemsee, a lake to the south-east of Munich, and the neighbourhood of Ettal – to be precise, a smaller valley called the

Graswangtal – became the site of a more modest building. In German the word *Schloss*, which means both 'castle' and 'palace', is used to refer to all of Ludwig's buildings. English speakers would tend to think of Neuschwanstein as a castle and of Linderhof and Herrenchiemsee as palaces, but for convenience I use the two terms here almost interchangeably.

Linderhof was the name of a royal hunting lodge to which Ludwig had been taken as a child. It had formerly belonged to the monastery and was named after the Linder family who had been its tenants. Their name in turn was said to be derived from the fact that a linden, or lime, tree had stood in the grounds. In fact a tree which some claim to be the original is still there. Although it interrupted the formal design of the garden, it was carefully tended on Ludwig's instructions and a garden seat was placed around it.

The palace began as an extension to the hunting lodge, and its walls, like those of the lodge, were originally built of wood. But in 1872 the lodge was dismantled and rebuilt further to the west, and at the same time the palace was faced with white ashlar stone. In place of the homely wooden building with its traditional Bavarian design there now emerged a compact but highly ornate structure, its elaborate façades adorned with decorative detail and allegorical sculptures. They include figures representing learning, soldiery, music, poetry, sculpture, architecture, agriculture, trade, science and industry. The portico, with its gilt balcony and rusticated columns, is surmounted by a statue of Atlas holding up the globe. The whole exterior is therefore a kind of all-embracing emblem of civilization as Ludwig saw it. Linderhof is a small palace, comparable in size to the Grand Trianon at Versailles on which it is partly modelled. The eclectic Baroque style of the exterior is highly effective and the abundance of detail is not oppressive. The building stands out like a delicately moulded wedding cake against the steep green background of the hillside behind.

The gardens are laid out in commensurately elaborate style. In front some steps lead down to a pool, in the centre of which is a fountain, adorned with gilded figures of the nymph Flora and two putti. The jet rises up to a height of thirty metres, its white spray echoing the foamy façade of the palace. Beyond the fountain and facing the building to the south is an Italianate double stairway, zigzagging up through a series of terraces to a little circular classical temple in which stands a marble statue of Venus. On the slope to the north of the house there is a water cascade flanked by pergolas. The boundaries of the formal garden merge into a wilder environment, more in the English manner of gardening, and this in turn merges into the untamed setting of the wooded hillside. The gardens, therefore, like the house, are a skilful blend of different styles.

The interior of the building is something of a surprise. One enters through an intimate little hallway with pink marble pillars and a small double staircase leading up to the first floor. Here all restraint ends, and the eye is accosted by a lavishness of furnishing and decoration which is completely out of proportion to the size of the building. The music room is lined with Gobelins tapestries and equipped with what must surely be one of the most ornate pianos ever made – a frothy mass of white and gold, covered in cupids and swags of carved foliage. Among the other *objets d'art* in the room are a life-size peacock in Sèvres porcelain and a marble group over the fireplace entitled 'The Apotheosis of King Louis XIV of France'.

More echoes of the Sun King are found elsewhere in the building. There is a statue of him, for example, in the oval, white and gold Audience Chamber. Although Linderhof was not intended as a copy of Versailles, an attempt was made in the interior to convey something of the atmosphere in which Louis

XIV might have lived. This is most apparent in the bedchamber, the largest room in the house, with its great canopied bed, surrounded by a gilt balustrade and overlooked by a ceiling fresco of the Sun god in his chariot. A curious feature of the dining-room is the so-called *Tischleindeckdich* (table, lay yourself), a table which could be lowered mechanically through the floor and down to the kitchen below, so that Ludwig could avoid having his reveries disturbed by servants while he was eating. A similar contraption is to be found in the unfinished wing of Herrenchiemsee. As one goes from room to room one becomes jaundiced by the surfeit of opulence. Everywhere the eye is dazzled by the brilliance of gold leaf, painted Meissen porcelain, brightly coloured silk wall panels and huge glass chandeliers. Nevertheless, in its entirety Linderhof is a place of great charm.

In the vicinity of the palace stand the original hunting lodge and a Chapel of Saint Anne, which was built in 1684 by the Abbot of Ettal. To these Ludwig added a number of other buildings which provided him with a variety of exotic settings. There was the Hunding Hut, which was built around the trunk of a tree and where Ludwig and his companions sat on bear skins drinking mead. This has now disappeared, along with the Hermitage of Gurnemanz where the King was able to immerse himself in the atmosphere of the Parzival story. In sharp contrast to these rustic hideaways was the splendour of the Moorish Kiosk with its throne flanked by figures of peacocks, its sumptuous 'Turkish' furnishings and its brilliant stained-glass windows. This building was bought by Ludwig in 1876 from the owner of a castle in Bohemia, but it probably came originally from Paris, as did the Moroccan House which Ludwig bought in 1878 and which was later moved to Oberammergau nearby where it is now in private possession.

The most remarkable of the buildings at Linderhof is the artificial Grotto of Venus, situated on the hillside above the palace and intended to represent the interior of the Hörselberg, where the first act of *Tannhäuser* is set. The grotto was built in 1876–7 under the direction of the 'landscape sculptor' A. Dirigl. It was created with enormous technical ingenuity. A basic framework of iron girders and pillars was skilfully covered with cement, sometimes laid over canvas, which was sculpted to give a convincing impression of a natural grotto, complete with stalactites. The grotto was also given a lake, an artificial waterfall and mechanically created waves. On the waters floated a boat shaped like a cockleshell, in which Ludwig sometimes sailed dressed as Lohengrin. In addition the grotto was equipped with a device which could produce a programmed sequence of five different lighting effects, lasting for ten minutes each and concluding with the appearance of a rainbow over the painted tableau from *Tannhäuser* which formed the backdrop of a small stage set into the wall. The electrical machinery that produced these effects consisted of twenty-four dynamos, one of which is now preserved in the German Museum in Munich as one of the earliest examples of its kind. The light with its changing colours was produced by twenty-four arc lamps which shone through rotating sheets of tinted glass, and the place was heated by seven furnaces to keep it at a temperature of exactly 20° Centigrade. Although the equipment has now been brought up to date, the grotto was a remarkably advanced piece of engineering for the age in which it was built – a Disneyland creation nearly a century ahead of its time.

One of the things that gives Ludwig's castles their charm and impact is the fact that in each case the environment was brilliantly chosen. Like a master jeweller who instinctively knows the ideal setting for a stone, he had an outstanding flair for placing his buildings in such a way as to create an effective and dramatic blend of architecture and surroundings. And this applies also to the views obtained from inside the castles. Look, for example, at the snow-covered plain of the river Lech framed in the Romanesque arch of one of the windows at Neuschwanstein.

Herrenchiemsee, Ludwig's last and most sumptuous palace, has a quite different environment from the other two. It stands on the Herren island in the Chiemsee, Bavaria's largest lake, which lies some fifty miles to the south east of Munich. It is easy to see, when one goes there, why this place was chosen, in preference to the Ettal area, for Ludwig's Versailles project. The atmosphere and terrain blend with the Louis XIV style of architecture in a way that a mountainous environment would not have done. In the vicinity of Neuschwanstein and Linderhof, wrapped in the brooding silence of the mountains, one's gaze directed upwards to the distant peaks, one feels solitude heavy with mystery and with the presence of the Nordic gods.

At Herrenchiemsee the vistas open outwards and not upwards, and the lines of the landscape are horizontal in emphasis, save for the towering wall of the Alps in the hazy distance to the south. Here one's vision seems compelled to move in wide sweeps along the reedy shoreline and over the great placid expanse of water and sky. The silence here is also of a different quality. It is not the mysterious silence of the mountains but a clear, expansive silence, broken only by the gentle lapping of water or the cry of a seagull. There is a potent magic here, but it is not the magic of Wagner. Even in the woods near the palace one feels the presence not of Wotan but of Pan.

Echoing the flatness of the surroundings, the palace is, like Versailles, a building of horizontal emphasis. To the west it presents a marble courtyard flanked by projecting wings, and to the east a single sweep of yellow stucco and ornate stonework, facing a formal garden of parterres, fountains and statues. When one stands here in front of this magnificent façade and looks down the great triumphal avenue stretching away from the palace one is struck by a paradox, for this avenue ends abruptly at the shoreline. Versailles was meant to be approached by admiring throngs. But at Herrenchiemsee the pomp and magnificence were essentially for the King alone.

There are two main islands in the Chiemsee: the Herrenwörth and the Frauenwörth. Both are the sites of old religious houses, one for men, the other for women, as the names imply. The Frauenwörth still has its convent, as well as a number of holiday houses. On the Herrenwörth (or Herreninsel), however, monastic life ceased in 1803 and the island went into private hands. The seventeenth-century Baroque monastery building remains and is now called the Old Palace. It was here in 1948 that a conference was held to lay the ground plan for the Federal Republic of Germany.

In 1873 there was public alarm at a proposal to cut down the splendid woods that cover most of the Herreninsel, and in order to prevent this piece of vandalism Ludwig decided to acquire the island as a site for a new palace. Within a month after the purchase Ludwig's architect Dollmann was taking measurements for the building, and in February 1874 he was sent on a trip to Versailles to obtain ideas. The same year the King himself also visited Versailles, for the second time.

It took nearly five years of preparation before the foundation stone for the new palace was laid on 21 May 1878. Thereafter the building proceeded under an increasing shortage of money as the King's financial position deteriorated. In 1884 he quarrelled with Dollmann when the latter was unable to progress with the work as fast as Ludwig wished on account of the lack of cash. Dollmann's associate Julius Hofmann took over as architect. The gardens, also modelled on those of Versailles, were the work of Karl von Effner, who had created the gardens at Linderhof. The layout succeeds in evoking the spirit of the Versailles park on a smaller scale.

By 1885 the palace was sufficiently far advanced for Ludwig to stay there from 7 to 16 September. This short sojourn was his only one at Herrenchiemsee. Soon afterwards the money ran out completely and building work ceased. One of the curious things about Herrenchiemsee, however, is that from the start it was planned to remain unfinished in the sense that only certain rooms were intended to be made habitable. The rest of the interior was to be merely a skeleton structure. Many owners of large houses shut off suites of rooms when the upkeep becomes too burdensome. Ludwig is rare, if not unique, in having built a house whose façade conceals many rooms that from the beginning were mock rooms. Since his death, all of the rooms that Ludwig planned, with the exception of the chapel, have been completed.

The rooms of Herrenchiemsee divide into two groups: the state apartments and the private apartments. The former include the State Bedroom and the Gallery of Mirrors, closely based on its counterpart at Versailles, but considerably longer (Mansard's original is 240 feet long, whereas Ludwig's version is 330 feet). These are in the opulent style of Louis XIV, whereas the Private Apartments are in the more intimate style of Louis XV. The latter include the King's Private Bedroom and the Dining Room which, like the one at Linderhof, is equipped with a *Tischleindeckdich*. Interestingly, although the palace is full of paintings and statues of the Sun King, it is his great-grandson Louis XV whose bust stands in the Private Bedroom.

The division of the rooms into these two groups reflects a dichotomy in Ludwig himself. Two kings lived within him: the Sun King that he would like to have been and the Night King that he knew he was. The contrast is reflected in the colour schemes of the rooms. The State Bedroom, for example, with its huge canopied bed fenced off by a balustrade and overlooked by a ceiling painting of the sun god Helios, is red in emphasis. In the Private Bedroom, similarly designed but on a smaller scale, the key colour is blue, Ludwig's personal favourite. Appropriately, the 'solar' State Apartments are approached sun-wise – from the east around through the southern wing – whereas the 'nocturnal' Private Apartments are entered from the west, the direction of the setting sun, and lie in the northern wing. A symbolic link between the two groups of rooms is provided by the ceiling painting in the anteroom known as the Salle de l'Oeil de Boeuf. This depicts the dawn goddess Aurora, in a golden horse-drawn chariot and loosely draped with a red cloth, greeting her husband, Astraeus, god of the starry night sky, who is draped in a star-spangled blue cloth. The former is arriving and the latter departing. To the right is Cronos, the god of time, holding up an hour glass. Between the heads of Aurora and Astraeus shines the morning star, said in mythology to be the offspring of the two. These figures reappear, charmingly metamorphosed into Rococo putti, in a Meissen porcelain group in the Oval Salon. They stand on either side of a clock, at the base of which is a figure of Cronos, his hands bound by chains forged by Vulcan.

This imagery becomes clearer when we remember the possibility, mentioned earlier, that Ludwig believed in reincarnation. An interesting piece of evidence for this is a small document written in French and now preserved in the Secret Archive.[8] It is an order to himself 'never again to fall into the same fault on pain of losing the crown'. The document is dated 24 February 1880 'of our fifth reign' and is signed 'Louis'. If he considered his incarnation as Louis XIV to be his first reign, then the period of Louis XV would have been his second, that of Louis XVI his third, and that of the post-Revolutionary King Louis XVIII his fourth, since the so-called Louis XVII, the ill-fated Dauphin, never reigned. Thus, if Ludwig had been next in line he would have been the fifth Louis. If he thought he was Louis

XIV reborn, either literally or in spirit, then Herrenchiemsee becomes much more than just a copy of Versailles. It can be seen as a magical place where the centuries that separated Ludwig from his namesake shrank to the brief and eternally repeated moment between night and day, a place where time was forever immobilized, just as the hands of Cronos are chained by Vulcan.

In terms of Ludwig's mythology, Herrenchiemsee and Linderhof represent, as I have said, the world of the Sun, Neuschwanstein that of the Grail, and the Moorish Kiosk and Moroccan House that of the Moon. Another building in the Moon category is the Schachen hunting lodge, high up in the mountains near Garmisch-Partenkirchen. Externally it is a simple wooden structure: The interior, however, is of the utmost opulence and embodies all of Ludwig's passion for the Orient. In this area, as with the court of Louis XIV, Ludwig was extremely well informed.

Another of Ludwig's oriental creations was the Winter Garden, begun in 1867 and built on the roof of the north wing of the Residenz in a sort of vast greenhouse made of glass and iron. It had an artificial lake, a profusion of tropical plants and a huge backdrop of a Himalayan scene painted by Christian Jank. A description of this place has been left by the Spanish Infanta, Maria de la Paz, whose husband was a relative of Ludwig. She writes:

> I saw an enormous garden, lit in the Venetian manner, with palms, a lake, bridges, pavilions, castellated buildings. 'Come,' said the King, and I followed him fascinated, as Dante followed Virgil to Paradise. A parrot swinging on a golden hoop cried 'Good evening!' to me, while a stately peacock strutted past. Crossing by a primitive wooden bridge over an illuminated lake we saw before us, between two chestnut trees, an Indian town . . . Then we came to a tent made of blue silk covered with roses, within which was a stool supported by two carved elephants and in front of it a lion's skin.

The King conducted us further along a narrow path to the lake, in which was reflected an artificial moon that magically illuminated the flowers and water-plants . . . Next we came to an Indian hut, from whose roof native fans and weapons were hanging. Automatically I stopped and the King urged me forward. Suddenly I felt as if I had been transported by magic to the Alhambra: a little Moorish room, in the centre of which was a fountain surrounded by flowers, carried me to my homeland. Against the walls were two splendid divans, and in an adjoining circular pavilion behind a Moorish arch supper had been laid. The King invited me to take a centre seat at the table and gently rang a little hand-bell . . . Suddenly a rainbow appeared.[9]

In this Hollywood creation Ludwig could forget the raucous, beer-swilling city outside. Alone, or with some specially favoured guest, he could summon up rainbows and inhale the scent of exotic flowers, blissfully unaware that this garden, like his entire way of life, was resting on a structure that was too weak to carry it. The vast weight of earth, trees, water and iron girders was far too heavy for the palace walls, and after the King's death the whole thing had to be dismantled for reasons of safety. Ludwig's cook, Theodor Hierneis, relates in his entertaining memoirs, *The Monarch Dines*, how as an apprentice he occupied a room directly under the lake, whose water would drip down through the ceiling so that he had to sleep under an umbrella.

In addition to the buildings that were actually constructed, Ludwig planned many more that remained unrealized. In the grounds of Linderhof there was to have been a theatre for private performances, and not far away, across the Austrian border, he intended to erect a Hubertus Pavilion modelled on the Amalienburg at Nymphenburg. The latter reached the stage of a brickwork skeleton, but this was pulled down after the King's death. The other projects remain only in the form of drawings and watercolours. Among these are two versions of a Byzantine palace, the first designed by Dollmann, the second by Hofmann. This was to have been built near Linderhof. There is also a design by Hofmann for a Chinese Palace, based on the imperial Winter Palace in Peking. Here Ludwig envisaged setting up a court where Chinese ceremonial would be observed and the servants specially trained in the appropriate etiquette. He himself had carefully studied books on the customs of the Chinese court.

Ludwig's last project was for a castle similar to Neuschwanstein but in the Gothic manner, which was to be called Falkenstein. Once again the indefatigable and versatile Christian Jank was called upon to create an artist's impression of the building. He began with a comparatively restrained design but finally produced something that looked like an illustration to one of Grimms' fairy tales – a great cluster of pinnacles and battlemented towers, clinging to a rocky hilltop and approached by a gateway with a portcullis. The architectural work was entrusted to Max Schultze and later to Eugen Drollinger, who was at work on the design when the King died. One of the building's features was a room which took the form of a bedchamber and chapel combined, with the bed set into an apse painted with the Virgin Mary and the Christ Child flanked by angels.

One other unrealized idea is worth mentioning. This was for a cable car suspended from a gas balloon which would have been used as a means of conveyance between Herrenchiemsee and the mainland. It was to run at a height of 160 feet for a length of 4,000 feet, and the car was to travel at ten feet per second, whisking the traveller over the lake in a journey into the past lasting six minutes and forty seconds. The King commissioned Dollmann to draw up a report on the possibility of such a scheme, but the architect was obliged to conclude that it was impracticable and dangerous. If a storm blew up the wire might break and the balloon float up into the sky taking its passenger with it. The picture of Ludwig making his final farewell in this way is curiously appropriate.

It might be thought that with the passage of time Ludwig's architectural creations would have come to be seen as vain exercises in nostalgia, pomposity and pseudo-historicism, and it is true that some people do see them in this light. But there are many more who have a genuine admiration for the castles. Why is it that, when many other mock historical buildings of the nineteenth century now appear absurd, Ludwig's have grown in stature? The answer lies partly in the fact that, behind the eclecticism of the buildings, one always senses the underlying sincerity and strength of the vision which called them into being. Moreover none of them ever descends to mere pastiche. Even Herrenchiemsee, which is so closely modelled on Versailles, has a character of its own. Ludwig's rigorous demands, combined with the efforts of skilled designers and craftsmen, produced work of a bold and original stamp that often foreshadows later styles in a remarkable way.

A vast army of artists, craftsmen, designers and decorators worked on the buildings, their abilities constantly stretched and challenged by Ludwig's unusual requirements. Many businesses had reason to be grateful for the King's patronage. Two textile firms, for example, worked for seven years on the State Bed at Herrenchiemsee. In addition there were furniture makers, wood carvers, goldsmiths and representatives of countless other crafts. In this way not only a great deal of employment was provided, but also a tremendous impetus was given to the decorative arts in southern Germany. Whatever else Ludwig may have achieved, his greatness as a patron of architecture is assured.

13

Dreams of El Dorado

In March 1873 a distinguished Bavarian public servant left Munich bearing instructions from the King for what must have been the strangest assignment of his life. His task was to find a piece of foreign territory where Ludwig could set up a new kingdom. This was no superficial whim on the King's part. If he could not make Bavaria live up to his ideals, very well, he would not be content with creating retreats for himself in the country. He would start all over again somewhere else. He would find some unspoilt tract of land across the sea – a *tabula rasa* on which he could write his dreams afresh. Here he could be the kind of ruler he had always wanted to be, a Grail King in his own Monsalvat. Perhaps when he thought about the prospect Wagner's words from *Lohengrin* echoed once again in his mind: '*In a far country, out of reach of your footsteps . . .*' And perhaps he remembered too the legend of Prester John, son of Parzival's half-brother Feirefiz. This mysterious figure had become a mighty priest and king, and was said to reign over a wondrous kingdom somewhere in the East.

As his scout for this project, Ludwig chose Franz von Löher, director of the Bavarian state archives and a well-known figure in his own right. Löher had been a democratic politician, distinguished lawyer and university professor, and was the author of many books on history and law. He was 54 years old at the time and, with his spectacles and bewhiskered face, the image of the dignified German 'Herr Professor'. On the face of it he was a strange choice for the job – rather as though a British monarch were to entrust such a mission to the Keeper of Public Records or the Garter King of Arms. Yet Löher entered into the task energetically and conscientiously.

His first voyage took him via Spain to the Canary Islands, along the north African coast to Constantinople, around the Greek and Turkish islands and then home, a journey lasting from March to July 1873. On his return he drew up a detailed report which he presented to the King at the beginning of August. This and subsequent reports of a similar kind are preserved in the Secret Archive of the Royal House.[1]

Löher describes vividly the difficulties and hardships he encountered: waiting for days for the arrival of unreliable steamships, trying to find people who could give him the information he needed for the King's purposes without giving away the reason for his mission, travelling on horseback over the volcanic mountains of Tenerife, 'a horrific ride of fourteen hours', in order not to miss the post boat to Parma. Considering his age, Löher appears to have endured all this with remarkable good humour. He made a close inspection of many different sites, ascertained the legal problems involved in buying property in the various places, and made some very practical suggestions as to how Ludwig's plan might best be accomplished.

'From the start the main goal to be borne in mind,' he wrote, 'is to make his Royal Majesty completely independent of seasons, men and needs of all kinds.' To this end, he went on:

'I have suggested that property be acquired on three islands at the same time and the necessary buildings and facilities installed so that residence can be taken up now here, now there, as is desired and as the season permits. In this way there need be no interruption in the supply of fresh food products.' In order to live comfortably and conveniently, he continued, it would be necessary to acquire not only several residences but also several estates producing different types of food.

Such practical details were probably less interesting to Ludwig than Löher's tempting descriptions of some of the sites he visited. In Tenerife, for example, he found a place called El Palmas on the higher part of the island, which he described as follows:

> This is a lonely area, covered with shrubby woodland but easily cultivable. The heights above afford a magnificent view the like of which the respectful author has never seen before. On both sides, beyond the wavy contours of the mountains one has a view of the ocean, and one can see Palma as though it were sketched in the air, and Gomera clear in its outlines, both against the enchanting blue of the water.

As for specific properties that could be bought, there was a villa belonging to an Englishman called Smith which was 'magnificently situated and charmingly appointed, but in the long run rather too small for a royal residence'. Another, belonging to the Marquess of Guadalcaso, was somewhat more suitable. Löher also pointed out, however, that to acquire part of the Canary Islands as a kingdom would be no easy matter, since the islands were not a colony but a Spanish province.

Löher found some equally enticing sites when he came to the Greek islands. He was particularly taken by one on Samothrace, of which he wrote the following description:

Right in the middle of the north coast are hot springs, and an hour's walk higher up are the ruins of the Christos monastery. All the way to the shore stretches a vista of shrubland and groves of trees, enlivened by the presence of finches, thrushes and nightingales. A woodland stream, like those found in our own alps, which even in summer is full of water, gushes down to the sea.

In the case of these islands, which were under Turkish control, it was particularly important to acquire sovereignty. 'The Turkish régime,' Löher explained, 'is either lethargic or brutal, and the lowest official can use his position for all sorts of chicanery and blackmail that would be unthinkable in our country ... It would therefore be out of the question for a King to be under the jurisdiction of a Turkish official.'

Several times Löher insisted that Ludwig should visit any prospective site himself before a final decision was made. He also emphasized the need for great secrecy in the proceedings. 'The whole undertaking,' he wrote,

> is so full of interest and novelty that, as soon as the tiniest hint of it leaked out, not only the German but also the foreign press would seize on it with loud cries and lengthy pronouncements. Opportunistic entrepreneurs would thrust themselves forward uncalled for, so that the acquisition of land and the entire project would be rendered much more difficult and costly.

In 1875 Löher made a second journey, this time to Cyprus and Crete. On the same trip he also made inquiries in Constantinople as to whether a suitable piece of land might be available in the Crimea. Once again he turned in a lengthy report of his investigations, but still Ludwig was not satisfied. So the search was widened. Löher could not undertake any more journeys himself, so he began to compile reports from the accounts of other travellers. One of the places considered was Afghanistan.

'The foothills of the Hindu Kush towards the south,' wrote
Löher,

> have a certain similarity to our beloved Alpine landscape. Friendly
> villages are built in terraces on the slopes. An excellent, world-
> famous wine is cultivated here. Apricots, almonds and numerous
> other fruits grow wild. The valley that stretches out towards Kabul
> is, thanks to the protection of the snowy mountains, a landscape
> of meadows and gardens . . . Imagine what could be made of such
> a place under an orderly regime!

This makes curious reading in the light of recent events
in Afghanistan. As Löher pointed out, the two rival powers in the area, Russia and England, might have welcomed
the establishment of a neutral regime in the heart of Asia.
Would the history of that troubled region have been different, one wonders, if Ludwig had set up his kingdom there?
And what would the wild Afghan tribesmen have made of the
aesthete King?

Another exotic place suggested by Löher was Egypt. In a
comparison which he knew would please Ludwig he wrote:
'The sixty-seven-year reign of Ramses II (the Great) in the
fourteenth century B.C., with its flourishing of literature and its
creation of mighty architectural monuments, can be compared
to the era of Louis XIV.'

South America, the Pacific islands, Persia, Norway – all were
considered as possible locations for the new kingdom. But finally
Löher was forced to come to a regrettable conclusion. In his
final report he wrote:

> I have myself visited a large part of the inhabited world and have
> read and researched in countless books. Yet I could find only very
> few places which might be remotely suitable, and in not a single
> case – with the possible exception of Norway – would I like to
> guarantee that the enterprise could really succeed . . .

On the whole earth there is not a single spot which totally fulfils the conditions for a satisfactory outcome. The goal can be only partly attained and certainly not without great sacrifice and trouble.

It must have been a depressing revelation for Ludwig that on the entire globe there was not one place where he could pursue his dreams undisturbed.

At the end of his last report Löher made a quite sensible suggestion:

If it were a question of acquiring a stretch of land or an island with total or half sovereignty it would be worth considering whether to seek the help of the German foreign service . . . In nearly every foreign country the government of the German Reich is treated with great consideration, and its diplomats and agents are so active that the matter would be hard to conceal from them once negotiations with the foreign government had begun. Now the powers in Berlin would not wish such an undertaking to succeed unless it had won the favour and support of Kaiser and Chancellor. On the other hand, if it were a matter of acquiring a large private estate, for example in Norway or Brazil, then the project could be pursued fully independently.

Ludwig's pride would never have allowed him to seek Bismarck's help in finding a new kingdom for himself. Nor would he content himself with merely having a private estate in a foreign country. He therefore resigned himself to abandoning the scheme.

No word of the project reached the public until after Ludwig's death. When it became known Löher was severely criticized for having, as it was thought, taken advantage of Ludwig's strange notions to obtain for himself two trips abroad. In fact Löher could hardly be blamed for conscientiously carrying out

Ludwig's wishes nor for making the best of it by publishing two travel books on his journeys.

If the plan had leaked out at the time it was conceived it would undoubtedly have caused a major scandal in Bavaria and probably brought about Ludwig's removal from the throne even earlier. Its failure must have caused Ludwig to turn with greater energy towards his other consolations: his buildings and his activities as a theatrical patron, which we shall examine next.

14

Ludwig II and the Theatre

In 1872 fuel was added to the growing rumours of Ludwig's mental instability by reports of a new aberration: the King had taken to having plays performed solely for himself and his occasional guests. These private performances deserve to be examined in some detail because, in their own way, they were remarkable events, not without artistic value and certainly not mere exercises of self-indulgence or insanity. Like his architectural activities, they must be seen as part of an attempt to create for himself a vivid illusion of the ideal world that he longed for. The desire to sit alone in a theatre can be easily understood when one remembers that in those days theatres were fully lit during a performance, and there were often irritating interruptions from the audience who, in any case, would have been just as interested in the King as in the play itself.

The idea for the private performances appears to have taken root in Ludwig's mind in 1871. In that year he ordered a production of a play entitled *Un Mariage sous Louis XV*, a comedy by Alexandre Dumas *père*, and before the first public performance he commanded a full dress rehearsal, something that was then very unusual, except in the case of a Wagner opera. He found this an enjoyable way to see a play and subsequently attended other rehearsals. Another foretaste of the private performances came on 25 September of the same year when he attended a special performance of the Oberammergau Passion Play, put on at his request after the last public performance and attended only by the King and four companions, including Prince Ludwig of Hesse. The King was much loved and revered in the Oberammergau district, and hastily raised flags were flying from nearly every house as he entered the village in a carriage at nine o'clock on a beautiful sunny morning and made his way to the festival theatre. In the interval the King returned for lunch to Linderhof where he was staying, and came back to the theatre for the continuation of the play in the afternoon. He was deeply moved by the performance, and a few days later he invited the main actors and the mayor of Oberammergau to a meal at Linderhof. He also had a huge Crucifixion group sculpted in marble and erected on a hill near the village as a testament to his admiration for the performance he had attended.

The private performances proper started in the following year. The actor Ernst von Possart, a leading member of the court theatre company for many years, describes how they began in his memoirs *Erstrebtes und Erlebtes (Aspiration and Experience)*:[1]

> The King's liking for attending performances as the only spectator developed logically and consistently.
>
> I remember clearly the audience . . . at which His Majesty declared to me with visible annoyance: 'I can experience no illusion in the theatre as long as people stare at me incessantly and follow my every gesture with their opera glasses. I want to be a spectator, not a spectacle for the crowd!'
>
> It was in our small auditorium, the enchanting Residenz Theatre, that the monarch felt himself especially restricted by the proximity of the public.

To protect the King from the gaze of the curious, silk curtains were hung on the side pillars of the royal box. But unfortunately the theatre-goers . . . made even more diligent efforts to penetrate the half-darkness of the royal box, and continued to point their opera glasses towards it.

One evening the infuriated monarch walked out of a performance in the middle of an act, determined never again to show himself before the public in a theatre.

Shortly afterwards the King attended a rehearsal of Schiller's *Maria Stuart*, but this time found the experience unsatisfactory and thereafter did not attend any more rehearsals. Instead one day he commanded the theatre company to perform a short play, *The Countess du Barry*, a comedy by Ancelot translated into German by L. Schneider, at the Residenz Theatre for himself alone. This took place at 3.00 p.m. on 6 May 1872, the first of the real private performances. Possart continues:

The ease with which the King was able to devote his attention to this performance, without being molested by the probing eyes of other spectators, filled him with deep satisfaction.

The performance was repeated soon afterwards in a similar manner. And what could be more natural than that the King should then wish to enjoy a larger drama, produced with the advantages of the imposing stage at the Court Theatre, stylishly performed and with the main roles as well cast as possible?

Thus arose the series of performances that were to be given every year for fourteen years (1872–85), taking place in the spring and autumn. Altogether there were 209 such performances: 154 plays, forty-four operas and eleven ballets. Forty-seven of them took place in the Residenz Theatre and 162 in the Court Theatre. The total cost of the whole series was 987,609.55 marks.

Ludwig's theatrical tastes were more wide-ranging than one might suppose. It comes as something of a surprise, for example, to learn that he appreciated the work of Ibsen and took a keen interest in the Norwegian dramatist during his stay in Munich. The plays put on for the private performances, however, reflect very strongly his particular obsessions. Here again we find the three worlds of the Sun, the Grail and the Moon which we encountered in the case of his buildings. The works of the Sun group were those dealing with the life at the French court under Louis XIV and his successors. Those of the Grail group were the operas of Wagner. Many of these were staged as private performances, including the *Ring* which was put on three times (twice in the year 1879). As for the oriental world of the Moon, this was represented by a number of plays including two by Kalidasa, the fifth-century writer who is considered by many to be India's greatest dramatist. It was a sign of Ludwig's fastidiousness that he rejected two existing German translations of one of Kalidasa's works and commissioned the poet Karl von Heigel to make a new one for a fee of 750 florins. The oriental theme was also present in Massenet's opera *The King of Lahore*, which Ludwig had performed in 1879.

Not all of the private performances, however, were linked to Ludwig's special obsessions. For example, there were works with a classical theme, such as Gluck's *Iphigénie en Aulide* and Shakespeare's *Pericles, Prince of Tyre*. The latter, before being staged privately, was given a public performance in Munich on 20 October 1882. Before that it had been unknown to German audiences. There were also historical plays by Schiller and Victor Hugo.

As in the case of Ludwig's buildings, a whole army of people was kept busy in these productions. To begin with many of the plays were specially written or translated for the King by such writers as the indefatigable Karl von Heigel, who wrote ten plays which were staged as private performances. Ludwig also commissioned Heigel to make a translation of Victor Hugo's trilogy of plays, *Cromwell*, insisting that it be written in rhyming alexandrines. Heigel spent about a year at this task, the hardest of his life as he described it, but Ludwig's death prevented it from being performed. Another writer who worked for Ludwig was August Fresenius, who translated many plays from the French and also wrote two original ballets for the private performances. The playwrights Hermann von Schmid and Ludwig Schneegans also wrote plays for the King. In some cases the King had special accompanying music written.

The performers included many famous names and ones that were to become famous: actors such as Ernst Possart and Josef Kainz (of whom we shall have more to say shortly), actresses such as Hermine Bland and Marie Dahn-Hausmann, singers such as Heinrich Vogl. The versatile Possart was also frequently called upon to act as director, which meant something rather different from what it does today. On the Munich stage at that time visual accuracy and effect were given priority, and dramatic presentation was a secondary consideration. The director, therefore, had to take great pains over details of scenery and costume. Other theatre staff included set and costume designers, stage engineers, musicians and conductors. All of these people were conscious of the standards demanded of them, and the result was a high level of achievement.

It must be remembered that all this effort did not go merely for the enjoyment of one man. Many of the productions, such as *Pericles*, had already been seen publicly. Others went to the public stage after being tried out privately. An example of the latter was Kalidasa's *Urvasi*, which was remarkable not only for its lavish and realistic scenery – with rich vegetation and ornate palace rooms – but also for the ingenious transformation effects achieved by the theatrical engineer Karl Lautenschläger.

When it was performed publicly in 1887, after Ludwig's death, it caused a sensation. The Munich stage at that time was the envy of Germany, and this was due in no small measure to the effect of the private performances, a fact that is corroborated by the Director-General of the royal stage, Karl von Perfall, in his book *A Contribution to the History of the Royal Theatre in Munich* (1894):

> Despite the untold trouble that they cost and the deep inroads that they made into the regular programme, these performances were of tremendous profit to the Munich royal stage. The company felt itself to be striving for and achieving great aims, for the tasks set by the King were hard and could be carried out only by an artistic institution of the very first rank.[2]

The course of a typical private performance is described by Kurt Hommel in his detailed book on the performances.

> The Director-General von Perfall usually sat to the right or left in front of the stage.
>
> Shortly before the beginning of the performance the King left his apartments, 'preceded by a gentleman-in-waiting carrying torches, and made his way through the Nibelung Corridor at such a fast pace that the torch-bearer had difficulty in keeping an appropriate distance'. Immediately after the appearance of His Majesty in the large central box . . . the overture began or the curtain was raised. This box remained softly lit even during the performance so that the King could study sketches for the sets and costumes and compare them with the way in which they had been carried out on the stage. He also often consulted the text of the play, for he expected his performers to be word-perfect. In the box below the monarch there were places for members of his Cabinet and specially invited guests, to whom, however, he was not visible. In the interval he sent his adjutants on to the stage to convey recognition, thanks or a word of criticism.

At the end of the performance the King might applaud, then the curtain would drop. He would reward the main performers with often extravagant presents which he sent to their dressing-rooms. He, however, would often remain sitting reflectively in his box. Only after his departure were the members of the orchestra allowed to leave their places. Until then they had to remain motionless and not look around. The performance was not considered ended until the King stood up. The artists who had received presents were obliged to thank the King in writing the same night.

All participants were strictly forbidden to allow any reports about the private performances to come before the public. And it was exactly this which led to the vulgarized accounts that circulated after the death of King Ludwig II.[3]

It might be thought that these performances would have been a painful or embarrassing ordeal for those who took part in them. In fact the opposite was the case. Ernst von Possart, who participated in nearly all the private performances, writes of them as follows: 'I still consider these performances the most sacred and serene that I have ever experienced in all my fifty years on the stage.'[4] He also declared that 'nothing unworthy was ever performed and nothing was ever unworthily performed'.[5] Frau Therese Vogl, who often sang with her husband Heinrich, in private Wagner performances, was of the same opinion. 'We artists,' she wrote, 'had the indescribably joyful feeling that the King was attending with his whole heart and soul.'[6]

One of the actors who took part in the private performances was a handsome young Austro-Hungarian Josef Kainz, who was twenty-two years old when he came to Munich in 1880. The following year he took part in a private performance of Victor Hugo's play *Marion de Lorme*, playing the part of Didier, an idealistic young man of humble birth who redeems the courtesan Marion. This led to an intense, turbulent and shortlived friendship between the King and the actor, which constituted the last really close human tie of Ludwig's life. The performance of *Marion de Lorme* took place on 30 April 1881, and the King was deeply impressed by Kainz's melodious voice and sensitivity as an actor. The play was repeated twice at Ludwig's request, on 4 and 10 May, and after each of the three performances he sent Kainz an expensive present: first a ring set with diamonds and sapphires, then a golden chain with a swan, and finally a diamond-studded watch. He also invited Kainz to attend two private performances as a guest, though the actor sat in a separate box and the two did not meet.

At length the King decided that he wished to meet Kainz, and normally when a wish was conceived by Ludwig it had to be instantly fulfilled. Thus during a rehearsal at the Residenz Theatre on 30 May, Ludwig's emissary Hesselschwerdt, Quartermaster of the royal stable, arrived with the message that Kainz was invited to come immediately to Linderhof and spend three days there as a guest. Kainz was delayed in leaving Munich because of the need to keep his visit secret, and he arrived by train at Murnau at seven o'clock in the evening to find that the royal carriage had been waiting there for most of the day. At about two o'clock in the morning he arrived at Linderhof, cold and exhausted, and was ushered to the Grotto where the King was waiting for him and where a table was laid for supper. It was four o'clock before they emerged from the Grotto into the first-light of dawn, but Ludwig was disappointed. He had expected Didier. Instead he saw a rather skinny young man, shivering with cold and temporarily robbed of his impressive voice by awe at his host and his surroundings. At first Ludwig wanted to send the actor home, but the Court Secretary Bürkel persuaded him to let Kainz stay on.

Kainz, on Bürkel's advice, began to play the role that was expected of him. When he next met the King he put on his stage personality and his best Didier voice. Ludwig was once again enchanted. Together they toured the surroundings of Linderhof, visiting the Hunding Hut, rowing on the lake in the Grotto, drinking coffee in the Moroccan House. Far into the night Kainz had to recite long passages from Victor Hugo or read from Byron or Calderón, knowing that Ludwig, with his extraordinary verbal memory, would jump on him whenever he made a mistake. It was all a terrible strain for poor Kainz, especially as he was never quite sure where he stood in his relations with the King. Sometimes Ludwig would suggest that they address each other by the familiar 'du' and would insist that Kainz should forget he was in the presence of a King. But when Kainz took him at his word and became over-familiar Ludwig would bristle and scold him. It was like walking a tightrope. Ludwig, however, was on the whole delighted by his guest.

Kainz's stay was extended to twelve days. He returned to Munich laden with more expensive presents but utterly worn out from lack of sleep and the strain of the visit. Ludwig, however, was already planning a new venture for himself and the actor. At first he wanted to make a trip to Spain, but it turned out that this was too difficult to arrange at that time of year. Instead he decided that they should go to Switzerland to visit the sites associated with William Tell in the region of Lake Lucerne. He was planning a new production of Schiller's play about the Swiss hero, with Kainz in the role of Tell's comrade Melchthal, and he was keen that the actor should prepare for the part by immersing himself fully in the atmosphere of the Tell country. It was also a good excuse for Ludwig to pay another visit to the area that meant so much to him.

With his passion for travelling incognito, Ludwig arranged for passports to be issued for Kainz and himself bearing the names of Didier and the Marquis de Saverny (another leading character from Hugo's play), and the two set off, accompanied by a small retinue, on 27 June. Almost at once irritating things began to happen. Travelling by way of Lucerne, they arrived at Kastanienbaum on the shore of the lake expecting a private steamer to be waiting. Instead there was a vessel decked out in flags, whose captain greeted Ludwig as 'Your Majesty'. So much for the incognito. Furthermore the 'castle' in which Ludwig had expected to be accommodated turned out to be a hotel. More publicity. More prying eyes. Ludwig grew increasingly vexed, until he was placated when a Swiss bookseller named Benzinger lent his country house, the Villa Gutenberg, for the King's visit, and the authorities of the canton placed a steamer at the disposal of the royal party.

For the next few days the group toured the district visiting all the places mentioned in Schiller's play, and once again Kainz was required to recite endlessly and at all hours of the night. The actor grew more and more tired and irritable. But Ludwig was only just getting into his stride. For the sake of extra realism he decided that Kainz should make a journey over the mountains which Melchthal took in the play and which he describes in a memorable passage in the second act. Kainz set off bravely on the two-day climb, accompanied by bearers with a liberal supply of champagne and Mosel wine to quench his thirst. After walking for twelve hours over snow and ice he arrived, sore-footed and ill-tempered, at Engelberg, the half-way stage, where he spent the night. The following morning he flatly refused to go any further. Instead he returned to the lake by carriage. When the King asked him eagerly what it had been like he replied: 'Terrible.' Ludwig was dismayed, but not for long. He now decided that Kainz must recite the Melchthal speech standing on top of the Rütli mountain. After one vain attempt to persuade him even to make the climb, Ludwig finally dragged him to the summit at two o'clock in the morning and commanded him to recite the passage. Kainz, tired out from an exhausting day on the lake, adamantly refused and promptly fell asleep. This was too much for Ludwig. He left Kainz where he was and returned to the villa in disgust.

The following afternoon Kainz learned that the King had left without him to return to Munich. Kainz, now repentant, caught up with Ludwig in Lucerne and there was a scene of apparent reconciliation. The two were even photographed together, Kainz sitting down and looking embarrassed and uncomfortable, while Ludwig stood towering beside him, a distant look in his eyes. But Ludwig's infatuation with the actor was now over. Some communication did pass between them after this, but the friendship was destroyed for ever. Soon after this Kainz married, and the following summer repeated the journey to Lake Lucerne. In the visitor's book of the hotel where he stayed he entered the words: 'Josef Didier, together with his mother and bride.'[7]

The subsequent lives of the two men were very different. Kainz continued to perform on the Munich stage, unhampered by his falling into disfavour with the King, and he later went on to become one of the most successful and distinguished actors of his day. While Kainz's path went upwards, Ludwig's henceforth went downwards into increasing isolation and mental decay.

15

Forbidden Longings

The Kainz episode and other similar events in Ludwig's life will have raised in the reader's mind the questions that must now be tackled. Was Ludwig a homosexual? And if so, to what extent? In answering these we must bear in mind that homosexuality encompasses a wide spectrum, ranging from those who feel sexual attraction exclusively towards their own sex, to those who feel only occasional or temporary homosexual leanings. All the evidence we have about Ludwig points to the fact that his sexual nature was nearer to the former than to the latter. Many things that corroborate this have already emerged in earlier chapters. I have mentioned his enthusiasm for the young woodcutter on the Watzmann, his sudden infatuations with men such as Paul Taxis and Josef Kainz, his excessively cold behaviour towards his fiancée, his panic at the very thought of marriage. But to say merely that Ludwig was a homosexual is not enough. We need to consider his homosexuality in the light of current attitudes and also in the context of his character as a whole if we are to understand the extreme anguish that his leanings caused him.

In Germany in Ludwig's time, as in most other European countries, homosexuality was officially and publicly reviled, even though there were many homosexuals in all strata of society, as there have been throughout history and in all nations. Furthermore, Article 175 of the Imperial Criminal Code (which replaced the old Prussian Criminal Code when the Reich was formed) declared that: 'Unnatural vice between two persons of the male sex, or between a man and an animal, is punishable with imprisonment; it can also be punished with loss of civil rights.'[1] This did not, however, prevent the capital of the Reich from being one of the most flourishing centres of homosexuality in Europe. According to one writer of the time, the city was the scene of many social gatherings of homosexuals – 'dinners, suppers, evening parties, five o'clock teas, picnics, dances, and summer festivals'.[2]

Germany's homosexuals were, moreover, beginning to rebel against their ostracism, and there was a strong movement for greater tolerance in this field. One of the leaders of this campaign was the Hanoverian writer Karl Heinrich Ulrichs (1825–95), himself a homosexual. Writing under the pseudonym of Numa Numantius, he issued a series of polemical works in favour of his cause under the general title of *Anthropological Studies in the Sexual Love of Man for Man*, which appeared between 1864 and 1879. He also wrote poetry on the same theme. Ulrichs maintained that homosexuals, although in a minority, are normal in the sense that they have a defensible and rightful place in the human scheme of things. A similar view was held by the Berlin sexologist, Dr Magnus Hirschfeld. Ulrichs used the term 'urnings' to describe homosexuals, while he referred to heterosexuals as 'dionings'. The word 'homosexual' was not coined until 1869. The popular term in Germany was and still is *warme Brüder* (warm brothers), for which Hirschfeld gave the rather bizarre explanation that 'the skin of the urning almost always feels warmer than his environment'.[3]

Despite the efforts of men like Ulrichs and Hirschfeld, and despite the relative openness of 'urning' activity in Berlin, homosexuality remained, to the majority of Germans, a thing to be abhorred. Most homosexuals were ashamed of their condition, and even those who came to terms with it were normally at pains to conceal it, especially if they occupied a position of any standing in the community. Fear of exposure and of prosecution among homosexuals made them easy and frequent victims of blackmail. It is easy, therefore, to imagine the feelings of a King who discovered that he was a homosexual. He would feel himself especially vulnerable to public ignominy and to blackmail. In Ludwig's case this fear would have been accompanied by an acute sense of guilt as a result of his repressed upbringing, his religious piety and his highly idealized view of human love.

Here it is important to point out that, side by side with true homosexuality, and to some extent overlapping with it, there existed in Germany a tradition of passionate friendship between members of the same sex. We find, for example, the novelist Jean Paul (J. P. F. Richter, 1763–1825), who was not a homosexual, writing to his friend Christian Otto: 'Ah, my friend, if I could only once more clasp your form to my breast.'[4] This type of sentiment was derived partly from an emulation of the ancient Greek attitude towards love between males. Goethe, who was also no homosexual, understood this well. In a letter to his patron the Duke of Weimar from Rome in 1787, he wrote of the 'remarkable phenomenon of the love of men for each other', and he went on:

Let it be admitted that this love is seldom pushed to the highest degree of sensuality, but rather occupies the intermediate region between inclination and passion. I am able to say that I have

seen with my own eyes the most beautiful manifestations of this
love, such as we have handed down to us from the days of Greek
antiquity; and as an observant student of human nature I was able
to observe the intellectual and moral elements of this love.[5]

True homosexuals, like the poet Count August von Platen-
Hallermünde (1796–1835), often took refuge in this sentimental and idealized view of male attachment. Thus Platen was
able to write that until he met a young lieutenant nicknamed
'Federigo' 'he had not realized that there could be such a thing
as guilty relations between men and that bodily pleasure could
be included in such feelings'.[6]

For a while Ludwig, like Platen, was able to see his predilec-
tion for the male sex as belonging to this sentimental tradition.
And indeed his relationship with Wagner was of this nature, as
I have already pointed out. But there must have come a time
when he became aware that his feelings for men went beyond
the limits of this convention. Even after this, however, he strove
to keep his friendships on a spiritual plane.

I have mentioned some of the men who played a part in his
life. Paul Taxis, it will be remembered, was his close companion
during the early part of his reign. Taxis, however, fell from
favour towards the end of 1866. The equerry Richard Hornig
fared better, remaining on friendly terms with the King until
1886, despite the fact that he greatly upset Ludwig by marrying.
Another person who must be mentioned in this context is a
cavalry officer named Baron von Varicourt, whom Ludwig made
his aide-de-camp in 1873 and for whom he had a short-lived
infatuation. Because of Varicourt's name, Ludwig imagined
him to possess an illustrious genealogy, with forebears who
had rendered distinguished service to France and the French
monarchy. Varicourt tried to tell the King that this was not
so, but Ludwig would not listen. As with all his friends, he

had a fantasy image of Varicourt, and a romantic genealogy was part of it. Three days after their first meeting Ludwig invited Varicourt to a private performance, and the usual florid exchange of letters followed. Soon they were dining together in the Winter Garden, taking long drives in the moonlight and talking together far into the night. Then, about a month after they had met, they quarrelled. The cause is not known, but Varicourt evidently took offence at something Ludwig had said. The reconciliatory correspondence that followed included a curiously revealing letter from Ludwig to Varicourt, written on 25 April 1873:

> There is something in your letter I keep wondering about. You write that you appreciate most highly – as you express yourself – my favours of a purely spiritual nature. Please explain to me why you emphasize that particularly, as it is a matter of course that they were of a purely spiritual nature. But you emphasize it specially; please write me the reason why. It is an enigma to me which I absolutely cannot understand; that is why I ask for an explanation of this curious and *completely incomprehensible* phrase. It would hurt me deeply if only the shadow of a doubt were to come between us.[7]

Here Ludwig gives himself away by 'protesting too much'. He was still perhaps clinging to the idea of romantic friendship and shying away from the knowledge of his physical yearnings.

The friendship continued for another two months. Then it was abruptly broken off when Varicourt offended the King by falling asleep while Ludwig was reading to him. No doubt Varicourt found it difficult to keep pace with Ludwig's nocturnal existence, just as in the case of Kainz who also fell from grace through going to sleep in the King's presence.

Apart from his infatuations with men like Taxis, Varicourt and Kainz, Ludwig also showed favour towards more humble members of his retinue. As early as the first year of his reign there were comments about his friendliness towards his valet, Voelk. As his reign progressed he resorted more and more to the company of men of the servant class, until at the end they formed almost his only companions. Chapman-Huston describes how, in about 1871, 'Ludwig started getting groups of foresters, peasants and grooms together in a tent at night for feasting, drinking and crazy horseplay of one sort or another'; he adds that these gatherings 'naturally caused unending gossip'.[8] Towards the end of his life Ludwig had a stormy relationship with another lackey, Alfonso Welcker, who served him for about eight to ten years and in the end betrayed him by giving evidence to the commission investigating the King's insanity.

If and when Ludwig crossed the threshold from sentimental friendship to physical gratification is difficult to establish, but it is arguable that he did cross it. The evidence for this rests chiefly on the Secret Diary and on various oaths written on scraps of paper preserved in the Secret Archives. The relevant part of the diary (that is, the part referred to as 'secret') was begun in December 1869 when Ludwig was twenty-four and was continued until a few days before his death. The original manuscript was destroyed, but parts of it survive in the unreliable pirate version issued by 'Edir Grein' at Liechtenstein in 1925 and the passages quoted by certain authors, notably by Desmond Chapman-Huston in his biography of the King. As Chapman-Huston was given full access to the original version for his research I rely here on his quotations. He comments on the diary as follows:

> It is one of the most fantastic and extraordinary documents of its kind in existence. When a Catholic introvert, by persistence in what he knows to be evil, cuts himself off from his Church, his

Priest and his Confessional, he is almost bound to turn elsewhere
for relief. Hence such documents as the secret diaries of Ludwig
II and Roger Casement.

Ludwig's, like that of Casement, has only incidental his-
toric importance and no literary value or significance whatever.
Yet it is not merely a pathological study; it has intense psychological interest and, meagre though it be, it is the secret record of a
mind in torment . . .

The first entry, which is undated, displays certain characteristics
which repeatedly occur. The most notable is the fixation of the
King's obsession by Louis XIV and all that concerned that monarch.
The motto of Louis, 'Nec pluribus impar' [roughly, 'a match for
the whole world'], and the French royal lilies, seem to have given
Ludwig courage and hope only second to that inspired in him
by the sign of the Cross. The reference to Oberon, King of the
Elves and the guardians of the Treasure of the Nibelungen in the
Nibelungen Lied, is equally characteristic . . .

Psychologically, and biographically, the most important admis-
sions made in this first Diary entry are that the writer has, in the
past, indulged in sensual love, that he has repeatedly 'fallen', thus
betraying his ideals; that, sick of such love, and longing to achieve
its psychic counterpart, he is continuously failing, and ever crying
out for help and strength to overcome the evil within. This indeed
is the burden of the Diary throughout which opens, as it is to end,
with an account of one of many 'falls'.[9]

The diary not only reveals an acute sense of carnal guilt; it
also betrays the writer's mental deterioration. The following
quotations will give an idea of the flavour of the document. On
29 June 1871 he wrote in the diary:

Drive to Schlux . . . Sworn in memory of the oath in the Pagodenburg on 21st of April . . . Soon I will be a spirit; heavenly airs are
around me . . . I repeat it, and as truly as I am the King, I will keep
it, not again until the 21st September. Then to try it otherwise;
at the third time it succeeds. Remember the 9th of May 3 times

3! – Feb. – April – June – Septemb. Fragrance of the lilies! The King's delight . . . This oath has its binding power, as well as its potency by

De Par le Roy

LR

DP LR

Solemn oath before the picture of the Great King. 'Refrain for 3 months from all excitement.' 'It is not permitted to approach hearer than one and a half paces.'

Louis

Given at Hohenschwangau in the year

of our Salvation 29 June 1871,

Of our Reign the eighth.[10]

Why he describes his reign as the 'eighth' is a mystery. Unlike his reference in another place to a 'fifth' reign (see Chapter 12), it does not seem to make any sense even in terms of a reincarnation theory.

The first entry for the year 1872 refers to Richard Hornig:

. . . Reconciliation with Richard beloved of my soul . . . On the 21st, the anniversary of the death of the pure and exalted King Louis XVI. Symbolically and allegorically the last sin. Sanctified through his expiatory death, and that catastrophe of the 15th of this month, washed of all mire, a pure vessel for Richard's love and friendship. – The ring, consecrated and sanctified in the water, gives the wearer the strength of a giant, and the power of renunciation. – Kiss holy and pure . . . only once. I the King. The 21 Jan. 1872 – *Vivat Rex et Ricardus in aeternum – Pereat malum in aeternum.*[11]

Then, on 3 February, he found it necessary to make another vow:

Hands not once more down on penalty of severe punishment. In Jan. Richard was with me here three times . . .! On 31 Court Ball

Ride with R. in Nymphenburg, (Amalienburg). *De Par le Roy*. It is sworn by our friendship, on no account again before 3rd June . . .[12]

There are many entries in this vein, often invoking the name of Louis XIV to aid him in keeping his vows, and sometimes referring to the royal bed, which seems to have been a particular fetish of his. In his New Year entry for 1873, for example, he wrote:

> I swear and solemnly vow by the pure and holy sign of the Royal Lilies inside the impassable, invulnerable balustrade enclosing the Royal Bed, during the year just begun as much ever possible bravely to resist every temptation, and never to yield if at all possible either in acts or in words, or even in thoughts . . .[13]

As time went on the entries became more and more incoherent, and often strange numerological observations were mingled with the vows and resolutions. For example, here is part of the entry for 28 July, 1877:

> 1877 year of Redemption! – The Royal Lily triumphs and makes any relapse quite impossible! – July 30 days still, then never, never, never more. (Symbolic, allegorical significance) 1877 year of Redemption! (30 to 31 years) 1866 time of Lilies (year of the *Nibelungen* R. W. and L. R.). Once more a risk of that fall and the right to the Crown and the Royal Throne has to be forfeited.[14]

More numerology comes in the New Year entry for 1878:

> Before number XII of the year of my reign was completed, and therefore the miserable fatal number 13 was still in the ascendant, the 'last' fall occurred! – Shortly before I became 33 years of age.

He goes on to remark that the digits of 33, multiplied by one another, give 9, 'the number of the steps of the *throne* power of self-command achieved when I have reached this number . . .'[15]

Some of the guilty outpourings in the diary could refer to fantasies and auto-erotic activity. But it is difficult to interpret the entry for 13 September 1877 in that light:

Au Roy

In this letter is given the *order* and with it also the necessity and possibility of fully abstaining from kisses, *anathema* in *aeternum*! Therefore conquered at the age of 32 and not quite 3 weeks, the last misfortune. Terribly near the brink of a complete fall, night of the 12–13 Sept. 77 . . . [16]

The same applies to the very last entry in the diary, made on 7 June, 1886:

1st June definitely the last full 2 months and 3 weeks before the 41st birthday

You remember Sire

Remember

Remember

From henceforth never!

From henceforth never!

From henceforth never!!!

Sworn in the name of the Great King

now invoking the puissant aid of the Redeemer.

Linderhof

(Also from kisses strictly to abstain

I swear it in the name of the King of Kings.) [17]

This pledge was signed jointly by Ludwig and Alfonso Welcker and sealed with the royal cypher and crown.

Whatever realities lie behind Ludwig's words, the Secret Diary remains a poignant testament to the anguish of sexual guilt and repression.

The whole subject of Ludwig's homosexuality has been widely discussed in recent years, and has often been treated in a sensationalist way. An example is the book by Robert

Holzschuh, *Das verlorene Paradies Ludwigs II* (The Lost Paradise of Ludwig II).[18] Holzschuh quotes extensively from a collection of 'original letters' from Ludwig to his equerry Karl Hesselschwerdt, which had come up for sale at a Munich auction house. On the basis of these, Holzschuh concludes that in the latter part of his life Ludwig repeatedly had homosexual contact with cavalry soldiers and other young men of lower social standing. The authenticity of these letters has been questioned, and the possibility has been raised that they were forged in order to provide ammunition for Ludwig's dethronement. However, there is abundant proof that the issue of his homosexuality was perceived as a serious problem in many quarters, including the Bavarian government. For example, on 5 May 1886 the Council of Ministers sent a message to the King in which they expressed deep concern about the matter of the cavalry soldiers and saying that the presence of a large number of these in his entourage was being talked about everywhere.[19] In this connection, the cancelling of his engagement and his alleged aversion to the company of women have often been mentioned. However, the latter allegation is not borne out by the facts. As I show in Chapter 9 of this book, there were many women whom he admired and whose company he enjoyed, including the sculptress Elisabeth Ney. Of course, many homosexuals are fond of the company of the female sex, so these friendships with women are of no great significance in this regard. If Ludwig was a homosexual, as much evidence indicates, it is surely time to take a more balanced view of the matter.

16

Farewell to Wagner

Ludwig's last decade began with Wagner once again in the forefront of his life. For eight years they had not seen each other, although their correspondence had continued. Then, in August 1876, they were brought together again when the *Ring* was at last given its première, though not in Munich as Ludwig had originally envisaged.

Wagner, Cosima and the children had regretfully bidden farewell to Triebschen in April 1872 and had established themselves at Bayreuth, an attractive little town in northern Bavaria which Wagner had chosen six years earlier as the site for the central temple to his art. A combination of reasons had led him to choose this particular place. He did not, if possible, want to offend Ludwig by going outside Bavaria, but had rejected Munich mainly because of the difficulties and enmity that he had encountered there in the past. Bayreuth was conveniently situated within the Bavarian borders but in a Protestant region where he felt at home, and it happened to be geographically more or less at the centre of the German-speaking world. The town also had an old opera house which, surprisingly enough, possessed the largest stage in Germany. Altogether Bayreuth seemed ideal for Wagner's purposes, and he was in any case charmed by the place.

There was, however, an awkward problem to be overcome if the complete *Ring* was to have its première at Bayreuth. It will be remembered that in 1864 Wagner had signed an agreement under which the score of the *Ring* was to be the property of King Ludwig, and he had already reluctantly abided by this agreement in the case of *Das Rheingold* and *Die Walküre*. But he knew that if he delivered the two remaining parts, *Siegfried* and *Götterdämmerung*, Ludwig would insist on their being performed in Munich as had happened, to Wagner's chagrin, with the two earlier operas. Wagner therefore decided simply to break the agreement and withhold the scores from Ludwig. At the end of 1870, when the King pressed him for the score of *Siegfried*, he pretended that he had postponed finishing it until he had completed the first act of *Götterdämmerung*. This, however, was a barefaced lie, as the score of *Siegfried* was already complete. By the spring of 1871 the King had become aware of what lay behind Wagner's prevarication. 'I dislike Wagner's plan very much,' he wrote to Düfflipp on 19 April. 'It will be a pure impossibility to produce the whole Nibelung cycle in Bayreuth next year.'[1] But five weeks later he was writing to Wagner describing the scheme as 'magnificent'[2]. It is a measure of his devotion to Wagner's work that he was willing to forgive yet another example of deceit and dishonesty on the part of his old friend. By early 1872 he had given way completely to Wagner over the question of the *Ring*. It must have been galling for him to see his early hopes shattered in this way on top of all the other disillusionments that he had suffered, and it would not have been surprising if he had felt bitter and resentful towards Wagner. Yet on 3 January 1872 he wrote to the composer:

In spite of every tempest that appears to divide us, in spite of all the cloud-racks that pile up between us, our stars will yet find each other: even when the profane eye cannot pierce through the thick veil to the radiant brightness of them we two will recognize each other; and when we have at last reached the holy goal we had set ourselves from the beginning, the central sun of the eternal godhead, that light and life for which we suffered and fought undaunted we will render an account of our doings, the meaning and aim of which were to spread that light over the earth, to purify and perfect humanity with its sacred flames, making it the sharer in eternal joys.[3]

At first Wagner planned to produce the entire *Ring* at Bayreuth in 1872, but when he visited the Bayreuth opera house in April 1871 he realized that the auditorium was much too small and that a reconstruction was impossible. Nevertheless he was more enthusiastic than ever about Bayreuth and its environs, and he decided that there was no alternative but to build a new opera house, specially designed for Wagnerian purposes. He announced that the *Ring* would be performed in the new theatre in the summer of 1873. Once again he was being wildly optimistic, and he soon discovered that the theatre would not be ready until 1874 at the earliest. The foundation stone was laid on 22 April 1872 in pouring rain – even in the midst of his triumphs the gods seemed to go out of their way to test Wagner's endurance.

Ludwig subscribed 25,000 thalers towards the cost of the theatre, but later he agreed that the money could be used for the building of Wahnfried, Wagner's house at Bayreuth. Wagner gratefully erected a bronze bust of the King in front of the house, but adroitly manoeuvred Ludwig into paying for it. Meanwhile Wagner and Cosima had been travelling around Germany raising money for the theatre. Everywhere he was now fêted as a great German artist, but the fund-raising proceeded with frustrating slowness. Some money trickled in from the Wagner societies that had been set up in many parts of the country, and generous donations came from the Sultan of Turkey and the Khedive of Egypt, but the German princes on the whole behaved with extraordinary meanness. Because of this disappointing response the building work proceeded much more slowly than had been anticipated. In a desperate attempt to speed up the fund-raising Wagner went on a gruelling concert tour, but there was still not enough.

By midsummer 1873 it had become clear that, although the shell of the building could be completed, only a large loan would make possible the installation of the necessary fittings and stage equipment. For such a loan a guarantor would be required, and the only possible candidate was King Ludwig II. When, however, Wagner sent an impassioned letter to Ludwig, a reply came from Düfflipp to the effect that the King was not prepared to help any further beyond the 25,000 thalers already subscribed – he had evidently forgotten that this money had in the end been used for Wagner's house. After launching a fruitless nationwide appeal through booksellers and music dealers, Wagner turned in desperation to the idea of appealing directly to the Kaiser via the Grand Duke of Baden. The Grand Duke refused to help, but by this time Ludwig had changed his mind. Probably he had heard about Wagner's plan to approach the Kaiser and had revolted against the idea of Prussia stepping into the breach. On 25 January 1874 he wrote to Wagner:

> From the depths of my heart I beg you to forgive me for my long delay in writing to you . . . Do not be angry with me on that account dearest Friend. It is my consolation that you know me and can have no doubt that my true and genuine friendship for you and my enthusiasm for your divine, incomparable works are so deeply implanted in my soul that it would be lunacy to believe in any

decline of my ardour for you and your great undertaking. No, No and again No! It shall not end thus! Help must be given! Our plan must not fail. Parsifal knows his mission and will do everything that lies in his power . . . Do not despair, but make me happy at once with a letter.

I must unfortunately confess to you that my finances are in anything but a brilliant condition at the moment; I was forced to hesitate although this is not normally in my nature.[4]

The result was that Ludwig lent Wagner 100,000 thalers which was to be repaid within a year and a half. If it had not been for this loan the Bayreuth festival theatre might have remained a shell. As it was, Ludwig's intervention saved the future of what Newman calls 'the greatest of all monuments to German art'.[5]

It was ironic that Ludwig, who had always hoped that Bavaria would be the focal point of the German cultural revival, now found himself rescuing an institution that finally annihilated this cherished ambition; for Wagner's new centre, although technically in Bavaria, was in fact a national phenomenon in a totally new sense. In retrospect the creation of the theatre can be seen as an event of supreme importance for the German people. Here, for the first time, was a temple of art where the whole of Germany could worship, a place that symbolized a new national artistic consciousness. The founding of the Bayreuth theatre therefore represented on a spiritual and cultural plane what the founding of the Bismarckian Reich represented on a practical and political plane.

After many delays the theatre was finally ready to open its doors in the summer of 1876, and for the first performance a galaxy of German notables descended on Bayreuth, including the Kaiser. Ludwig, of course, came as well, but he did not go to the opening public performance. Instead he attended a general rehearsal on the 6th, 7th, 8th and 9th August. As always, he

was anxious to avoid prying eyes, and on 12 July he had written
to Wagner:

> Oh, how I am looking forward, after such a long period of sep-
> aration, to seeing you again at last, my sincerely loved and truly
> honoured friend! Anything bordering on an ovation from the pub-
> lic I wish strenuously to avoid; I will, I hope, be spared from
> banquets, audiences and visits of foreign people of rank; all such
> things I hate with all the force of my soul. I come to be revived and
> enthused by your great creation, to refresh my heart and soul, not
> to show myself to inquisitive gapers and to make myself available
> as an object for ovations.[6]

On 4 August the royal train set out for Bayreuth. The town
was expecting Ludwig's arrival, and the station was richly decorated. But the King did not alight there. At about 1.30 a.m.
the train stopped outside the town at the small Rollwenzel halt,
where Wagner was waiting. As the King stepped out of his
carriage it must have struck Wagner how heavy he had grown
during their eight years of separation. Wagner, by contrast, was
looking small, frail, thin and grey. The strain of the Bayreuth
preparations had taken their toll. There were tears in the older
man's eyes. He felt an impulse to embrace the King, but instead
they shook hands. They then mounted a carriage and were taken
to the Hermitage, a lovely rococo mansion near the town where
the King was to stay during his visit. Here the two men talked
until three in the morning.

The impression made on Ludwig by the performances he saw
is evinced in the letter that he sent Wagner very shortly after
his arrival back at Hohenschwangau.

> I came with great expectations; and, high though these were, they
> were far, far exceeded. I was so deeply moved that I might well
> have seemed taciturn to you . . .

Ah, now I recognize again the beautiful world from which I have held aloof; the sky looks down on me again, the meadows are resplendent with colour, the spring enters my soul with a thousand sweet sounds . . . You are a god-man, the true artist by God's grace who brought the sacred fire down from heaven to earth, to purify, to sanctify and to redeem! The god-man who truly cannot fail and cannot err![7]

As a result of experiencing the words and music of the *Ring*, Ludwig adds, he has been put into a state of 'blessed intoxication never before experienced'. He was now, he said, longing to see the *Ring* for the second time, even though this would mean attending a performance with a full audience. Once again, however, he repeated his desire to avoid publicity.

He returned to Bayreuth on 26 August, the day after his thirty-first birthday, and attended the third and last *Ring* performance on the succeeding four days, for once overcoming his aversion to public events. At the end of *Götterdämmerung*, he came to the front of his box and joined in the applause as Wagner stepped on to the stage to address the audience. In his speech Wagner said that the festival had been 'embarked upon in trust in the German spirit and completed for the glory of the King of Bavaria, who had been not only a benefactor and protector to him but a co-creator of his work'.[8] The last phrase must have made Ludwig particularly pleased. He returned to the Hermitage for a short rest, then drove to his waiting train. This time there was no getting away from the throng that lined the route, but Ludwig did not seem displeased by this. He appeared relaxed and happy. It was, however, his last appearance before a crowd and also his last visit to Bayreuth. His loan for the theatre was not repaid in the stipulated time. On the contrary, the 1876 festival ended with a deficit, and Wagner had to make yet more demands on Ludwig's generosity. Not until 1882, the year before Wagner's death, did Bayreuth start to show a profit.

In November 1880, the year in which Bavaria celebrated the 700th anniversary of the Wittelsbach dynasty, Wagner paid a visit to Munich. At a private performance of *Lohengrin* on 10 November he and the King sat together in the royal box. It was their last face-to-face meeting. On the 12th Wagner conducted the prelude to *Parsifal*, attended by the King, Cosima and the painter Franz von Lenbach. According to Lenbach's account, re-layed at second hand, this occasion was marred by disharmony. It is said that Ludwig irritated Wagner by arriving late, then annoyed him still further after the prelude by demanding a rep-etition. Finally, when Ludwig asked for the *Lohengrin* prelude so that he could compare the two, Wagner reportedly handed the baton to the Kapellmeister, Hermann Levi, and walked off in a huff. The story has probably been exaggerated, for Ludwig made no mention of any unpleasantness when he recorded the event in his diary. A few weeks later, at Christmas, Ludwig sent the composer a small gold model of Hohenschwangau, to serve as a paperweight, as well as a beautiful little Renaissance cabinet of ebony inlaid with silver. Moreover the two men con-tinued to correspond as warmly as before, though Wagner was temporarily aggrieved when Ludwig declined to come to the première of *Parsifal* at Bayreuth in 1882, pleading illness.

The *Parsifal* performance was conducted by Levi, who had remained faithful to Wagner despite the latter's contentious pronouncements about Jews. It galled Wagner to have such a Christian work conducted by the son of a rabbi, but Levi's outstanding ability as a conductor was indispensable to him.[9] It is interesting to note that Ludwig did not suffer from racial or religious prejudice, as is shown by a letter he wrote to Wagner on 11 October 1881:

I am glad, dear Friend, that in connection with the production of your great and holy work you make no distinction between

Christian and Jew. There is nothing so nauseous, so unedifying, as disputes of this sort: at bottom all men are brothers, whatever their confessional differences.[10]

Ludwig finally saw *Parsifal* at a private performance in 1884, repeated the following year. By then, however, Wagner was dead. One February evening in 1883 Ludwig received a telegram from Venice giving the news that the Master had been struck down by a heart attack. In his sudden grief Ludwig is said to have stamped so hard that he smashed a floor tile. Henceforth the pianos in all his castles were covered over with crape. 'Wagner's corpse belongs to me,' he declared. But when the train carrying the coffin back to Bayreuth stopped at Munich for a few hours, Ludwig was not among the vast crowd that gathered at the station to pay homage. He contented himself with sending his aide-de-camp with a large wreath of palm leaves. Nor did he attend the burial at Wahnfried on 18 February. Throughout their long association Wagner had caused him both joy and anguish. Now that he was gone Ludwig must have felt more alone than ever before.

17

The Twilight Years

'Next to great joy,' writes Henry James in *A Most Extraordinary Case*, 'no state of mind is so frolicsome as great distress.' In the months after Wagner's death Ludwig, instead of immersing himself in his sorrow, seemed to blossom forth with a new gaiety, spending a great deal of time in the company of his first cousin, Prince Ludwig Ferdinand, and the Prince's new bride, Maria de la Paz, Infanta of Spain. The Prince, a qualified doctor, was someone whom Ludwig admired and enjoyed talking to about the details of his profession. And he was charmed by the Infanta, an attractive, lively woman, who wrote poetry. After their wedding in April he went out of his way to entertain the couple. He gave them a romantic supper party in the Winter Garden[1] and invited them to Herrenchiemsee – a privilege accorded to few other people in Ludwig's lifetime. During their meetings Ludwig's conversation sparkled. He dazzled and charmed his guests with his brilliant talk of literature and drama. Even so, he still insisted that they show proper respect towards him. The Princess was reprimanded through an intermediary for not bowing low enough, and the Prince was sent a letter in which Ludwig asked him not to behave in quite such a free and cousinly manner. But the Princess did not find Ludwig the aloof and inaccessible figure that she had been led to expect. 'This man,' she later wrote, 'has something great and poetic about him, and has powers of imagination such as one rarely finds in anyone.'[2]

During those spring months of 1883 Ludwig seemed to throw off some of the cobwebs that had gathered during his years of isolation. For a brief spell Munich was hopeful that the King might have turned over a new leaf. But his gaiety was superficial. In his heart he was as lonely as ever.

The number of people whom he could call friends was rapidly diminishing. Wagner's death had removed his greatest friend, but just before that he had lost another when his Cabinet Secretary, Friedrich von Ziegler, resigned for the second and final time after serving the King for nearly seven years. Ziegler became Cabinet Secretary in 1876 after the dismissal of Eisenhart, which was carried out in the abrupt manner so often displayed by Ludwig when someone fell from his favour. On 11 May 1876 the royal retinue was preparing to accompany the King to Berg. As Eisenhart was packing, Düfflipp arrived and told him that no carriage had been provided for him and that the King appeared to be contemplating changing his Cabinet Secretary. Eisenhart was offended at this indirect way of dismissing him but took it philosophically. Later, when Düfflipp tried to change the King's mind, Ludwig replied: 'Leave me alone; I can't think how I put up with that idiotic face for so long.'[3]

Until then Ludwig had never felt any close mental kinship with any member of his Cabinet staff, but Ziegler was cast in a different mould from the others. A lawyer by training, he was a painter and poet in his leisure time and understood the world of culture and art. Ludwig at first accepted him grudgingly on the recommendation of Düfflipp, but rapidly came to judge him as the best Cabinet Secretary he had ever had and to feel a strong personal liking for him. He even invited Ziegler to call him by the familiar 'du', though the Cabinet Secretary tactfully never made use of this privilege. Ludwig sent the usual fulsome letters to Ziegler, often supplemented by poems. Ziegler was not as carried away by the friendship as Ludwig was, but he reciprocated as best he could.

Despite the King's protestations of friendship towards his Cabinet Secretary, he still made Ziegler's job extremely difficult. As Ludwig became more and more of a recluse and spent increasingly shorter periods in Munich, the Cabinet Secretary became virtually his sole channel of communication in affairs of state and thus took on the role of a kind of unofficial prime minister. The importance thus thrust upon the Cabinet Secretary was totally unconstitutional and placed a terrible burden on the occupier of the post. For example, if a minister wanted an important document signed by the King it would be left to Ziegler to obtain the signature, when it should have been up to the minister to insist on an interview with the King and to resign if no signature was forthcoming. A few ministerial resignations might have brought Ludwig to his senses. As it was, ministers continued to take the line of least resistance and to rely on the hard-pressed Cabinet Secretary to be their intermediary.

Zeigler's duties came to extend far beyond his official function. For instance his handwriting pleased Ludwig so much that Ziegler was often asked to act as an amanuensis or to copy out illegible documents. His aid was also enlisted to help satisfy Ludwig's voracious appetite for literature. Baron Walter von Rummel, Ziegler's son-in-law, has left an account of this:

> King Ludwig read . . . a great deal and on all sorts of subjects. All this reading matter had to be obtained by Ziegler, whether it had

to do with medieval or modern German literature or with long-forgotten French works. The main requirement was for books of the seventeenth and eighteenth centuries dealing with the time of Louis XIV and XV. As the King did not want to read everything himself Ziegler was required to give detailed expositions of these works and to make extracts . . .

He alone could not manage the task. His wife sprang to his aid and made extract after extract. Even just the titles of these countless works filled whole volumes.[4]

These onerous duties were not all that Ziegler had to put up with. The long-suffering Cabinet Secretary also had to endure Ludwig's strange whims, his irrational likes and dislikes, his unpredictable moods, his fussiness about trivialities. Once the King reprimanded him for using the words 'already mentioned' in a report. Things were not 'mentioned' to a King but 'announced'; 'mention' was a 'reprehensible' word.[5] On another occasion, while the Cabinet Secretary was speaking, the King casually picked up a revolver from a table and pointed it at Ziegler's temple. Ziegler, after a momentary shock, realized that the King would not dare to shoot him, and he calmly went on talking. Several times Ludwig lowered the revolver then took aim again. Finally the King, slightly irritated at having failed to unnerve Ziegler, put the weapon down. 'Amazing,' he remarked, 'the sort of things they make nowadays. See how convincingly this has been made to look like a revolver, and it's only a thermometer!'[6]

It was small wonder that Ziegler eventually found the job of Cabinet Secretary too much for him. Pleading illness, he resigned in the autumn of 1879. The following April the King, after inviting him to a private performance and to dinner at Berg, pleaded with him to return. Ziegler agreed, but henceforth relations between them were marked by increasing friction, and Ziegler resigned for good in January 1883. He was replaced by Alexander Schneider.

In the same year, 1883, Holnstein fell into disgrace because of his refusal to continue trying to raise loans. He and the King had never really liked each other. Now Holnstein became openly hostile and was to play a major part in Ludwig's downfall.

Ludwig was strangely contradictory in his treatment of those who worked for him. At times he was kind and considerate, at other times thoughtless to an extraordinary degree. He expected people to serve him unconditionally, and was outraged when anyone found his demands excessive. In this way he lost many loyal friends who might otherwise have been at his side when his enemies were gathering against him.

One such friend was his equerry, Richard Hornig, who served him with self-sacrifice for eighteen years. One of his duties was to follow Ludwig's carriage or sleigh on horseback, even in the most bitter cold. Sometimes he would have to dismount and, bare-headed and with freezing fingers, adjust the King's ermine rug or peel an orange for him. Often only a liberal supply of spirits enabled him to stay upright in the saddle. It was only in 1878 that he was given permission to ride behind in a carriage. On his journeys the King would take open-air picnics, even in vile weather, and Hornig was obliged to serve him. As a result he often suffered from bad throat inflammations. Because Hornig was an intelligent and educated man, Ludwig often entrusted him with assignments which had to be kept secret or which the King's secretariat was unwilling to handle. Consequently Hornig often found himself in conflict with the staff of the secretariat, but if he refused an assignment he incurred the King's displeasure.

Hornig persistently refused offers of a title from Ludwig. He did, however, accept the gift of a house and large grounds at Seeleiten on the Starnberg lake. Once a week when at Berg Ludwig would go there for dinner. Despite his initial opposition to Hornig's marriage, he came to like Frau Hornig and would enjoy playing with the children and giving them presents. In the relaxed domesticity of the Hornig household he got a glimpse of the life that he himself could never have.

The relationship between the two men was marred by periodic rows. In 1871, for example, Ludwig wrote to a member of his staff that Hornig had 'behaved shamefully towards me, revealing his deceitful, hypocritical character in all its hatefulness'.[7] This breach was soon healed, but there were other quarrels between them. In 1883, for example, there was a noisy scene at Herrenchiemsee when Hornig tried to restrain the King from using his umbrella to smash some ornaments which had been carried out in plaster instead of in marble.

Hornig sadly watched his friend's mind deteriorate and his behaviour become increasingly grotesque. He observed the unscrupulous and scheming people who increasingly came to dominate the King's entourage. He saw the often brutal way in which Ludwig treated his servants. He himself was ordered to raise money in preposterous ways. Other members of Ludwig's staff humoured him and pretended to obey these far-fetched orders, but Hornig was evidently not willing to do this. One day early in 1886 he declared that he could no longer go on searching for money. At this Ludwig flew into a rage and told him to leave the house. They never met again, but Hornig was not totally disgraced as he subsequently became head of the royal stud at Rohrenfeld on the Danube. He did not relinquish his house at Seeleiten.

Meanwhile there had been many changes in the royal secretariat. The Court Secretary Düfflipp had resigned in 1877, mainly because he had been unable to persuade the King of the need to spend less money. He was replaced by the former police lawyer, Ludwig von Bürkel. Düfflipp estimated that Bürkel would not be able to hold out for more than two years before the King's finances collapsed altogether. In fact Bürkel lasted for five years, though at the end of that time the royal purse was in debt to the tune of $7\frac{1}{2}$ million marks. Bürkel was replaced by Philipp Pfister, who in turn was replaced after five months by Hermann Gresser, a retired army captain. Gresser fared little better, and was ousted in favour of Ludwig von Klug. The latter was more astute than his predecessors and retained his position until after Ludwig's death.

Towards the end of his reign Ludwig was spending only about three months of every year in Munich. The brash life of the capital became increasingly unbearable to him in comparison with the serenity of the mountains, woods and lakes. And so he spent more and more time travelling, often at night, through the countryside surrounding his castles and hunting lodges. Sometimes he would walk for hours along the shore of Lake Starnberg, a group of lackeys following ten minutes behind. Sometimes he would travel in a gilt coach festooned with Baroque carving and surmounted by angels supporting a crown. In snowy weather he would take to an ornate open sleigh, likewise gilt, with a great curving prow ending in a pair of putti holding up a lantern, and with a seat at the back for the King's footman. The sleigh would be pulled by four magnificent white horses steered by two outriders. The figure of the King, half-hidden by an ermine rug and wearing the familiar black overcoat and bowler hat, looked slightly out of place in comparison with the powdered wigs and elaborate livery of the footmen and outriders. In the darkness these journeys could be hazardous, especially as the King liked to travel at high speed. Sometimes they would lose their way, and on one occasion one of the outriders nearly plunged over a precipice. The peasants were filled with wonder when they caught sight of this fairy-tale conveyance passing their windows on winter nights, and the King's nocturnal excursions rapidly became legendary among the people of the Bavarian Alps.

Whereas in Munich Ludwig would take every precaution to avoid even being glimpsed by the public, in the country his behaviour was quite different. In Munich there were socialist elements hostile to the monarchy, and he even feared assassination, but among the deeply conservative alpine people he could feel safe and at ease. Secure in their respect and affection, he was able to display exactly the right mixture of dignity and easy informality, instead of having to hide behind a rigid barrier of protocol as he did with people nearer to his own rank.

The peasant families who gave him shelter by their firesides during his outings were afterwards rewarded by presents such as large bouquets of flowers. Giving presents had always been one of his great passions, and it continued until the end of his life. Each year, as Christmas approached, Hohenschwangau became an Aladdin's cave of jewellery, books, pictures and objets d'art waiting to be presented as gifts. Birthdays were also not forgotten. One young cavalryman, whose birthday fell during a period of duty at Hohenschwangau, was astonished to be summoned into the King's presence and given an enormous cake, two bottles of wine, cigars and other luxuries. Reports of such gestures and of Ludwig's friendly encounters with peasants spread rapidly, and during his last years he was loved by the country people of Bavaria as few of his predecessors had been.

Many stories are also told of his kindness towards animals. One day a wild chamois burst into the mirror room at Linderhof and did considerable damage, but when a servant tried to chase the animal out Ludwig ordered that it be left alone. 'At least he doesn't tell lies,' the King remarked.[8] On another occasion he invited his favourite grey mare to dinner and had her served a sumptuous meal on the best crockery, which she afterwards proceeded to smash. Not since Caligula made his horse a consul had such a bizarre scene been witnessed.

For many years there had been doubts about Ludwig's sanity. Now these were reinforced by increasingly numerous reports of his odd behaviour. By this time he preferred to live by night, waking up at around seven o'clock in the evening, having lunch at about midnight, supper in the early hours of the morning and going to bed when most people were rising. This in itself was not evidence of madness, but the strange things he did at night were another matter. As early as February 1868 it was reported that Ludwig would sometimes spend an entire night riding around the Court Riding School in Munich. Imagining that he was travelling to, say, Innsbruck, he would calculate how many laps were necessary in order to cover the equivalent distance. At the half-way stage he would dismount and have a picnic, then continue until he had reached his imaginary goal. Curiously enough, Albert Speer, Hitler's former armaments minister, resorted to a similar practice while serving a twenty-year sentence in Spandau prison after the Second World War. In order to overcome boredom he walked repeatedly around the prison yard, calculating the distance he covered each day and imagining – that he was progressing on foot around the world. Interestingly, he knew at the time about Ludwig's nocturnal rides.[9]

Perhaps Ludwig's 'mania' had just as logical a basis as Speer's. It is less easy, however, to explain away some of his other oddities. The orders he issued became progressively far-fetched. In 1879 we find him writing to Bürkel demanding that the latter organize a kind of country-wide spy network to 'combat the bad elements that are spread everywhere'.[10] More fantastic still was the order he gave to his stable quartermaster, Hesselschwerdt, to travel to Italy and recruit some bandits to capture the Prussian

Crown Prince during a visit to Mentone and to keep him chained in a cave and fed on bread and water.

His treatment of his servants became increasingly tyrannical. Although he would sometimes show great kindness, as in the case of the cavalryman's birthday, the slightest offence would bring sudden and violent retribution on these unfortunate lackeys. He would box their ears, kick them or even empty washbasins over their heads. They had to follow an elaborate set of rules. For example, if they unexpectedly met the King in a corridor or anteroom they were to bow as low as possible and on no account look him in the face. For breaking this rule the valet Mayr had to wear a black mask in the King's presence for more than a year. As Ludwig explained to Ziegler: 'He has to wear a mask so that I don't see his criminal countenance.'[11] In the royal presence it was also forbidden to clear one's throat, cough, sneeze or speak Bavarian dialect. Sometimes the King went so far as to order those who had offended him to be flogged, locked up or executed. These orders were fortunately ignored, but had Ludwig been a medieval king it is likely that quite a number of people who had displeased him might have been killed before he was finally removed from the throne. It is worth mentioning here, however, that when he was his true self he detested the thought of capital punishment, and he commuted nearly every death sentence that was passed to him for signing.

There is no doubt that Ludwig was now living more and more in a world of total fantasy. Sometimes he would dress up as Louis XIV, sometimes he would don his Lohengrin costume and float around the Venus Grotto in his cockleshell-shaped boat. On occasions his servants would pass the door of his dining-room and hear him carrying on a conversation with imaginary dinner guests of the French court. His veneration for Queen Marie Antoinette was so great that whenever he passed a statue of her on the terrace at Linderhof he always took off his hat and stroked the cheeks of the statue. It was in imitation of Louis XIV that he cultivated his extraordinary manner of walking. Among the many people who commented on this was Gottfried von Böhm, who described it as follows: 'This walk was a total mockery of nature. Taking great strides he threw his long legs out in front of him as if he wanted to hurl them away from him, then he brought the front foot down as though with each step he was trying to crush a scorpion.'[12]

The King also suffered from hallucinations. He would hear imaginary sounds in an adjoining room and demand to know what they were. To pacify him the servants would pretend that one of them had accidentally made a noise while carrying out some duty and would apologize for the disturbance. The bluff Hornig refused to admit to hearing these noises, to which the King declared that he must have lost his hearing in the artillery. Ludwig would also see imaginary objects. Once he told Mayr to put away a knife, and when Mayr objected that there was no knife in the room the King blurted out: 'But there should be one there. Where have you put it? Why have you put it away? Put it back immediately.'[13]

This mental deterioration was accompanied by a physical one. He now suffered increasingly from severe headaches which went on for long periods. Toothaches also continued to bother him. His appearance in these last years is typified by a photograph taken in 1884; it shows a man of massive build with a flabby-cheeked face and a wispy moustache drooping mournfully down to his chin. His eyes stare absently out from beneath the faintly comic bowler hat with upturned brim which seemed to have become his favourite headgear. His weak health had forced him to give up riding. In any case even the stoutest horse would by now have found it hard to carry him. This worsening of his looks must have been one of the reasons for his dislike of being looked at and his shunning of company.

A heart-rending anecdote illustrating his loneliness is related by Bürkel, who came one day to bring the King an invitation to a function in Munich.

> Naturally he refused. I pressed it on him and said how much his people loved him and with what rejoicing he would be greeted in Munich after all this time. 'I cannot! I cannot!' he replied, rubbing his forehead. 'It is frightful, but I can no longer bear to be stared at by thousands of people, to smile and extend greetings a thousand times, to ask questions of people who mean nothing to me and to listen to answers that do not interest me. No! No! There is no longer any escape from my solitude!' Then, softly and sadly he added to me in a whisper: 'Sometimes, when I have read myself to exhaustion and everything is quiet, I have an irresistible urge to hear a human voice. Then I call one of the domestic servants or outriders and ask him to tell me about his home and his family.' And, with a sadness that pierced my heart, he concluded: 'Otherwise I would completely forget the art of speech.' There was no other explanation: a terrible demon in him held him back from returning to the world; he wrestled with this dark power and was overcome.[14]

Ludwig had given his last dinner party in 1884, with the Prince and Princess Ludwig Ferdinand as guests. It was a year of farewells. In June Elisabeth of Austria was staying on Lake Starnberg and one day rowed with her daughters Gisela and Valerie across to the Roseninsel. She was unable to see Ludwig, but left him a poem she had written comparing herself to a seagull and him to an eagle and sending greetings 'from foam-crested billows to thee in thy kingdom of snow'. In the autumn of the same year he saw his mother for the last time. They spent a happy day together in the old castle of Hohenschwangau. After that he communicated with her only in writing. All his life Ludwig had loved writing letters to people he cherished. Now most of these people were gone, including his dear Sibylle von Leonrod who had died in 1881. Now his mother was one of the few to whom he could pour out his heart. On 9 March 1886 he wrote to her from Hohenschwangau:

> In remembrance of tomorrow's anniversary of Father's death, and because I am not in Munich as usual at this time of year, I feel urged to get in touch with you in this way. During the near future I shall remain here anyhow, as what ought to have happened has not yet happened. Because of profoundly sad experiences I am unhappy and in a bad temper and must wait until the reason for it (the earlier the better) disappears. It is disagreeable to write or say more about it, and I beseech you not to say anything to anybody – even about these pointers. I very much enjoyed the magnificent winter here and would rather like to go to town as usual now . . . The throne room of the new Castle is not quite finished yet, but the pictures, which are very beautiful, are finished . . . Just now the mountains are reflecting the morning sun. I am sending you a little Russian altar; I shall remember you in my prayers. In inmost love I kiss your hand, dear Mother,
>
> Your grateful son,
> Ludwig.[15]

Two days later he wrote to her after she had visited Otto:

> I do hope that you found Otto well. Today I dreamt I spoke to him for a long time. It is deplorable that it is not possible in reality. I thank you heartily for your dear wishes that I should be happy. That I have not been happy for months has to do with the buildings.[16]

Ludwig was here alluding to the money problems that were holding up his building projects. Generously his mother wrote offering to place at his disposal all the money under her control, but he wrote back on 23 March 1886:

I feel urged to send you my warmest thanks for your charming offer, which is too kind of you; but I would like to ask you to allow me to decline. Through some sort of manipulation the head of the Secretariat must succeed in adjusting this matter in time . . . For some days I have been suffering from a heavy catarrh and pains in my eyes, which I got from reading too much.[17]

In his letters to his mother Ludwig concealed the full extent of his despair. But to Dürckheim and others he increasingly spoke of suicide and repeatedly asked to be provided with a supply of poison. It was not only the money problems that depressed him, but also his bad health, his disillusion with the world and the feeling that his whole life was somehow sliding towards an abyss. At one time he had been able to count on many loyal friends and helpers. Now most of them had gone. The trusty Dürckheim still remained, but increasingly Ludwig relied on men like Hesselschwerdt, whom Böhm met in 1885 and described as follows: 'He did not exactly represent the noblest incarnation of the Bavarian type, but he spoke in a businesslike manner and behaved suavely. I do not know why he nevertheless filled me with a certain mistrust.'[18] With such people around him Ludwig was in a dangerously vulnerable position. As mentioned in Chapter 15, it was Hesselschwerdt who allegedly procured cavalry soldiers and other young men as sexual partners for Ludwig in his latter years.

One of the most serious consequences of this lack of trustworthy advisers was that there was now no one who could prevent Ludwig from losing all sense of reality where money was concerned. As long as he had people likeDüfflipp around him there was at least some restraint on his ever-mounting debts, but Düfflipp had resigned as Court Secretary in 1877, mainly because his pleas for economy had fallen on deaf ears, and since then the King had been spending with increasing abandon. As it was Ludwig's financial crisis which triggered off the plot against him, it is necessary to understand the whole background to the crisis and the ways in which Ludwig had raised money in the past.

One particular source of money, which was not publicly known about until many years after Ludwig's death, is of great importance to the whole story. From the early 1870s Ludwig received a series of payments from Bismarck, and it has been maintained (though not proved) that these were a reward for the writing of the *Kaiserbrief*, the crucial letter from Ludwig in 1871 inviting Wilhelm I of Prussia to become Emperor of Germany. These payments remained a well-kept secret throughout the Bismarck era, but in 1892 it leaked out that the new Imperial Chancellor, Count Leo von Caprivi, had made the puzzling discovery that a sum of 300,000 marks had been sent annually to Munich over a number of years. No record had been made as to whom or what the money was intended for, but it was rumoured that it had something to do with Ludwig's part in the founding of the Reich.

For many years German historians were reluctant to believe that this story was true, because of the discreditable light which it threw not only on Ludwig but also on the genesis of the Reich. For example, when Böhm published the first extensive biography of Ludwig in 1922 he wrote:

> I have always doubted the veracity of this account because Ludwig II was at that time not yet in financial need, and such a comparatively trivial sum must have seemed to him a poor compensation for partial surrender of the sovereignty to which he held so firmly.[19]

Ludwig's subsequent biographers, relying largely on Böhm, have played down the whole affair and thereby missed the very important implications it has, both for our judgement of Ludwig and in a wider historical context. But since Böhm's work appeared, research has reopened the possibility that the payments in question were indeed made, and for precisely the reason that so many people found embarrassing: that is to say they were a form of bribe from Bismarck to Ludwig in return for his help by way of the *Kaiserbrief*. Böhm is also wrong in saying that Ludwig was not in financial need at the time, for he had by then spent large sums on Wagner and had already embarked on his costly building programme.

Conclusive evidence about the payments was discovered by Robert Nöll von der Nahmer, who tells the whole story in his book *Bismarcks Reptilienfonds* (Bismarck's Reptile Fund, 1968). Nöll discovered in the German Federal Archives at Koblenz the diaries of Prince Eulenberg, who in the early 1890s was Prussian envoy in Munich, and these provided the documentary proof that had so far been lacking.

It appeared that in 1892, when the puzzling discovery about the payments was made in Berlin, the Bavarian envoy to Prussia, Count Lerchenfeld, hastened to Munich to warn the Prime Minister, Crailsheim, and to tell him that, to make matters worse, a publisher in Zürich was threatening to issue a booklet exposing the whole affair. Curiously enough, it was only then that the Prussian envoy Eulenberg heard anything about the payments. When he indignantly asked for an explanation from the Prussian Foreign Minister he was told that he had been deliberately kept in the dark to avoid encumbering him with knowledge that might place him in an embarrassing situation. Now that the cat was out of the bag Eulenberg hurried off to Crailsheim to ask for a full account of the whole business. In his diary he recorded what Crailsheim told him:

The payments began in 1871 after Ludwig II agreed, on Holnstein's suggestion, to give his approval to the proclamation of King Wilhelm as Kaiser in return for recompense in cash. This is stated by Ludwig in a letter to Holnstein which the latter, in his own justification, has placed in the files. The payments continued annually until 1884. The sum amounted to 300,000 marks per year. A larger payment is supposed to have been made in 1871. This is not apparent from the list and available receipts.

The instalments of 300,000 were listed by Holnstein as only 250,000. He always (that is each year) kept ten per cent and maintained that he had been authorized to do so by the King because in the legacy of Prince Karl of Bavaria (his wife's grandfather) he had not been given sufficient consideration. The King wished to compensate him (this sounds rather improbable).[20]

As Holnstein had delivered 250,000 marks each year and kept 30,000, this left 20,000. This sum was evidently placed in a special fund for paying Ludwig's barber and dentist. Eulenberg remarked that the latter demanded 'horrendous fees' for his frequent treatment of Ludwig's decay-ridden teeth. Holnstein went on drawing from the 'reptile fund' until 1888. When the story leaked out in 1892 he resigned from the court service pleading illness. The regent Luitpold, Ludwig's uncle, in any case did not wish to retain him. Before 1892 Luitpold knew nothing of the payments. One puzzling piece of the whole jigsaw puzzle is the fact that on 5 June 1886, just over a week before Ludwig's death, the sum of 250,000 marks was paid out from the reptile fund, but no record has been found of its having been received, and it is not known for whom the money was destined.

Was Ludwig guilty of writing the *Kaiserbrief* for a bribe or not? Nöll claims that he was, but it is only fair to say that since Nöll's book appeared in 1968 further research has once again thrown doubt on the matter. Professor Hans Rall, a leading expert on Ludwig II, has pointed out that the payments began not in 1871, as Nöll's quote from Eulenburg stated, but in 1873, and that the sum which Ludwig received was minute in comparison to the amount paid to the state of Bavaria. There is, he maintains, no causal connection between the *Kaiserbrief* and the payments that began two years later.

Clearly, however, suspicious minds might have assumed a causal connection had the payments become public knowledge, and this could have given rise to an immense scandal. Therefore, whether there was genuine bribery involved or not it was necessary to keep the matter secret. The potential scandal gave Bismarck a secret hold over Ludwig. Probably this remained implicit and no direct blackmail was ever exerted, but Ludwig knew that it would be dangerous to go against Bismarck's wishes. Twice he obliged Bismarck by removing envoys to Berlin of whom the Chancellor disapproved. 'You cannot believe,' Ludwig wrote to Wagner, 'how difficult it sometimes is to be a Prussian prefect.'[21] It is significant that this letter came to the notice of the Prussian envoy and was reported back to Berlin in January 1883. That this should happen with a private letter shows that someone close to Ludwig was acting as a Prussian spy. The most likely candidate was Holnstein, but by that time the royal entourage was full of spies.

Ludwig had every reason to dislike and fear Bismarck. Yet it is a curious fact that towards the end of Ludwig's life an apparently warm friendship by correspondence existed between the two men, although the only time they had ever met each other face-to-face was when Bismarck had been a guest at Nymphenburg in 1863 when Ludwig was eighteen. In his memoirs Bismarck recalled the occasion as follows:

> At the regular meals which we took during our stay at Nymphen-burg on August 16 and 17 the Crown Prince, afterwards Ludwig II, sat opposite his mother, and next to me . . . Our conversation did not go beyond the ordinary Court subjects. But even so, I thought I recognized in his remarks a talent, a vivacity, and a good sense realized in his future career . . . He made a sympathetic impression on me.[22]

Bismarck always kept a high regard for Ludwig's intelligence and he maintained that there were only two men for whom the King had any real respect: himself and Wagner. Ludwig, for his part, was strangely divided in his attitude to Bismarck. When writing to Wagner he referred to the 'miserable German Reich' under the leadership of 'that Junker from the marches'.[23] But, despite all his anti-Prussian feelings, he sensed the greatness of the Iron Chancellor and must have felt a personal sympathy for him. He knew that his hated cousin, the Prussian Crown Prince, was at loggerheads with Bismarck, and this might have prejudiced him in the latter's favour. He also remembered Bismarck's profession of 'vassalship' to the house of Wittelsbach. On a deeper level he probably felt that, like himself, Bismarck was a man motivated by a grand vision and by the dictates of a powerfully felt destiny. In addition there was the factor of Bismarck's secret payments to him. Perhaps he felt the need to maintain good relations with Bismarck, or possibly he was genuinely grateful to the Chancellor. At any rate when Bismarck went, as he regularly did in the summer, to take the waters at Kissingen – the town that had once been so devastated by his troops – Ludwig placed his best coach horses at the disposal of his old adversary and sent enormous bunches of flowers to the Chancellor's wife. They never repeated their meeting of 1863, but they conducted a lively and wide-ranging correspondence.

Despite the money from Prussia, Ludwig's financial position became steadily worse. And still his building mania continued. By early 1884 his debts had reached a level of $7\frac{1}{2}$ million marks, and the situation became so desperate that an appeal to Bismarck for more funds was necessary. Accordingly the Court Secretary Pfister was dispatched to Berlin incognito. Bismarck was willing to help, and the matter was discussed with his banker, Bleichröder. Before, however, an agreement could be reached with Bleichröder word came that the Bavarian finance minister, Emil von Riedel, had recognized the seriousness of Ludwig's position and its implications for the country and had taken over negotiations for a loan for the King. He was particularly anxious for Bavaria to avoid the undignified spectacle of Ludwig's creditors suing the royal treasury, as they were entitled to do under Bavarian law, and possibly confiscating some of the King's property in lieu of payment. As a result of Riedel's negotiations a loan of $7^{1}/_{2}$ million marks was granted by a south German consortium of banks.

For the time being disaster was averted, but the money was only enough to clear Ludwig's debts. He continued to build as though his coffers were full to overflowing. It was now his chief pleasure in life. Inevitably he soon needed more money. In December 1884 Klug, who was now Court Secretary, found a financier named Söhnlein who was prepared to lend Ludwig 400,000 marks towards the building of Herrenchiemsee on condition that he be given a title. Ludwig at first had scruples about selling a title in this manner, but eventually he agreed. Söhnlein's loan, however, did not go nearly far enough, and by the summer of 1885 the King's debts had taken a further jump of over 6 million marks, bringing the total to nearly 14 million. He therefore calmly wrote to Riedel demanding that the Finance Minister arrange another loan for him so that he could continue his building without hindrance.

This time Riedel was not so accommodating. He wrote to the King pointing out to him the urgent necessity of introducing the strictest measures of economy into his financial affairs. He went on to say that the predicament of the royal treasury had become the subject of comment in the press, especially abroad, in a way that presented a danger to King and throne. Riedel had, he said, done his utmost to find a way of helping the King, but in vain. He could only advise His Majesty to introduce the suggested savings and to avoid any payments which could not be covered. Ludwig, indignant that Riedel should dare to lecture him in this way, declared his intention of finding a new Finance Minister. The other ministers, however, threatened to resign if Riedel were sacked, and Ludwig had to back down.

The crisis had now ceased to be merely a financial matter and had taken on a serious political dimension. The Prime Minister Lutz, who until now had remained fairly aloof from the affair, decided to intervene. He sent a letter to Klug setting out the facts as he saw them. The royal treasury could not hope for any more support from private sources, nor could any money be provided from state funds without special legislation. To obtain that legislation would involve laying the whole question before Parliament. According to Lutz's inquiries any such appeal to Parliament would end in defeat, thus seriously damaging the prestige of the crown. To avoid legal action by the King's creditors and the possible confiscation of his property it was necessary for Ludwig to suspend his building programme, have a precise list of his debts drawn up and allow an examination of the running of his household to see where savings could be made.

Ludwig was now in a panic at the thought of his castles being seized and desecrated by a swarm of creditors. But still he was not willing to follow the economies suggested by Lutz. Instead he wrote to Dürckheim on 28 January 1886:

> If a certain sum is not obtained (in about four weeks) Linderhof and Herrenchiemsee, my property, will be legally confiscated! If this is not forestalled in good time I shall either kill myself promptly or else leave immediately and for ever the accursed land where such an abominable thing could happen. I now ask you, my dear Count, and urgently enjoin you to assemble an armed force which will be true and loyal to me, will not be intimidated by anything and will be able, if the worst comes to the worst and the required

sum does not materialize, to throw out the rebellious mob of legal scoundrels.[24]

Dürckheim beseeched the King to give up this idea, as it could have serious consequences for his authority and might lead to fateful proceedings in Parliament and in the Reichstag. To this Ludwig wrote back a peeved letter saying that it was no concern of Parliament and the Reichstag and that whoever had put these ideas into Dürckheim's head was clearly 'of a democratic turn of mind'.[25]

Next he wrote to the Minister of the Interior, Baron von Feilitzsch, repeating his fear of the possible confiscation of his castles and stating that he needed 20 million marks. A sum that would merely cover his debts was no use at all. What he needed was enough to continue building. Feilitzsch wrote back that a loan of 20 million was outside the realms of possibility. Rich people who could lend such sums were not to be found, and there was no hope of help from Parliament. Only a few weeks earlier, he said, a prominent member of the Patriotic Party, which held the majority in the assembly, had mentioned the subject at a public meeting and had hinted at the unwillingness of his party to support financial aid for the King.

Ludwig, in desperation, now turned to increasingly far-fetched schemes of his own for raising money. Dürckheim, in a memoir, describes one of these schemes, which Holnstein had told him about. The King had heard that in Persia there lived an infinitely rich man who would be able to lend or give the required millions. Accordingly a member of the royal stable staff was ordered to go to Persia to find the mysterious million-aire and ask for a loan. The emissary, realizing the futility of the quest, remained in Munich and, after a plausible interval, reported to the King at Hohenschwangau that the rich Persian had recently died of cholera.

Dürckheim himself was ordered to go on a similar wild goose chase. He was to travel to England and ask the Duke of Westminster for a loan of 10 million marks. When this order was relayed to him by Hesselschwerdt, Dürckheim replied: 'All right, tell the King that you have given me the order and that I shall report to him about it in writing tomorrow.' Hesselschwerdt answered that he could not do that as he himself was supposed to have travelled to Naples to find a loan for the King but had not gone as he knew the mission was useless.[26]

Other servants were ordered to seek loans from the King of Sweden, the Sultan of Turkey, and the Shah of Persia and other foreign potentates. One of them was told to go to Brazil. Hesselschwerdt was also asked to make an indirect approach to the Austrian emperor. None of these ideas, however, came to anything, and Ludwig decided to resort to more desperate measures. A group of trusted servants was sent to Frankfurt with instructions to rob the Rothschild bank. The group travelled to Frankfurt but had no intention of carrying out their orders. They remained there for a few days and then returned to Munich, where some representatives of the King were waiting at the station to hear the result of the mission. The men reported that they had prepared the robbery most carefully but that a last-minute hitch had prevented their carrying it out.

Then the dreaded blow fell. In April the company supplying gas and water to Ludwig's castles, which was owed over 100,000 marks, decided to take their claim to court. The hearing was fixed for 9 May. This was the first legal action on the part of the creditors. Others would surely follow. This brought Ludwig to his senses, and once again he consulted Bismarck. The Chancellor sent a sensible reply, saying that he should appeal to Parliament. If he did this, the Chancellor said, he was confident that the Bavarian people would grant their King enough money not only to pay his debts but also to finish the building work that he had already embarked upon. Ludwig decided to follow this advice and issued instructions that the matter was to be put before Parliament.

The ministers of the government, however, did not share Bismarck's view that an appeal to Parliament would succeed. And they knew that the failure of such an appeal would do great harm to the crown. They sent a message to the King telling him this and urging him instead to return to Munich and take in hand personally the regulation of his finances. Ludwig was incensed and began once again to plan a change of government. Hesselschwerdt and Ludwig's barber Hoppe, who by then had evidently become one of his main advisers, were entrusted with the task of finding the new ministers. The former Cabinet Secretary Ziegler was asked to organize the dissolution of Parliament and the change of government. He refused, and strongly advised against any such course of action.

The whole affair had now blown up into a major political crisis. Lutz was not willing to see his government replaced by one chosen by Ludwig's barber and quartermaster. And even if this could be averted it was clear that there was going to be a never-ending conflict between the King and the government over Ludwig's chronic over-spending. Reports of His Majesty's strange behaviour gave Lutz and his colleagues the opportunity that they needed. If the King could be proved insane then he could legally be deposed and replaced by his brother Otto. As Otto was already insane there would have to be a Regency under Prince Luitpold, Ludwig's uncle. It was this plan that was now set in motion.

18

The Trap Closes

The events leading up to Ludwig's deposition are recounted by Dürckheim in a revealing personal memoir[1] which is worth quoting extensively. Dürckheim writes:

> It was a great misfortune for the King that in the autumn of 1885 he did not go to Munich as he normally did at that time of year. On the evening of 10 November he was already on his way [presumably from Hohenschwangau] when he suddenly gave the order to turn back and proceeded instead to Linderhof. After a few days there he went to Hohenschwangau.

Dürckheim says that he never learned the reason for Ludwig's fateful change of mind, but speculates that it might have had something to do with the fact that some private performances that he had been looking forward to had been cancelled because of expense. The memoir continues:

> This not coming to Munich in the late autumn of 1885 was a decisive turning point – the beginning of the end. The consequence was . . . that the King also did not come to Munich in the winter (February 1886). If he had come the whole course of the crisis

would have been different . . . the catastrophe of 1886 would not have happened – or at least not in the way that it did.

Dürckheim describes how Hesselschwerdt and other people surrounding the King did their best to isolate him more and more so as to gain increasing control over him. He goes on:

During the winter and spring of 1886 there was a sudden disappearance of the loyalty and discretion that had hitherto been shown when the King's private affairs were discussed. Newspaper articles began to appear with increasing frequency – at first only abroad but then also in the Bavarian press. There was public discussion and criticism in all the beer houses, and no longer just about the financial calamities of the privy purse and the King's buildings but about all His Majesty's habits, manner of living, and so on. There were insinuations of the worst kind about the cavalrymen who for some time had been acting as lackeys, and the most exaggerated stories were told about presents to these people, about His Majesty's maltreatment of them, and so on. Remarkably enough, the police never intervened, although in public hostelries the crudest kind of *lèse-majesté* was continually being uttered. As always in such cases, relatively few people were the instigators. The majority listen, agree or disagree, go home and repeat what they have heard. It is very easy to create a mood when no hindrance is placed in the way!

It must occur to the impartial observer that there was a deliberate intention to create sentiments of hostility towards the person of the King. This would never have succeeded to the same extent if the King had been in Munich as usual from the middle of February to the middle of May.

But there he stayed, far away and isolated in Hohenschwangau. What person could (or would) disprove the things that were being said about his mental condition?

Dürckheim mentions a dinner party given by the Saxon envoy at which a Bavarian government minister was overheard to say: 'If he (i.e. the King) does not give way, then we shall make short shrift with him.' This was a reference to the demands for Ludwig to cut down his spending. Dürckheim goes on to describe a conversation with Count Holnstein at a race meeting one day in May 1886:

Count Holnstein took me by the arm and went with me behind the grandstand as fewer people were circulating there than in front. Then the following conversation ensued:

Holnstein: 'Things are getting worse all the time with the King; there's no holding him any more; he's a complete lunatic.'

I: 'Come now, you're exaggerating. I don't believe it.'

Holnstein: 'No, no, it's true. You don't know all the details that I do. The King is also physically ill. He suffers from terrible congestion and headaches. He's always having to put an ice-pack on his head. None of the people around him can stand it any more. He mistreats them all. In the matter of money he just won't listen to reason. And his behaviour borders on treason . . .'

I (interrupting): 'How so? What do you mean by that?'

Holnstein: 'The business with Orléans, from whom he wanted to ask for a loan in return for an assurance of Bavaria's neutrality in a Franco-German war. [This evidently referred to Prince Ferdinand of Orléans, the husband of Ludwig's former fiancée Sophie.] Fortunately the whole thing was thwarted before it could be carried out.'

I: 'That I absolutely refuse to believe. I'm sure it's untrue.'

Holnstein: 'Yes, yes, it is true. And now it really is high time that something was done. If anyone can help to throw light on the King's mental state, either through his own observations or through the possession of letters from His Majesty and so forth, he should no longer hold back. You should also make yourself heard. You must have recent letters from the King.'

I: 'Certainly I have, but they most emphatically do not prove that the King is mentally ill, on the contrary. In any case what you ask is quite impossible; it goes against my position and my duty.'

Holnstein: 'Aha! But I am of a quite different opinion. I am a good Bavarian.'

Holnstein then hinted at the danger of Prussia intervening if something were not done. His statement that he was 'a good Bavarian' was of course pure hypocrisy.

By the time of this conversation the plot to depose Ludwig was already well advanced. The sixty-five-year-old Prince Luitpold had agreed to the ministers' plan that he should step in as Regent. Immediately after this the Bavarian envoy in Berlin, Count Lerchenfeld, had told Bismarck what was afoot. In a report to the Foreign Minister, Crailsheim, he described his two conversations with Bismarck as follows:

> I explained briefly to the Imperial Chancellor that the mental condition of the King did not permit that the ruling of the country should be left in his hands any longer. I pointed out that, although it was the financial question that had given the impetus towards grasping a speedy remedy, this was in itself a secondary consideration in comparison with other sad things. I described the mood in the country and the impossibility of an orderly regime under the King. I told the Prince that the person next in line to the throne, in agreement with the ministers of government, had decided that the country could no longer be exposed to incalculable dangers. Things had come to a limit in Bavaria . . .
>
> The Imperial Chancellor expressed his deep regret at this sad state of affairs. He found it deeply painful as the King had always been a gracious benefactor to him. But . . . if the King was unfit to rule because of mental illness, then, in all conscience, he could see no reason to keep him on the throne.[2]

Lerchenfeld then showed Bismarck a letter from Ludwig ordering that one of his servants be deported to America. This somewhat slender piece of evidence was apparently enough to convince Bismarck that Ludwig should be deposed. It is important to realize, however, that the process of deposition was in no way started on Bismarck's initiative. Furthermore, the way in which it was carried out went against the Chancellor's advice. In his discussion with Lerchenfeld he urged that the ministers should seek the authority of Parliament for what they were planning, so as to avoid the appearance of a secret *coup d'état* and the odium that might then fall on Prince Luitpold. This advice was not followed, and the plot proceeded in a highly clandestine manner.

On 23 March Lutz had held a discussion about the King's mental condition with Dr Bernhard von Gudden, a distinguished expert on mental illnesses who was Professor of Psychiatry at the University of Munich and director of the District Mental Hospital of Upper Bavaria. Gudden was a short, bearded man, nearly sixty-two years old. He was evidently a humane and enlightened person who had done much to advance the study of psychiatry and believed in handling insane patients with the minimum of physical restraint. Gudden listened carefully to what Lutz told him and agreed that the evidence seemed to indicate that the King was suffering from a form of paranoia or what was then called 'primary madness', a condition which would nowadays be classified as a variety of schizophrenia. According to a psychiatric textbook published in 1883, this form of insanity was characterized by 'a pathologically false conception of the relationship of oneself to the environment' in which 'healthy perception is impaired to a high degree by sensory illusions of all kinds as well as through subjective interpretation of normal impressions'.[3] Following this meeting it was agreed that Gudden would prepare a medical 'appraisal' (*Gutachten*) to provide the legal basis for Ludwig's deposition. Gudden had the reputation of being a careful and rigorous researcher, but in this case he made a serious professional blunder by agreeing to make his diagnosis without seeing the patient. Since it was inconceivable that the King would allow himself to be examined by a psychiatrist, it was necessary to prepare the appraisal on the basis of documents and of other people's observations. A search was now instigated to provide Gudden with the necessary information. Hence Holnstein's request to Dürckheim for letters from the King.

Those who joined Dürckheim in refusing to cooperate included Bürkel and Mayr – despite his undignified treatment at the hands of Ludwig, Mayr did not testify until after the King's death. Many, however, came forward with documentary or eye-witness evidence. All of Ludwig's strange habits, his mal-treatment of his servants, his rages, the gruesome punishments he ordered, his far-fetched schemes for raising money, his hallu-cinations – all these were raked together and fed to Gudden and his colleagues. Some of this evidence was no doubt maliciously exaggerated by those of the King's entourage who had a grudge against him, but not all of it can be dismissed on those grounds. Hornig, for example, only agreed with great reluctance to help with the inquiry. He had nothing personal to gain by testifying against the King and was not the kind of man to bear a grudge. The inclusion of his evidence, therefore, lends at least some weight to Gudden's appraisal.

In drawing up the appraisal Gudden was aided by three other doctors: his son-in-law, Dr Hubert Grashey, and Drs Hagen and Hubrich. It was dated 8 June 1886 and pronounced the following judgement about the King's condition:

> The mental powers of His Majesty are disrupted to such an extent that all judgement is lacking, and his thinking is in total contradic-tion with reality . . . Gripped by the illusion that he holds absolute power in abundance and made lonely by self-isolation, he stands like a blind man without a guide at the edge of the abyss.

The report concluded with the following three observations:

1. His Majesty is in a very far advanced state of insanity and is suffering from a form of mental illness which is well known

to alienists by experience and is designated by the name of paranoia (madness).

2. In view of this form of the illness, which develops gradually and progressively and extends over a large number of years, His Majesty must be declared incurable, and a further decay of his mental capacities is to be expected with certainty.

3. Because of the illness free volition on the part of His Majesty is impossible. Consequently he must be regarded as incapable of exercising government; and this incapacity will last, not only for longer than a year, but for the entire remainder of his life.[4]

It is now generally recognized that the medical appraisal was a rather shoddy piece of work and that there is grave doubt as to whether the King was really insane as the term is understood by modern psychiatry. Clearly, however, he was far from healthy either in mind or in body, and we must at this stage ask the question: what precisely was the matter with him?

During the Nazi period a booklet on the mental illness of Ludwig and Otto, by a certain Dr Brewitz, was published by the Party Information Office.[5] This was part of a propaganda campaign to discredit the princely families of Germany by claiming that they suffered from hereditary illness. It does, however, cite some genuine instances of madness on both sides of Ludwig's family. Two of Queen Marie's ancestors, for example, the Landgrave Ludwig IX of Hessen-Darmstadt and his daughter Karoline, both suffered from hallucinations and shared Ludwig's habit of living a nocturnal existence. On his father's side, Ludwig's aunt Alexandra suffered from the firm conviction that she had once swallowed a glass piano and spent many years in a mental home. Brewitz also mentions that it was said of Ludwig's father, Maximilian II, that he had contracted syphilis in his youth and suggests that this could have been a contributory factor to the illnesses of both Ludwig and Otto. Chapman-Huston, in his biography of Ludwig, also mentions the possibility that Maximilian suffered from syphilis, but does not draw any conclusions from it as to Ludwig's illness. Might the syphilis theory provide a convincing explanation of Ludwig's condition? This can almost certainly now be discounted, but it may be worth considering some of the evidence for and against.

The question was examined in the early 1970s in an article by Dr Christoph Biermann in a German medical journal.[6] Although the family history, Biermann writes, shows a certain tendency to schizophrenia, 'the postmortem findings point without doubt to an organic disease of the brain'. Biermann goes on to suggest that this disease was in fact a late development of syphilis. 'I think,' he says, 'that the description of Ludwig II's complaints, his mental symptoms and his manner of behaviour towards the end of his life can easily be attributed to late-syphilis.' Biermann then asks whether the disease was contracted early (i.e. congenitally, during pregnancy or in early infancy), or later in Ludwig's life. An early infection could have been transmitted by his father or possibly by his wet-nurse who, it will be remembered, died when he was seven months old of 'typhoid fever', possibly a euphemism for syphilis. An infection in adulthood would be most likely to have occurred through homosexual contact. But the infection could have come about in many other ways, for, contrary to popular superstition, the disease can be acquired quite independently of sexual intercourse. In England, for example, the custom of kissing a Bible when taking a judicial oath repeatedly led to syphilitic infection. If the illness had been contracted in adulthood any abnormal psychological tendencies or other symptoms which he showed in adolescence would have to be accounted for by other factors, such as the history of mental disturbance in the family. On the other hand a congenital or childhood infection would probably have developed sooner. On balance Biermann is inclined to think that 'syphilis acquired in adulthood is more likely, but an infection in early childhood cannot be ruled out'.

If Ludwig did suffer from syphilis it would, as Biermann points out, explain the veil of silence that has obscured the full truth about the case ever since Ludwig's death. Had it become known the prestige of crown and state would have suffered. As Lutz stated in 1886 after Ludwig's death, the publication of certain facts would injure public esteem for His Majesty and be disrespectful to the dead. To suppress these facts would have been in the interests not only of the government and regent but also of those who saw Ludwig as a hero and wished to preserve his memory as unblemished as possible. Furthermore, any disclosure about syphilis would inevitably have opened up the whole question of the King's sex-life in general. As Böhm writes:

> Things that were long kept secret were related one day by the Court Secretary Klug at a hunting party given by Baron K. I do not feel myself called upon to repeat here details that belong properly to medical history. They give a historical basis to the good and bad jokes that were circulating about this matter and proved how justified was the wish of the Master of the Horse that the investigations of the King's illness should not extend to sexual relations. Von Gudden agreed to this request all the more readily as more than enough incriminating evidence was already available.[7]

Since the publication of the previous edition of this book, the question of Ludwig's illness has been much discussed. One person who has done so is the distinguished German psychiatrist Prof. Heinz Häfner, who argues in his book *Ein König wird beseitigt* (A King is Removed) that Ludwig was not mentally ill and that the psychological assessment was a travesty. Häfner examines the evidence for the syphilis theory and essentially rejects it. Whereas he says that Otto's acute mental and physical deterioration were very likely to have been due to syphilis contracted in his youth, Ludwig's symptoms were entirely different. He had none of the dementia and progressive paralysis from which Otto suffered. On the basis of a close examination of the autopsy report on Ludwig, Häfner concludes that Ludwig had suffered an attack of meningitis at the age of seven months, 'resulting in lifelong and often severe headaches'. He adds that probably the King's insomnia and extreme touchiness were due to the presence of scar tissue on the meninx.[8]

Häfner acknowledges Ludwig's tendency to live in a fantasy world, his *folie de grandeur*, his homoeroticism and his self-isolation, but he argues that none of this amounted to mental illness. The move to declare him insane was, he argues, essentially motivated by the ambition of Prince Luitpold to assume the regency.

To return to the deposition, once Gudden and his team had completed their medical appraisal events moved swiftly. On 10 June a proclamation was issued announcing the Regency. It was signed by Prince Luitpold and the leading members of the government, and explained that as the King was suffering from a serious illness which prevented the exercise of his duties as monarch, and as Prince Otto was suffering from a similar illness, Luitpold was taking over as Regent in conformity with the Bavarian constitution. In fact the constitutional legality of the move was questionable. Although the constitution provided for a Regency during the minority of a monarch or in the event of the monarch being unfit to rule for a prolonged period, it did not state who was entitled to initiate the establishing of a Regency.

Meanwhile, on 9 June, a commission had set out for Hohenschwangau to inform Ludwig of the steps that were being taken and to place him in medical custody. The commission consisted of the following members: Baron von Crailsheim, the minister responsible for the royal house and for foreign affairs; Counts Holnstein and Törring, who had been named as joint legal guardians of the King; Dr Karl Rumpler, secretary to the commission; Lieutenant-Colonel Baron von Washington who was to act as a sort of aide-de-camp to the deposed King; Dr von Gudden, his assistant Dr Franz Carl Müller, and a number of medical orderlies.

The commissioners arrived at the old castle of Hohenschwangau late in the evening and at about midnight sat down to supper to plan how they would tackle the King, who was staying up the hill in the new castle (which I shall refer to by its present name of Neuschwanstein). It was decided that first of all a message from Luitpold would be read to him, then Gudden would step forward with his assistant and orderlies and explain to the King that he was to be taken into medical care. They would then proceed with the King to Linderhof castle, where he was to be kept under supervision. Later Berg was decided upon as a more suitable place of confinement.

At about one o'clock in the morning Holnstein found Ludwig's coachman, Fritz Osterholzer, harnessing the horses to the royal carriage, as he normally did at this time in case the King wished to go for a night ride. Holnstein told him to put the horses away again, and when Osterholzer remonstrated that this would go against the King's command, Holnstein replied that it was now Prince Luitpold and not the King who was in command. Realizing what was afoot, Osterholzer slipped off and made his way up to Neuschwanstein. The King was pacing up and down the Singers' Hall declaiming verses from Schiller when the coachman, breathless and incoherent, was ushered in. When Ludwig finally understood Osterholzer's message he was incredulous, and at first refused to accept that there could be any danger. If there were, he said, Hesselschwerdt would have warned him. He did not know that Hesselschwerdt had been zealously cooperating in the conspiracy. At length, however, Ludwig ordered that the entrance to the castle be barred and that his own guard be reinforced by a contingent of police from Füssen. At the same time he asked that the local fire brigades be alerted.

The commissioners, in the meantime, had learned that the King had been warned of their presence and decided that there was not a moment to lose. Towards four o'clock in the morning they drove up the steep, winding road to Neuschwanstein through cold, driving rain. Slowly the dawn began to break and the looming outline of the castle came dimly into view against the mist-laden slopes beyond. They arrived at the gateway to find it guarded by gendarmes who stoutly refused to admit them.

At this point bizarre comedy intervened in the shape of an eccentric old lady of Spanish descent named Baroness Spera von Truchsess, a famous figure in Munich society for her colourful personality and lavish parties. She was already known to Dr Gudden, as she had been an inmate of his asylum on a number of occasions. The Baroness was an ardent admirer of the King, and often stayed at the Alpenrose inn at Hohenschwangau in the hope of catching an occasional glimpse of him. Now, accompanied by her landlady and a female servant, she appeared brandishing a parasol and proceeded to berate the members of the commission for their shameful disloyalty. Gaining access to the castle, where the commission had failed, she was taken to the King. She implored him to travel at once to Munich and offered to accompany him. Ludwig politely refused, and it was several hours before the Baroness could be persuaded to leave.

At about half past five in the morning the commissioners climbed back into their carriages and returned to Hohenschwangau castle feeling disconsolate and humiliated. But an even worse humiliation awaited them. Soon after their arrival back at the old castle a detachment of local police arrived with orders from the King to arrest them. They were then marched in two groups up to Neuschwanstein again, passing on the way groups of local people who jeered at them. By now the whole neighbourhood knew what was happening.

On arrival at Neuschwanstein the commissioners were imprisoned in the gate lodge, where they learned that the King had ordered that their eyes should be put out and that they should be flogged and starved. These orders were not carried out, but the group spent a terrifying and uncomfortable two hours. Meanwhile Rumpler, alone of the commissioners, had managed to escape and report the plight of the others. A message was sent to the officer in charge of the police detachment at Neuschwanstein, informing him of the proclamation of the Regency and ordering him to release the prisoners. This he decided to comply with, and the commissioners were allowed to go. By late in the evening they were back in Munich feeling thoroughly foolish.

At this juncture Ludwig could still have saved himself by taking resolute action, but by now a sort of paralysis of the will had overtaken him. Shortly after the departure of the commissioners, Count Dürckheim arrived on the King's urgent summons and urged him to go to Munich where he was sure to be loyally received by the people. But Ludwig shook his head and said that the air of Munich did not suit him. Dürckheim then suggested that they go together across the border into the Austrian Tyrol, which was only an hour's carriage ride away. Again Ludwig declined. He was tired, he said; and anyway what would he do in the Tyrol? He did, however, consent to send a number of telegrams. One went to Bismarck, informing the Chancellor of his plight; another was sent to Baron von Franckenstein, who was to come for consultations about forming a new government of which he would be the head. Dürckheim prudently had these telegrams sent from Reutte across the Austrian border. Franckenstein duly received his in Marienbad and loyally set out to consult with the King, but he was intercepted in Munich and told that he would be allowed to go no further. Bismarck replied immediately with the same advice that Ludwig had been given repeatedly: he should go to Munich and rally the support of his people. But even the Iron Chancellor's advice failed to stir Ludwig into action.

Then came an order from the War Ministry that Dürckheim was to return to Munich immediately. When he asked Ludwig whether he should obey, the King did not directly countermand the order but begged him to remain. The Count was, he said, the only person left in the world whom he could trust. Dürckheim wired back that it was impossible for him to return. This brought another message from Munich, this time signed by Luitpold, threatening that Dürckheim would be tried for high treason if he delayed any further. Now Ludwig told him to wire Luitpold and ask for his permission to remain. It was the first tacit admission of defeat on Ludwig's part. A final telegram came back telling Dürckheim that the order from the War Ministry must be obeyed. At this Ludwig graciously told the Count to go, as otherwise his career and future would be ruined. Before Dürckheim left, the King begged him to obtain some poison from the nearest chemist. 'I can no longer live,' he declared.[9] It was a request which the aide-de-camp had to refuse. On his return Dürckheim was arrested, and told that he would be charged for his alleged part in a counter-proclamation which had been issued in the King's name but was later found to be of doubtful authenticity. He was soon released and the charge was later dropped. His subsequent military career did not suffer.

By the morning of 11 June the police watch on the castle had been dissolved and most of the servants had drifted away. To those who remained Ludwig railed bitterly against his uncle and talked repeatedly of suicide. 'Tell Hoppe,' he said, 'that if he comes tomorrow to attend to my hair he will find my head in the Pöllat gorge. I hope that God will forgive me this step.'[10]

Mournfully Ludwig wandered through the castle, up and down the stairways and even through the unfinished parts where gaps were spanned by makeshift bridges of boards. It filled him with sadness to think that he must bid farewell to this temple which he had planned and created so lovingly. He lingered in the great Singers' Hall with its murals from *Parzival*, and took his leave of the six Holy Kings in the empty alcove of the Throne Room. He stood in the colonnade and looked for the last time at the magnificent sweeping view over the plain of the river Lech. Occasionally he took up a book to read, then put it away again. Towards the end of the day he drank a great deal.

His coachman, Osterholzer, and his gentleman-in-waiting, Weber, still urged the King to take action to save his throne and to call upon the help of a loyal battalion of chasseurs who were stationed not far away. But by now Ludwig was resigned. 'No blood shall be shed for my sake,' he declared. 'I shall settle my account with Heaven.'[10] He kept asking his valet Mayr for the key to the great tower of the castle. Mayr, knowing his master's suicidal intentions, pretended that the key could not be found.

With Weber the King held a discussion about the immortality of the soul. Later he called Weber to his study and presented him with 1,200 marks and a valuable jewelled brooch. The young man, deeply moved, burst into tears.

Ludwig had declared his intention of dying at half past midnight, the same time at which he had been born. As the hour approached he kept asking for the key to the tower, and Mayr grew increasingly apprehensive. Perhaps the King would throw himself from another part of the castle. Then, at about midnight, a second commission from Munich arrived. It consisted of Dr Gudden, his assistant Dr Müller and five asylum orderlies. They were accompanied by a number of policemen. Müller has left a detailed account of what followed.[11]

This time there was no guard to prevent the entry of the commissioners. Instead Mayr came rushing towards them urging them to hurry as His Majesty was bent on suicide. An ambush was then planned. Medical attendants and policemen were to block the stairway leading to the tower above and below the point where it connected with a corridor to the King's apartments. Mayr was to give the key to the King, and when Ludwig emerged he was to be confronted by Gudden, with the police and attendants at the ready in case he made a dash up or down the stairs. All this went according to plan. When the King began to make for the staircase Gudden stepped out and intercepted him with the words: 'Your Majesty, it is the saddest task of my life that I am performing. Your Majesty's case has been appraised by four alienists, and following their pronouncement Prince Luitpold has assumed the Regency. I have the order to accompany Your Majesty to Berg tonight. If it pleases Your Majesty the carriage will depart at four o'clock.'

The blow had fallen sooner than the King had expected. He let out an exclamation of surprise, then looked around him with a bewildered expression. 'What do you want?' he kept repeating. 'What's all this about?' He staggered slightly as he was ushered back into his bedroom, where the orderlies stood by the windows. Gudden introduced the members of the group and reminded the King of an audience which he, Gudden, had been given in 1874. Ludwig remembered it clearly. A long conversation then ensued, during which Ludwig behaved with great dignity considering the shocked and humiliated state that he must have been in. He first inquired about the condition of Otto, then asked Gudden: 'How can you declare me insane when you have not examined me?' The doctor replied that this was not necessary in view of the abundance of documentary proof. Ludwig wanted to know how long the 'cure' would last. Gudden said that, according to the constitution, a Regency could be declared if the King were incapable of ruling for more than a year, therefore a year would be the minimum – an illogical reply since it assumed for constitutional convenience what had not yet been proved, namely that the King would be *non compos mentis* for more than a year. Ludwig then remarked: 'It could go quicker. They could do what they did to the Sultan. It's quite easy to dispatch a man from the world.' Gudden replied that his honour forbade him to answer this remark.

At length, in the early hours of the morning, the party descended to the forecourt where three carriages were waiting in the rain. On the journey to Berg the King sat alone in the middle carriage, whose doors had been fixed so that they could not be opened from the inside. As the dawn broke Ludwig caught a last glimpse of his Grail castle, 'sacred and out of reach'. Within a year would begin the incessant march of tourists through its rooms.

19

Prophecies Fulfilled

It is reported that the dying King Maximilian II breathed into the ear of his elder son a prophecy which is attributed to the sixteenth-century French astrologer Nostradamus but which does not appear in the standard editions of his work. It runs:

> *Quand le Vendredi Saint tombera sur le jour de Saint George,*
> *Pâques sur le jour de Saint Marc,*
> *Et la Fête Dieu sur le jour de Saint Jean,*
> *Tout le monde pleurera.*[1]

(When Good Friday falls on St George's day, Easter on St Mark's day and Corpus Christi on St John's day, all the world will weep.)

Perhaps because St George was considered the patron saint of Bavaria, this prophecy was thought to be of special significance to that country. Like his father, Ludwig II is said to have been haunted by it and to have mentioned it in tones of foreboding to a number of people.[2] Presumably he grew more apprehensive as 1886 approached, for in that year all the conditions of the prophecy were due to be fulfilled, if St John's day is taken to mean the day of John the Baptist, 24 June.

Waves had often beckoned Ludwig when he felt depressed. Now, on that gloomy June day when he was brought from Neuschwanstein to Berg, it was the waves of Lake Starnberg that beckoned – the same ones that in happier and sunnier times he had sailed over in a paddle-steamer named *Tristan*.

Ludwig and his captors arrived at Berg just after noon on Saturday 12 June. When the carriage door was unlocked the King stepped out surprisingly cool and composed. Jauntily he greeted the police guard on duty outside the castle with the words: 'Ah, Sauer, it's nice that you are in service here again.'[3] Then he went inside.

In the past few days a team of workmen, under the direction of Gudden's son-in-law, Dr Grashey, had been turning the little castle into a one-patient mental asylum. In the King's apartments the doors had been arranged so that they could only be opened from the outside with a key, peepholes had been cut into them so that the patient could be kept under constant observation, and sockets had been drilled into the stonework around the windows for bars to be fitted. To the King it must have seemed a terrible desecration of the place that had always been one of his favourite homes. But if he was upset he did not show it. He inspected all the arrangements as though he were a fastidious and important hotel guest. Finally he declared that everything was in order and retired to bed at three o'clock.

Meanwhile Gudden was delighted with the way things were going, as he told Grashey during a conversation over cigars late in the afternoon. The King was behaving in a gratifyingly reasonable manner. Nevertheless, Gudden was concerned about Ludwig's frequently voiced fear of an attempt on his life and also about the way in which his thoughts turned to suicide when he became over-excited. Gudden told the other doctors that the patient must be treated considerately and given as much freedom as possible. Müller, however, had misgivings about

Gudden's optimism and remarked to Washington that his chief was suddenly no longer the careful man that he used to be.

In the middle of the night the King woke up and wanted to get dressed, but was told by the orderlies that he could not yet have his clothes. This was part of Gudden's plan to return his patient to a normal pattern of waking and sleeping. Ludwig paced up and down the room in his night clothes. Then, having consumed an orange and some bread, he went back to bed.

The next day was Whit Sunday, 13 June. The King awoke at about 6.00 a.m. and called for Gudden, whom he asked if he could be allowed to attend Mass. The doctor refused, but still Ludwig did not lose his composure. He told the doctor that he was not angry at Prince Luitpold, who was only a tool of the plotters. He was, however, deeply offended at the choice of the perfidious Holnstein as one of the two guardians appointed to look after his legal interests. Next Ludwig held a long conversation with Grashey, during which the prospects for a recovery were discussed and he was assured that if a new medical appraisal pronounced him cured he would be restored to his former position. Meanwhile, Grashey said, he should live a well-regulated life, drink only a small amount of spirits, take plenty of exercise in the fresh air and choose a regular occupation. Ludwig seemed to agree to all this and asked Grashey to have his library transported from Neuschwanstein.

Gudden explained to Washington that he intended to try to break His Majesty's habit of solitude and to accustom him once again to being with people. It is open to question whether Gudden really held any hope of a permanent cure, for when Grashey remarked that he did not think the King's condition was irredeemable Gudden became annoyed and said: 'We'll talk about that another time.'[4]

Having eaten a hearty breakfast Ludwig called Gudden again, and after a while the doctor emerged from the King's room and announced that he and His Majesty would be going for a walk. Accordingly they set out shortly after 11 o'clock with one of the orderlies, Hack, following at a discreet distance. Over lunch afterwards Gudden reported to the other doctors that the walk had gone well, and told them that he and the King would be taking another walk in the evening, this time unaccompanied by anyone else. Müller and Washington tried to dissuade Gudden from taking such a risk, but he brushed their objections aside with a laugh and called them *Schwarzseher* (pessimists). Gudden had been impressed by the apparently calm and good-natured way in which Ludwig had been behaving. He did not know that the King prided himself on the art of dissimulation. Cabinet Secretary Ziegler once observed that 'His Majesty was at his friendliest when behind my back the order had gone out to find a successor for me.'[5] Ludwig had clearly been working skilfully on Gudden to gain his confidence.

In the early afternoon Ludwig was allowed a conversation with Friedrich Zanders, the head butler at Berg, but not before Gudden had made Zanders promise that he would not speak of escape plans or in any other way give the King hope of release. Zanders intended to gain Gudden's trust and wait for an occasion when the doctor would omit to extract such a promise from him, but what he proposed to do when the opportunity came is not known. His account of the incident was relayed at second hand in a work by Otto Gerold about the King's last days.[6]

'Do you think,' the King asked Zanders, 'that they will keep me locked up for over a year just like I am today?'

Zanders tried to reassure him by saying that his nervous affliction might be cured in a much shorter time and that there would then be no reason to keep him in medical care.

'Do you really believe that?' the King asked. 'L'appetit vient en mangeant. My uncle Luitpold will get used to ruling and come to like it so much that he will never let me out again.'

Ludwig then asked how many policemen were in the castle grounds and whether they would shoot at him. Zanders replied that there were six to eight policemen in the park but that they were not armed.

The interview with Zanders was followed by one with Müller, during which Ludwig asked the doctor about his medical training, his eyesight and his literary education. He appeared to take a liking to Müller, but told him that he did not trust the other doctors. One of them, he said, might find some unobtrusive means of killing him. When Müller had left, the King called for opera glasses and scanned the lake. Then he sat down to a late lunch, washed down with a mug of beer, five glasses of wine and two of arrack.

About an hour after he had finished this repast, the King sent for Gudden to go on the promised evening walk. The doctor told his colleagues that he would be back at about eight o'clock for supper. He and Ludwig donned hats and overcoats and armed themselves with umbrellas. When they emerged from the castle with one of the orderlies, Mauder, the rain had temporarily stopped, and Ludwig handed his umbrella to Mauder and politely asked him to roll it up. Mauder did so and gave the umbrella back to the King, who then walked on ahead. As Mauder turned back to the castle Gudden, who was a few paces behind, said quietly: 'No orderlies must go with us.' He then caught up with the King, and the two walked away from the castle, Ludwig towering so high above the doctor that if he had lifted his arm to a horizontal position Gudden could have walked underneath it. The departure of the incongruous pair was watched by Lauterbach, the policeman on duty at the castle, who was probably the last person to see them alive.

The two men began their walk at about 6.45 p.m., taking the lakeside path through the park in a southerly direction. There were three policemen on patrol in the grounds at the time, but they had not been told about the walk. Lauterbach saw one of these policemen, Klier by name, returning to the castle by an upper path some distance from the lakeside. Anxious that someone should keep an eye on the King and Gudden, Lauterbach told Klier to go back down the lower path and look out for the two men. About half an hour later Klier came back saying that he had seen no sign of either of them. Lauterbach told him to go and have another look. At about this time, that is between 7.45 and 8.00, Lauterbach noticed several boats travelling southwards down the lake quite close to the bank. Another half hour passed, and once again Klier came back having drawn a blank. The other two policemen patrolling the park happened to be nowhere near where the two walkers had gone. They later reported that they had heard nothing unusual.

By this time Müller had become alarmed and sent out more policemen to search the grounds. Still there was no result, and by 8.30 almost everyone in the castle, servants, orderlies and policemen, was scouring the area. Outside one of the gates of the estate some of the policemen noticed the fresh tracks of a carriage pointing in the direction of Munich, but of the King and Gudden there was no sign. Darkness fell and the rain grew heavy. The searchers armed themselves with lanterns and torches.

At about ten o'clock one of the search party spotted something black in the shallows near the edge of the bank. It proved to be the King's jacket and overcoat, the sleeves of the former inside those of the latter, indicating that they had both been thrown off hurriedly together. Another searcher found Ludwig's umbrella about three paces away on the bank. Gudden's umbrella lay nearby and the two hats were discovered on the shore line about 60 and 80 paces respectively towards the castle, lying as though they had been washed up by the waves.

The discoveries were reported to Müller, who now rushed down to the lake with Huber, the steward of the castle, and roused a fisherman who took them out on to the lake in his boat. They set off southwards, skirting the shore, and had not gone far before Huber cried out and pointed at something in the water. It was the King's body, floating face downwards. Gudden's body was a few paces away, his feet sunk into the muddy bed of the lake. With the help of some of the orderlies who had waded into the water, the bodies were hauled into the boat and then brought to the shore where Müller tried artificial respiration. But it was hopeless. Clearly both men had been dead for some hours. The King's watch had stopped at 6.54, Gudden's at 8.00, but the discrepancy is not as significant as has sometimes been maintained; watches can stop for a number of reasons, and in any case it was well known that Gudden frequently forgot to wind his.

The bodies were taken back to the castle, where the deaths were legally registered by a group of officials from Starnberg who had been summoned to the scene. Müller recorded in his book that the King's body showed no injuries, whereas Gudden's bore scratch marks on the forehead and nose and a bruise over the right eye as though from a fist blow; in addition the doctor's right middle fingernail was half torn off. These injuries to Gudden's body were also observed by Dr Grashey and by the Prussian acting chargé d'affaires, Eulenberg (later ambassador) who happened to be staying on Lake Starnberg at the time. But, strangely enough, the injuries did not feature in Müller's official record nor in the record made by the officers from Starnberg. Ludwig's face, according to Müller's book, bore 'a dark, domineering, almost tyrannical expression', whereas Gudden's had not lost 'the friendly smile that in his life had won over so many patients'.[7] When the doctor's death certificate was issued it recorded death by drowning. In the King's case, however, the cause of death was curiously left blank.

The corpses were ceremoniously laid in two rooms on the first floor. They were covered with blue silk sheets and surrounded by flowers. Two policemen kept watch over the King's body and four orderlies over that of Gudden. On the morning of Whit Monday a messenger arrived with a bunch of jasmine to be placed in the King's right hand. It was sent by Elisabeth of Austria, who was staying across the lake at Feldafing and had probably been unaware of the King's presence at Berg until his death was reported to her.

We must now try to reconstruct what happened on the fateful evening of 13 June. First of all we must examine the theory, particularly popular among present-day admirers of Ludwig, that his death was not suicide or an accident but murder. What might the motive for such a murder have been?

Let us suppose for a moment that there was a causal connection between the *Kaiserbrief* and the payments which Ludwig had been receiving from Bismarck. As long as Ludwig was on the throne the existence of these payments could only be an advantage to Bismarck, since Ludwig would never wish them to become public knowledge. Once off the throne, however, he had less to lose by telling the story, and if he had done so this would have been a great embarrassment to both Bavaria and Prussia. By a long stretch of the imagination this might have provided a motive for Ludwig to be murdered on the instigation of Berlin, but not a very strong one – for one thing there were other people, such as Holnstein, who knew about the payments.

A stronger motive might have been the threat of Ludwig's supporters organizing an armed rebellion and causing a civil war. It is known that there was widespread support and sympathy for the King. Therefore as long as he was alive this remained a possibility. Mary Queen of Scots was executed for a similar reason. A civil war would have been in the interests neither of Bavaria nor of Prussia, so it is conceivable that either Berlin or the government in Munich or both together could have instigated a murder plot. If Prussia was involved this again might explain the mysterious 250,000 marks.

Leaving aside the motive, let us turn to what we know of the actual death. A number of independent and official observers examined the scene afterwards and took special note of the footmarks on the bed of the lake. From their findings it appeared that what had happened was roughly as follows. Ludwig entered the water closely followed by Gudden. They proceeded out into the lake for perhaps twenty or thirty paces. At this point a struggle ensued (as shown by the churned-up mud) during which Gudden received injuries and drowned, possibly having first suffered a heart attack or collapsed for some other reason. The King then went further out, to the point where the floor of the lake drops abruptly into much deeper water. Here he drowned also. Subsequently both bodies drifted in a semi-upright position back towards the shore, as indicated by the marks left by the dragging feet. Hence the bodies ended up in water which, as has been rightly observed, was too shallow for them to have drowned in. At some point their hats came off and also drifted in.

This sounds plausible, but there are a number of things that are not clear. For example, was Ludwig trying to escape or to commit suicide? Hornig afterwards maintained that the King was heading for his (Hornig's) house at Seeleiten, about $2\frac{1}{2}$ kilometres ($1\frac{1}{2}$ miles) down the coast from Berg. According to an account quoted by Rupert Hacker, Hornig, his brother and a relative, Count Ramaldi, spent the whole morning and afternoon of 13 June travelling in a boat up and down the coast near Berg regardless of the rain. When the three men returned at dusk Ramaldi announced to his wife: 'We found a hat. It's all over!'[8] Probably their boat was one of those seen by Müller. If the account is true it certainly seems to indicate a rescue plan, of which Ludwig might or might not have been aware. The carriage marks outside the gates might also have been connected with a rescue attempt (or, for that matter, with an assassination attempt). So was Ludwig trying to escape?

A man bent on drowning himself does not have to throw off his jacket and coat. On the other hand Ludwig might have done this to get away from Gudden more quickly or because Gudden was clawing at his clothes. The physical evidence about Ludwig's intentions is therefore inconclusive. We can only say that, remembering his frequent talk in the past about killing himself, it seems likely that he did intend to commit suicide.

But was his death a result of that intention? And what was the actual manner of it? The doctors were not confident enough to record death by drowning. On this point it is also interesting to learn of the comments of two local people who saw the body, a fisherman named Jakob Lidl and a priest named Martin Beck. Both of them had seen many drowned corpses and both declared that no drowned man ever looked as the King did. So if he did not drown, how might he have died? Gudden is reported to have written to his relatives that he 'always had the wherewithal about him to overcome the King' even though he was Ludwig's physical inferior.[9] So it is likely that he carried chloroform and possibly used it on the King during the struggle, killing him in the process, since it is quite possible for chloroform to cause death, and then collapsing himself from a heart attack. This would not quite tally with the reported distribution of the footmarks, but the evidence regarding those is rather contradictory. If this is what happened it seems most likely that Gudden killed the King accidentally rather than intentionally. From what we know of the doctor it is hard to picture him in the role of an assassin. So we have the possibility that Ludwig's death was technically manslaughter, even if he entered the water with the intention of committing suicide.

As for the possibility of murder, this is very hard to sustain on the basis of what we know about the King's death. Gudden, as I have said, seems a most unlikely murderer, and it is hard to believe that he would even have been a party to such a crime. On the other hand, if another assassin was involved, why did he choose such an inopportune moment for his work, presumably involving the necessity of killing Gudden as well as the King? As Ludwig himself had observed, there were many much easier ways of doing away with somebody.

Whatever the cause of death, the news of it sent shock waves through Bavaria. 'O, what a noble mind is here o'erthrown!' declared the *Neueste Nachrichten* of 14 June, quoting *Hamlet*. The same issue of the newspaper carried a proclamation from Prince Luitpold announcing that, following the tragedy, Prince Otto was now the King. But, since Otto's own illness prevented him from ruling, he, Luitpold, would continue as Regent. When the news was brought to Otto he was unable to comprehend it and immediately began to talk about something else. He lived on until 1916.

After lying all of Whit Monday at Berg, Ludwig's body was taken in the evening to Munich where an autopsy was performed. The body was then placed in the chapel of the Residenz, where it lay in state surrounded by flowers and candles and dressed in the black velvet apparel of a Grand Master of the Knights of St Hubert. Around his neck were the collar and badge of the order. His left hand rested on a sword. His right still held Elisabeth's jasmine. The distorted expression on his face had been smoothed away by the embalmers, and the scars left on his skull by the autopsy had been carefully concealed.

The funeral took place on Saturday 19 June. All shops and businesses in Munich were closed, black flags were flying from many buildings, and vast crowds lined the route from the Residenz to the church of St Michael. A long procession wound its way through the town centre to the accompaniment of church bells and funeral music from military bands. In it marched soldiers, city officials, church dignitaries, schoolchildren and royalty. In the centre was the hearse, bearing the coffin and drawn by eight horses. It was surrounded by officers, gentlemen-in-waiting and members of the Order of St Hubert. Then came Prince Luitpold, walking with bowed head, followed by the Crown Princes of Austria and Prussia, the Princes of the Bavarian royal house and nobility from all over Germany. At 2.30 p.m. the procession reached the church, where the King's body was laid to rest in the crypt. Later his heart, encased in an ornate silver-gilt vase, was placed in the Votive Chapel at Alt-Otting, close to those of his father, grandfather and other members of the Wittelsbach family.

Those who watched the procession were witnessing not just the departure of a King but also the final passing of the old Bavaria. It is just possible that in the crowd was a seven-year-old Jewish boy named Albert Einstein, who lived with his parents in the suburb of Sendling. Thus the father of modern physics, the laser beam and the atomic bomb might have paid his last respects to the man whom Verlaine called 'the only true king of his century'.

The Queen Mother outlived Ludwig by three years, sustained by the Catholic faith which she had embraced in 1874. In memory of her son she had a wooden cross erected in the lake at the point where he drowned, and on the bank she had a rather ungainly chapel built in a neo-Romanesque style. The cross has since been replaced with one donated by the faithful members of the Ludwig II Society 'in memory of 13 June 1886', which they refer to as the *Todestag* (death-day). On this day every year a group of Ludwig's admirers gather by the shore of the lake. Prayers are said, and a wreath is placed on the cross. The legend of the Swan King lives on.

Epilogue: The Cult of the Swan King

This book would be incomplete if I were to end it at Ludwig's death. The Regency of Prince Luitpold lasted from 1886 until his death in 1912. Luitpold was succeeded by his son Ludwig, who in 1913 assumed the title of Ludwig III, even though the crown still belonged to the insane Otto who remained locked away at Fürstenried. Otto died in 1916, and Ludwig III ruled on until 1918 when he was dethroned. In subsequent years Bavaria saw the short-lived Soviet Republic of 1918–19, Hitler's abortive coup of 1923, the years of the Third Reich, and finally a respectable existence as one of the states of the Federal Republic of Germany. Even today, however, Bavaria retains a greater sense of independence than the other states, and there is still a vociferous monarchist movement, strongly fuelled by the legend of Ludwig II. Another volume could quite easily be written about the cult which has grown up around his legend. Indeed I can think of no other figure of recent history who has been the subject of so many novels, poems and plays and the object of so much hero-worship. In a way Ludwig is a nineteenth-century King Arthur – a real person who has been surpassed by his mythological persona.

His life was the stuff of which poetry and fiction are made, and novels about him began to appear even in his lifetime. A fascinating anthology of extracts from the vast volume of Ludwig II literature is provided by Ludwig Hollweck in his book *Er war ein König* (1979), which also contains an interesting introductory survey of the material.

Ludwig made his first appearance in fiction as early as 1875, in a work by Joseph Emruwe called *Die Königs-Schlösser. Ein Dichtertraum* (The Royal Castles: A Poetic Dream). Here the narrator is taken in his dream on a tour of the Bavarian royal residences by an old man representing the protective spirit of the House of Wittelsbach. At intervals Ludwig II also appears to the dreamer. Subsequent novels about Ludwig written while he was still alive include the gruesome story by the French writer Catulle Mendès, *Le Roi Vierge* (The Virgin King), published in 1884, in which the King is thinly disguised as Friedrich II of Thuringia, who dies playing the part of Christ in the Oberammergau Passion Play. As he hangs on the cross he has his servant Karl, dressed as a Roman soldier, pierce him with a lance.

After the King's death the literature mushroomed, and along with it the kitschy souvenirs: postcards of tearful Bavarian maidens kissing the King's statue or clasping his image to their breasts, painted busts and statuettes of him, beer mugs and brooches bearing his portrait. The trade in such objects continues unabated to this day.

Much of the writing about him is of the same quality as the souvenirs: cheap, sentimental and crude. And it is not confined to Germany and France. An English example is Max Pemberton's pasteboard novel, *The Mad King Dies* (1938). Characteristic of this work is the scene where Josephine Scheffsky sings the part of Venus in a private performance of *Tannhäuser*, given in the grounds of 'an ancient Schloss' where 'the Venusberg was a very bower framed in the woods – a great tent sheltering the amorous goddess from the night winds and all the tokens of her frailties artistically emphasized'. The ballet master instructs the singer to take her clothes off, telling her that 'Venus wears very little on these occasions and we expect such a true artiste as Josephine Schefzky [sic] to do real justice to her rôle'. Ludwig takes the part of Tannhäuser and, during the scene in the Venus-berg, cuddles Josephine 'as any ploughman might have cuddled a village maiden'. But when the scene is over the King flings his Venus from him and strides away 'as though the devil were at his heels'. Soon afterwards she learns that 'jumping upon his horse, he had ridden away to Munich with all the speed he could command'.

Not all the literature dealing with Ludwig is of this quality. He appears also in the work of more distinguished writers. For example, in Thomas Mann's *Doktor Faustus* (1948) the narrator and a friend visit Linderhof and have an argument over whether Ludwig was mad. In France, Verlaine celebrated Ludwig in verse, calling him 'le seul vrai roi de ce siècle' (the only true king of this century), and Louis le Cardonnel paid homage to him in a poem entitled *A Louis II de Bavière*. In 2004 the American poet Nick Norwood published a book of verse entitled *A Palace for the Heart: Laments for Ludwig II*, with an evocative picture of Neuschwanstein on the cover.[1] Biographies and historical books on him are legion – well over a hundred in German alone and many in other languages. Ludwig is even the subject of a Japanese *manga* (comic) in three volumes by the author and illustrator You Higuri. And, not surprisingly, a search of the internet under his name yields tens of thousands of entries.

Ludwig has also been the subject of at least six films. The first completed one was a silent film, made in 1920 with Ferdinand Bonn playing the part of Ludwig. In 1929 came a second film with Wilhelm Dieterle in the leading role, and in 1954 a third, starring O.W. Fischer with Klaus Kinski as Otto. In 1966 the subject was filmed by Frédéric Rossif, and in 1972 appeared two more films, directed by Luchino Visconti and Hans-Jürgen Syberberg. Other films in which he features include Tony Palmer's 1983 film *Wagner* with Richard Burton in the title role and the Hungarian actor László Gálffi as King Ludwig – the Wagner cult has of course fed into the Ludwig cult as has the cult of Ludwig's cousin, the Empress Elisabeth of Austria ('Sissi'). There have also been numerous plays about the King, an opera by the Swiss composer Heinrich Sutermeister, and two musicals: *Ludwig II. – Sehnsucht nach dem Paradies* (Ludwig II – A Yearning for Paradise), which opened in 2000 in a specially built theatre at Füssen near Neuschwanstein, and *Ludwig*^{2} (Ludwig 'squared'), which opened in the same theatre in 2005, but folded after a short time.

Then there are the Ludwig II clubs. In Bavaria alone there are dozens of such clubs and associations, such as the *Guglmänner* ('Men in Hoods'), who claim an ancient lineage and are organized like a chivalric order. They uphold the claim that Ludwig was murdered, demonstrate against instances of *lèse-majesté* and, on the anniversary of Ludwig's death, parade in black robes and pointed masks. Apart from these associations, there are numerous individual devotees of Ludwig. Among the most vociferous upholders of the murder claim is the Berlin author and publisher Peter Glowasz, who has written and published many books about the King.[2]

How are we to account for this extraordinary proliferation of legend, myth and fiction around Ludwig II, to the point of turning him into a cult figure? One reason, I believe, lies in the quality of mystery that surrounds his character and life – his wish 'to remain an eternal enigma to myself and to others' was amply fulfilled. Was he really mad? Was he a homosexual? Were there hidden reasons for the conspiracy against him? Did he drown himself in Lake Starnberg or was he murdered? These questions will continue to be debated.

Where there is mystery there are those who claim to have solved it, and this is another element in the Ludwig II cult. Many of his admirers believe themselves to be in possession of facts, especially about his death, which the general public does not know or refuses to believe; and this knowledge, this consciousness of being privy to secrets, gives them the sensation of belonging to a privileged group. Another factor which binds his supporters together is the feeling that they are championing someone who was a victim of injustice and philistinism.

More generally, Ludwig appeals to many people of the present day because of the world he created. The drab environment and processed culture that surround many of us today make us turn with delight to the visual riches of Neuschwanstein, Linderhof and Herrenchiemsee, and to the stories of Ludwig's colourful and eccentric life. Modern society, while starving us of so much vivid experience in the real world, encourages us to indulge our fantasies through the media and through the things that we consume. Therefore we can easily identify with a man who fulfilled his fantasies on such a grand scale. In Ludwig we detect a style and panache that are markedly lacking in modern public life. But there is something deeper as well. Behind the creation of Ludwig's castles, behind his patronage of Wagner, his private performances and his infatuations, behind the multiple tragedies and failures of his life, we sense the urgency of a mind on a quest, sustained by a bright and powerful vision.

Appendix: Monetary Values

S ome clarification is called for about the various units of German currency to which I have referred in the text. Before the unification of Germany in the early 1870s the south German states, including Bavaria, used gulden (florins), each of which was divided into 60 kreuzer. Prussia and the other north German states used marks and talers (one taler being equal to three marks, and each mark being divided into 10 groschen or 100 pfennige). After the unification, Bavaria adopted the north German system, and in 1873 one Bavarian florin was equal to 1.71 marks. In the same year one English pound was equal to about 12 florins (20.5 marks).

Notes

Preface

1. Quoted from the article on Wagner by Francis King in the encyclopedia *Man, Myth and Magic*, Vol. 106 (London, B.P.C. Publishing, 1971).

Chapter 1: The Northern Apollo Reborn

1. Edmund B. d'Auvergne, *Lola Montez: an adventuress of the forties*, (London, Werner Laurie, undated), p. 166. See also the amusing, if fanciful, portrayal of Lola Montez in George MacDonald Fraser's entertaining novel, *Royal Flash* (Barrie & Jenkins, 1970; Pan Books, 1971), and Max Ophüls's stylish and imaginative film, *Lola Montès* [*sic*], made in 1955 with Martine Carole in the title role.
2. d'Auvergne, op. cit., p. 218.
3. *Abendzeiting*, Munich, 16 October, 1991.
4. Munich, Buchendorfer Verlag, 2002.
5. Rupert Hacker, *Ludwig II. von Bayern in Augenzeugenberichten*, pp. 25–6.
6. ibid., p. 21.
7. ibid., p. 20.
8. Gottfried von Böhm, *Ludwig II., König von Bayern*, p. 2.
9. Desmond Chapman-Huston, *Bavarian Fantasy*, p. 15.
10. Böhm, op. cit., p. 3.
11. Frances Gerard, *The Romance of King Ludwig II of Bavaria*, p. 32.
12. Werner Bertram, *Der Einsame König*, p. 14.

Chapter 2: The Captive Years

1. Desmond Chapman-Huston, *Bavarian Fantasy*, p. 23.
2. ibid., p. 19.
3. ibid., p. 21.
4. ibid., p. 21.
5. Geheimes Hausarchiv 57.5.146.
6. Rupert Hacker, *Ludwig II. von Bayern in Augenzeugenberichten*, p. 26.
7. Desmond Chapman-Huston, *Bavarian Fantasy*, p. 36.
8. ibid., p. 44.
9. ibid., p. 47.
10. Ernest Newman, *The Life of Richard Wagner*, Vol. III, p. 206.

Chapter 3: From Cage to Throne

1. Desmond Chapman-Huston, *Bavarian Fantasy*, p. 53.
2. Gottfried von Böhm, *Ludwig II., König von Bayern*, p. 12.
3. Rupert Hacker, *Ludwig II. von Bayern in Augenzeugenberichten*, p. 43.
4. Böhm, op. cit., p. 15.
5. ibid., p. 16.
6. ibid., pp. 18–19.
7. ibid., p. 19.
8. ibid., p. 20.

Chapter 4: The Coming of the Friend

1. Otto Strobel, introduction to Vol. I of *König Ludwig II. und Richard Wagner, Briefwechsel*, p. xxvi.
2. ibid., p. xxxv.
3. ibid.

Chapter 5: The Second Lola

1. Rupert Hacker, *Ludwig II. von Bayern in Augenzeugenberichten*, p. 65.

2. Otto Strobel, *König Ludwig II. und Richard Wagner, Briefwechsel*, Vol. I, p. xxxvi.
3. *Richard Wagner's Prose Works*, translated by W. A. Ellis (London, Kegan Paul, 1892–9).
4. Desmond Chapman-Huston, *Bavarian Fantasy*, p. 72.
5. Hacker, op. cit., p. 46.
6. Strobel, op. cit., Vol. I, pp. 18–21.
7. ibid., p. 21.
8. Quoted by Ernest Newman, *The Life of Richard Wagner*, Vol. III, pp. 415–16.
9. ibid., p. 389.
10. Strobel, op. cit., Vol. I, p. 49.
11. ibid., p. 36.
12. Newman, op. cit., Vol. III, p. 240.
13. Gottfried von Böhm, *Ludwig II., König von Bayern*, p. 139.
14. Newman, op. cit., Vol. III, p. 370.
15. ibid., p. 353.
16. Wilfrid Blunt, *The Dream King*, p. 66.
17. Newman, op. cit., Vol. III, pp. 231–2.
18. Sebastian Röckl, *Ludwig II. und Richard Wagner*, Vol. II, 1866–83 (Munich C. H. Beck, 1920).
19. Newman, op. cit., Vol. III, pp. 343–4.
20. ibid., p. 241.
21. ibid., p. 242.
22. *Richard Wagner's Prose Works*, Vol. VII, p. 289.
23. ibid., p. 293.
24. ibid., pp. 293–4.

Chapter 6: A Triumph, an Idyll and a Parting

1. Otto Strobel, *König Ludwig II. und Richard Wagner, Briefwechsel*, Vol. I, p. 93.
2. Ernest Newman, *The Life of Richard Wagner*, Vol. III, p. 350.
3. Strobel, op. cit., Vol. I, p. 105.
4. Newman, op. cit., Vol. III, p. 386.
5. Strobel, op. cit., Vol. I, p. 108.

6. ibid., p. 143.

7. ibid., p. 161.

8. ibid., p. 165 n. 1.

9. ibid., Vol. IV, p. 74.

10. Newman, op. cit., Vol. III, p. 444.

11. Werner Richter, *Ludwig II., König von Bayern*, p. 88 n.

12. Newman, op. cit., Vol. III, p. 455.

13. ibid.

14. ibid.

15. ibid., p. 456

16. ibid., p. 458.

17. Strobel, op. cit., Vol. I, p. 226.

18. Newman, op. cit., Vol. III, p. 460.

19. ibid., p. 461.

20. ibid., p. 463.

21. ibid., p. 460.

22. ibid., p. 466.

23. ibid., p. 469.

24. Richter, op. cit., p. 104.

25. Newman, op. cit., Vol. III, p. 471.

Chapter 7: Germany in Turmoil

1. Werner Richter, *Ludwig II., König von Bayern*, p. 109.

2. ibid., p. 110.

3. Otto Strobel, *König Ludwig II. und Richard Wagner, Briefwechsel*, Vol. II, p. xiv.

4. ibid., p. 34.

5. ibid., pp. 37–8.

6. *Memoirs of Prince Hohenlohe*, translated by G. W. Chrystal (London, Heinemann, 1906), Vol. I, p. 150.

7. Strobel, op. cit., Vol. II, p. 63.

8. ibid., p. 65.

9. Rupert Hacker, *Ludwig II. von Bayern in Augenzeugenberichten*, break p. 121.

10. Strobel, op. cit., Vol. II, p. 73.

Chapter 8: Sophie

1. Rupert Hacker, *Ludwig II. von Bayern in Augenzeugenberichten*, p. 133.
2. Gottfried von Böhm, *Ludwig II., König von Bayern*, p. 363.
3. Hacker, op. cit., p. 138.
4. ibid., pp. 139–40.
5. ibid., p. 140.
6. ibid., p. 142.
7. Desmond Chapman-Huston, *Bavarian Fantasy*, p. 120.
8. Hacker, op. cit., p. 141.
9. Otto Strobel, *König Ludwig II. und Richard Wagner, Briefwechsel*, Vol. II, pp. 155–6.
10. Chapman-Huston, op. cit., p. 128.
11. Werner Richter, *Ludwig II., König von Bayern*, p. 173.
12. Hacker, op. cit., pp. 145–6.
13. British Public Record Office, FO.9.183.

Chapter 9: Lilla . . . and Others

1. Gottfried von Böhm, *Ludwig II., König von Bayern*, pp. 385–8.
2. This and other letters from Lilla von Bulyowsky which I have quoted are in Geheimes Hausarchiv, K 55.L4.52.
3. Böhm, op. cit., p. 391.
4. ibid., p. 397.
5. ibid., p. 398.
6. Rupert Hacker, *Ludwig II. von Bayern in Augenzeugenberichten*, p. 149.

Chapter 10: Wagnerian Strains

1. Otto Strobel, *König Ludwig II. und Richard Wagner, Briefwechsel*, Vol. II, p. 141.
2. Ernest Newman, *The Life of Richard Wagner*, Vol. IV, pp. 85–6.
3. Gottfried von Böhm, *Ludwig II., König von Bayern*, p. 148.
4. Strobel, op. cit., Vol. II, p. 185.

5. ibid., Vol. IV, p. 190.
6. Newman, op. cit., Vol. IV, p. 103.
7. ibid., p. 107.
8. Strobel, op. cit., Vol. II, p. 120.
9. ibid., p. 117.
10. ibid.
11. Newman, op. cit., Vol. IV, p. 44 and Desmond Chapman-Huston, *Bavarian Fantasy*, p. 143.
12. Strobel, op. cit., Vol. II, pp. 212–13.
13. ibid., pp. 213–15.
14. ibid., p. 216.
15. ibid., p. 217.
16. ibid., p. 229.
17. ibid., p. 232.
18. Newman, op. cit., Vol. IV, p. 147.
19. Strobel, op. cit., Vol. II, p. 239.
20. ibid., p. 283.
21. Newman, op. cit., Vol. IV, p. 222.
22. ibid., p. 224.
23. ibid., p. 237.
24. Strobel, op. cit., Vol. II, p. 310.
25. ibid., p. 311.

Chapter 11: A Crucial Decade: 1866–76

1. *Memoirs of Prince Hohenlohe*, translated by G. W. Chrystal (London, Heinemann, 1906), Vol. I, p. 259.
2. ibid., p. 261.
3. ibid., p. 262.
4. Gottfried von Böhm, *Ludwig II., König von Bayern*, p. 176.
5. Hohenlohe, op. cit., Vol. I, p. 368.
6. Böhm, op. cit., p. 224.
7. Werner Richter, *Ludwig II., König von Bayern*, p. 216.
8. ibid.
9. ibid., p. 219.

10. ibid., pp. 217–18.
11. Hohenlohe, op. cit., Vol. II, p. 15.
12. Richter, op. cit., pp. 223–4.
13. ibid., p. 248.
14. ibid., pp. 258–9.
15. See Walter Grasser's excellent biography: *Johann Freiherr von Lutz (eine politische Biographie) 1826–1890* (Stadtarchiv München, 1967).
16. Desmond Chapman-Huston, *Bavarian Fantasy*, pp. 166–7.
17. Hans Rall and Michael Petzet, *King Ludwig II* (English translation, 1980), pp. 47–8.
18. Hohenlohe, op. cit., Vol. II, p. 122.
19. Böhm, op. cit., p. 353.
20. Jean des Cars, *Louis II de Bavière*, p. 255.
21. Böhm, op. cit., p. 358.
22. Geheimes Hausarchiv, 55.3.39a.
23. ibid.

Chapter 12: Fantasies in Stone

1. Heinrich Kreisel, *Die Schlösser Ludwigs II. von Bayern*.
2. Otto Strobel, *König Ludwig II. und Richard Wagner, Briefwechsel*, Vol. II, pp. 224–5.
3. Hans Rall and Michael Petzet, *King Ludwig II* (English translation, 1980), p. 14.
4. Hyazinth Holland, *Lebenserinnerungen eines 90-jährigen Altmüncheners* (2nd edition, Munich, Parcus & Co., 1921). The quotations that follow are taken from pages 137–42 of this work.
5. Wolfram von Eschenbach, *Parzival*, translated by Helen M. Mustard and Charles E. Passage (New York, Vintage Books, 1961), p. 244.
6. Geheimes Hausarchiv, 755.
7. Desmond Chapman-Huston, *Bavarian Fantasy*, p. 147.
8. Geheimes Hausarchiv, 55.6.58.
9. Wilfrid Blunt, *The Dream King*, p. 92.

Chapter 13: Dreams of El Dorado

1. All the quotations that follow are taken from the Löher documents filed in the Geheimes Hausarchiv under reference number 55.6.57. For details of Löher's life see Karl Hüser, *Franz von Löher (1818–1892)*, (Paderborn, Verein für Geschichte und Altertumskunde Westfalens, 1972).

Chapter 14: Ludwig II and the Theatre

1. Quoted from Kurt Hommel, *Die Separatvorstellungen vor König Ludwig II. von Bayern*.
2. ibid.
3. ibid.
4. ibid.
5. ibid.
6. ibid., quoted by Hommel from Anton Memminger, *Der Bayernkönig, Ludwig II.* (Würzburg, 1919).
7. Paul Wiegler, *Josef Kainz. Ein Genius in seinen Verwandlungen* (Berlin, Deutscher Verlag, 1941), p. 48.

Chapter 15: Forbidden Longings

1. Iwan Bloch, *The Sexual Life of Our Time* (English version, London, Rebman, 2nd impression 1910), p. 520.
2. ibid., p. 517.
3. ibid., p. 499.
4. ibid., p. 550, n. 2.
5. ibid., p. 502.
6. Geneviève Bianquis, *Love in Germany* (English translation, London, Muller, 1964), p. 189.
7. Desmond Chapman-Huston, *Bavarian Fantasy*, p. 188.
8. ibid., p. 170.
9. ibid., pp. 156–8.
10. ibid., pp. 168–9.
11. ibid., p. 174.
12. ibid., pp. 174–5.

13. ibid., p. 179.
14. ibid., p. 209.
15. ibid., pp. 210–11.
16. ibid., p. 210.
17. ibid., p. 278.
18. Robert Holzschuh, *Das verlorene Paradies Ludwigs II*. (Frankfurt am Main, Eichborn Verlag, 2001).
19. Heinz Häfner, *Ein König wird beseitigt. Ludwig II von Bayern* (Munich, C.H. Beck, 2008), p. 497.

Chapter 16: Farewell to Wagner

1. Ernest Newman, *The Life of Richard Wagner*, Vol. IV, p. 284.
2. ibid.
3. ibid., p. 312.
4. Otto Strobel, *König Ludwig II. und Richard Wagner, Briefwechsel*, Vol. III, p. 29.
5. Newman, op. cit., Vol. IV, p. 397.
6. Strobel. op. cit., Vol. III, pp. 80–81.
7. ibid., p. 83.
8. Newman, op. cit., Vol. IV, p. 468.
9. The question of Wagner's attitude to Jews is complicated by the fact that his probable natural father, Ludwig Geyer, may well have been Jewish. It should also be noted that the anti-Jewish tone in certain of his writings was not reflected on a personal level. His relations with Levi, for example, were marked by great mutual warmth and respect.
10. Newman, op. cit., Vol. IV, p. 612.

Chapter 17: The Twilight Years

1. See the Princess's description of the garden in Chapter 12.
2. Desmond Chapman-Huston, *Bavarian Fantasy*, p. 236.
3. Gottfried von Böhm, *Ludwig II., König von Bayern*, p. 503.
4. Rupert Hacker, *Ludwig II. von Bayern in Augenzeugenberichten*, pp. 261–2.

5. ibid., p. 289.
6. ibid., p. 292.
7. Böhm, op. cit., p. 494.
8. Wilfrid Blunt, *The Dream King*, p. 167.
9. Albert Speer, *Spandau: the Secret Diaries* (London, Fontana, 1977), p. 408.
10. Bayerische Staatsbibliothek, Munich, manuscript collection, Bürkeliana 34, letter 11.
11. Hacker, op. cit., p. 302.
12. ibid., p. 264.
13. ibid., p. 305.
14. ibid., pp. 279–80.
15. Chapman-Huston, op. cit., p. 265.
16. ibid.
17. ibid., p. 266.
18. Böhm, op. cit., p. 532.
19. ibid., p. 280.
20. Robert Nöll von der Nahmer, *Bismarcks Reptilienfonds* (Mainz, v. Hase und Koehler Verlag, 1968), pp. 152–3.
21. ibid., p. 160.
22. Quoted by Chapman-Huston, op. cit., p. 39.
23. Werner Richter, *Ludwig II., König von Bayern*, pp. 310–11, n. 12.
24. Hacker, op. cit., p. 319.
25. ibid., p. 320.
26. ibid., pp. 322–3.

Chapter 18: The Trap Closes

1. Alfred Graf Eckbrecht von Dürckheim-Montmartin, *Notizen zur Königskatastrophe 1886*, written at Bamberg in March 1889 (a facsimile of Dürckheim's manuscript, edited by Dr Hans Keller, published under the auspices of Münchener Kulturkreis by Verlag der Grotius-Stiftung, Munich, in 1961).
2. Rupert Hacker, *Ludwig II. von Bayern in Augenzeugenberichten*, pp. 339–40.
3. ibid., p. 335.

4. ibid., pp. 343–4.

5. Dr Brewitz, *Die Erbkrankheit Ludwigs II und Ottos I von Bayern* (Informationsdienst der NSDAP-Reichsleitung, undated).

6. Dr med. Christoph Biermann, 'Leiden eines Königs'. *Deutsches Ärzteblatt*, No. 41, pp. 2685–91, No. 42, pp. 2949–2955 and No. 43, 3149–3154, 1973.

7. Quoted by Biermann, ibid.

8. Heinz Häfner, *Ein König wird beseitigt. Ludwig II von Bayern* (Munich, C.H. Beck, 2008), pp. 460–61.

9. Hacker, op. cit., p. 360.

10. ibid., p. 362.

11. ibid., p. 361.

12. Franz Carl Müller, *Die Letzten Tage König Ludwig II. von Bayern* (Berlin, 1888); quoted in the last two chapters of Hacker, op. cit.

Chapter 19: Prophecies Fulfilled

1. Hildegarde Ebenthal, *The Tragedy of a Throne*, pp. 18–19.

2. ibid.

3. Werner Richter, *Ludwig II., König von Bayern*, p. 386.

4. Rupert Hacker, *Ludwig II. von Bayern in Augenzeugenberichten*, p. 380.

5. ibid., p. 383.

6. Quoted ibid., pp. 383–5.

7. ibid., p. 400.

8. ibid., pp. 421–2.

9. Hans Rall and Michael Petzet, *King Ludwig II*, (English translation, 1980), p. 45.

Epilogue: The Cult of the Swan King

1. Lewiston, NY, Mellen Poetry Press, 2004.

2. E.g. *Herrlichkeit und Tragik eines Märchenkönigs* (Berlin, Peter Glowasz Verlag, 2004).

Select Bibliography

The literature on Ludwig II is vast and growing all the time, so there would be little point in attempting to provide a full bibliography here. The following is a slightly expanded version of my original selective list. Recourse to the internet will yield more comprehensive bibliographies, such as the one to be found on the website of the German National Library (Deutsche Nationalbibliothek): https://portal.d-nb.de. Information on recently published works can be found through the various internet bookselling services.

Bainville, Jacques: *Louis II de Bavière* (Paris, Perrin, 1900).

Bertram, Werner: *Der einsame König* (Munich, Herpich, 1936).

Biermann, Christoph: 'Leiden eines Königs', *Deutsches Ärzteblatt*, Vol. 45, 8 November 1973.

Blunt, Wilfrid: *The Dream King* (London, Hamish Hamilton, 1970).

Böhm, Gottfried von: *Ludwig II., König von Bayern* (Berlin, Engelmann, 1924).

Channon, Henry: *The Ludwigs of Bavaria* (London, Methuen, 1933).

Chapman-Huston, Desmond: *Bavarian Fantasy* (London, John Murray, 1955).

Des Cars, Jean: *Louis II de Bavière* (Paris, Editions J'ai Lu, 1977).

Ebenthal, Hildegarde: *The Tragedy of a Throne* (London, Cassell, 1917).

Gerard, Frances: *The Romance of King Ludwig II of Bavaria* (London, Jarrold, undated).

Glowasz, Peter: *Herrlichkeit und Tragik eines Märchenkönigs* (Berlin, Peter Glowasz Verlag, 2004). One of many works by Glowasz on the subject.

Grein, Edir: *Tagebuch – Aufzeichnungen von Ludwig II. König von Bayern* (Liechtenstein, Schaan, 1925).

Hacker, Rupert: *Ludwig II. von Bayern in Augenzeugenberichten* (Düsseldorf, Rauch Verlag, 1966).

Häfner, Heinz: *Ein König wird beseitigt. Ludwig II. von Bayern* (Munich, C.H. Beck, 2008).

Heigel, Karl von: *König Ludwig II. von Bayern. Ein Beitrag zu seiner Lebensgeschichte* (Stuttgart, Bonz, 1893).

Hierneis, Theodor: *Ein Mundkoch erinnert sich an Ludwig II.* (Munich, Heimeran, 1972). English translation, *The Monarch Dines* (London, Werner Laurie, 1954).

Hollweck, Ludwig: *Er war ein König* (Munich, Hugendubel, 1979).

Hommel, Kurt: *Die Separatvorstellungen vor König Ludwig II. von Bayern* (Munich, Laokoon-Verlag, 1963).

King, Greg: *The Mad King: The Life and Times of Ludwig II of Bavaria* (Secaucus, New Jersey, Carol Publishing Group, 1996).

Kobell, Luise von: *Unter den vier ersten Königen Bayerns. Nach Briefen und eigenen Erinnerungen* (Munich, C. H. Beck, 1894).

Kreisel, Heinrich: *Die Schlösser Ludwigs II. von Bayern* (Darmstadt, Schneekluth, 1954).

Lichtenfels, Matthias: *Ludwig II. König von Bayern*, novel (Düsseldorf, Deutsche Buchvertriebsund Verlags-Gesellschaft, 1960).

Newman, Ernest: *The Life of Richard Wagner* (4 vols., London, Cassell, 1933–47).

Pemberton, Max: *The Mad King Dies* (London, Cassell, 1928).

Petzet, Detta and Michael: *Die Richard-Wagner-Bühne König Ludwigs II.* (Munich, Prestel-Verlag, 1970).

Possart, Ernst von: (i) *Die Separatvorstellungen für König Ludwig II.* (Munich, C. H. Beck, 1901).

(ii) *Erstrebtes und Erlebtes* (Berlin, Mittler, 1916).

Pourtalès, Guy de: *Louis II de Bavière ou Hamlet-Roi* (Paris, 1928). English translation, *Ludwig II of Bavaria* (London, Thornton Butterworth, undated).

Rall, Hans: (i) *Die politische Entwicklung von 1848 bis zur Reichsgründung 1871*, in *Handbuch der bayerischchen Geschichte*, edited by M. Spindler, Vol. IV (1974).

(ii) *König Ludwig II. und Bismarcks Ringen um Bayern* (Munich, C. H. Beck, 1973).

Rall, Hans, and Petzet, Michael: *König Ludwig II.* (Munich, Schnell und Steiner, 1970. English translation, ibid., 1980).

Richter, Werner: *Ludwig II., König von Bayern* (Erlenbach and Leipzig, Rentsch, 1939). English translation, *The Mad Monarch* (Chicago, 1954).

Sailer, Anton: *Bayerns Märchenkönig. Das Leben Ludwigs II. in Bildern* (Munich, Bruckmann, 1961).

Strobel, Otto (ed.), *König Ludwig II. und Richard Wagner, Briefwechsel* (5 vols., Karlsruhe, Braun, 1936–9).

Tschudi, Clara: *König Ludwig II. von Bayern* (German translation from Norwegian, Leipzig, Reclam, 1911; English translation, 1908).

Wolf, Georg Jacob, *König Ludwig II. und seine Welt* (second edition, Munich, Franz Hanfstaengl, 1926).

Index